SILENT SCREAM

BY

YVONNE MASON

Silent Scream by Yvonne Mason

Published by Dressing Your Book

ISBN: 978-1-941912-04-1

Printed in the United States of America

ALSO BY YVONNE MASON

Stan's Story
A Touch of Love
Tangled Minds
Brilliant Insanity
Blood Alley
(Part of the "From the Shadows" Collection)

ACKNOWLEDGMENTS

Without these people this book would have never been born, first and foremost Jack Sewell, Retired, Executive Director/Criminal Investigator 19th Circuit State Attorney's Office Florida. He believes and supports my dream. He is the one who first told me about Gerard Schaefer as he took me on a tour of Hutchinson Island in 2006. It was one of the very first cases he worked.

State Attorney Robert E. Stone, 1973-1985, Retired He moved into private practice afterward. He fought tirelessly in uncharted waters to convict Gerard Schaefer. Rick McIlwain, Retired, State Investigator of the 19th Circuit State Attorney's Office Florida, who told me story after story. Roy Hazelwood, FBI Profiler who provided me with a pot of gold. State Attorney Bruce Colton of the 19th Judicial Circuit 1985-present for providing me with the human side of the circus, which was the Gerard Schaefer trial. Bruce was the Chief Assistant Public Defender during the trial. Robert Stone hired him as the Chief State Attorney in 1974 because Bruce had impressed him during the Schaefer trial

Robert Crowder, Sheriff Martin County, Florida. He saved Nancy Ellen Trotter and Pamela Sue Wells from the certain silent scream and certain death. Philip Shailer, Broward County State

Attorney, Co- Prosecutor, Retired, who helped prosecute Gerard Schaefer. He gave me his insight of Schaefer and his recollections of that time in history.

Danny Williams the custodian of evidence for the St. Lucie County Clerk's Office, who provided me with the mother lode of information, the box of evidence, which allowed the girls to have a voice.

Retired Captain Dave Yurchuck with the Broward County Sheriff's Office who met with me and filled in the gaps.

Charles C. (Chuck) Hemp retired Detective from Oakland Park Police Department who along with Dave Yurchuck and the late Pete Renje worked tirelessly in Broward County to make Susan Place and Georgia Jessup was heard.

These people either worked these cases or were involved in other important ways to see that justice was done and that the victims had a voice and no longer had to silently scream.

There is no way I could have made this book real without them. I am eternally grateful for their help, involvement, and support in making this dream real. I am honored for the help they gave me to give the victims a voice, for letting them know they have not been forgotten.

May we always support and believe in our justice system and those who serve. I personally salute each and every one of you.

Dedicated to

Jack

Without him this book would still be just a memory
and their screams would still be silent

"Silent Scream"

Forward by
Charles Hemp OPPSD ret.

When Gerard John Schaefer was perpetrating his evil in South Florida, and perhaps elsewhere as well, the term "Serial Killer" hadn't been coined. The crimes, which now fit into that category, have been documented throughout history but the label had yet to become part of the American lexicon.

The "Behavioral Science" unit of the FBI was non-existent and law enforcement in general had to rewrite the training manual when it came to dealing with these criminals, the crime scenes they left behind and the terrible void suffered by a family who lost a loved one under such monstrous circumstances.

In April of 1973 when the skeletal remains of Susan Place and Georgia Jessup were found in St. Lucie County the start of a joint investigation, which involved the Oakland Park Department of Public Safety, the Broward County Sheriff's Department and the St. Lucie County Sheriff's Department began. Numerous other law enforcement agencies, from Fort Lauderdale to Stuart also assisted and cooperated as south Florida detectives scrambled to determine if there was a link between this crime scene and other open cases.

By year's end exposure to Gerard John Schaefer's conversations, mind games, manuscripts and the story that unfolded with the investigation aged my fellow detectives and me 10 years. The terrible fear and cruelty that Schaefer's victims endured serves to illustrate a basic truth that homicide detectives come to understand. "There is nothing so inhuman, so bazaar or so painful that one person won't do to themselves or another human being.

I often think to myself that if this crime had to take place, I wish that it would have been later in my career when I was a more experienced, seasoned investigator and was better prepared to deal with the verbal games and manipulative tactics of this cold blooded murderer.

Although Schaefer was convicted of the heinous murders of Susan Place and Georgia Jessup, the voices of his other victims still cry to be heard. In her book, "Silent Scream," Yvonne Mason gives all of Schaefer's victims a "voice" and it is my hope that perhaps her work will allow them, their families and everyone connected to the evil of Gerald John Schaefer a lasting peace.

Preface

Normally I wouldn't do a Foreword and a preface in one book. However, this book merits both. As I researched this crime and the players involved many things that I already knew were reiterated and proved once again that there are no depths to which a human being will stoop.

There is no evil which man will not do. There are a myriad of excuses and platitudes a criminal will always fall back on when caught. They are not sorry for the crime they perpetrated, they are not sorry for the loss of life they caused. They are not sorry for the pain of the victim and the families as well. The pain, which never goes away. The questions, which always remain, unanswered. One question, which has haunted law enforcement and those who worked this case concerning Gerard Schaefer, has been "Did we do all we could?"

There is no answer. Sure they can play Monday Quarterback, they can continue to second-guess their abilities and their drive to put away one of the most vile and evil men who lived. But for what purpose does it serve? Who does it help at this junction? The answer to that question is no one and nothing. These players who worked so tirelessly to make sure that Schaefer was never able to perform his whore cleansing did the best they could with what they had.

At that time in law enforcement history there was no CSI (Crime Scene Investigations) to speak of, no DNA testing available, limited evidence techniques, and primitive lab/evidence analysis as compared to today's standards.

Schaefer was a genius. He knew the system of law. He knew how to manipulate and stage things to place him just on the edge of the crime without falling in. He always said he could never be tied to any of these crimes because he could never be placed at the scene. In that he was correct.

Schaefer's victims were never given a voice. Their screams have been silent for over thirty years. Their lives were taken at a time when they should have been planning their future. They were robbed of their youth and their old age. They were used as a tool for the sick and evil perversion of one human being.

Their story is between these pages. They now are heard.

You the reader decide what Gerard John Schaefer was.

For the victims!

CHAPTER ONE

HOW IT ENDED

At 9:40 A.M. Gerard John Schaefer's life drained from his body as he lay in a pool of bright red blood in his blood splattered cell at Starke Prison also known as Raiford, located in Starke, Florida just northeast of Gainesville. He had been stabbed by a fellow prisoner with a homemade knife, called a shank.

Schaefer's transgression included the fact that he had taken the last cup of hot water from a water fountain. Each inmate was allotted one cup. This was to insure that every inmate had access to the hot water. Schaefer took two. Maybe because he was the one who had been instrumental in getting the fountain installed in the first place he felt he was entitled to extra privileges. However, that appeared not to be the case. His worst transgression was that he made enemies and was not loyal to the code of prison conduct.

Gerard Schaefer had gained notoriety in prison by gaining the confidence of other well-known prisoners at Starke. He had gained the confidence of serial killers Ted Bundy, who killed girls at FSU as well as all across the country from

Washington State to Florida, Danny Rolling who killed girls at the University of Florida and Otis Toole who had been an accomplice to several serial killings starting out west and moving east. Schaefer would get these men to talk and then use their conversations to try and get leverage with law enforcement.

He wanted out of prison and thought if he was the confidential informant he would win his way out. He was the king pin at Starke, the celebrity who had been accused and convicted of savagely raping, killing and mutilating young women. He was the rogue cop who became skilled in the law by studying in the prison law library.

When Ted Bundy told Schaefer he had heard that Schaefer had killed up 28 young girls Schaefer's reply was it had been was closer to 34. Bundy's comment was that Schaefer had him by one. Schaefer more than likely was not happy that his status as a celebrity in his world was changing. Maybe he thought if he could get something on the "new kids" in the block he could regain his reign as king. The only thing it gained him was the loss of his life.

Schaefer's throat was savagely slashed and both of his eyes stabbed repeatedly. The viciousness of the attack was an act of sheer hatred. It also sent a message. This message was Schaefer and others like him who violated the code would no longer be able to see or talk. His eyes were blinded and his voice was silent. He endured the same silent scream, which his victims had endured. The attack was a statement of not only anger, but also territory.

Schaefer's life ended as he had ended the lives of so many women and young girls, in a pool of blood, created by a maniac.

Schaefer's demise came about as he lived, violently. December 3, 1995 was indeed a red-letter day for the man who never admitted to the slayings of at least nine, but as high as 34 females between 1966 and 1972. Even though he was only convicted for two in 1973 he spent the next twenty-two years eluding to the fact that he perpetrated other violent killings. He did it in television interviews; manuscripts he wrote which he sometime said were fiction and letters to people in law enforcement as well as his publisher Sondra London.

CHAPTER TWO

WHO WAS GERARD JOHN SCHAEFER?

Who was Gerard John Schaefer? It depends on who one asks. If one asks the criminal justice system they will tell you he was the first serial killer in the state of Florida. They will tell you he was a liar, a manipulator, and a disgrace to the uniform of law enforcement. If one asks the medical field they will tell you that he was narcissistic, a sexual predator and a psychopath. If one were to ask his family one will be told he was a loving son, brother and husband. If one asks the victim's families who lost daughters, they will tell you he was the most evil man they knew.

However, when Gerard John Schaefer was asked, he said he just wanted to leave good behind. He would say he was a great writer of fiction, an expert in the horror genre of sex, mutilation, pain and death. He would tell you he came from a good catholic family. He would say he was a good catholic man. Schaefer would tell you that he was a good cop who just wanted to protect those he kidnapped from becoming whores or being killed by others.

Schaefer would tell you that he was not the person who the media and the State Attorney's office had portrayed him to be. He would tell you he was betrayed by his attorney Elton Schwarz, his publisher Sondra London and by the media. He would tell you that he was innocent of all the charges and innuendos of which he had been accused.

Gerard Schaefer believed he was not the monster he was.

While in prison, he made a statement in an interview that he wanted to do something good with his life that exemplified the good as opposed to the bad. This statement was made after he had been convicted of murdering two young women from Ft Lauderdale, Fl. in 1972.

The "good" he chose to perpetrate was to kill young women who he thought were whores; their death released them from a lifestyle which was out of their control. He felt they believed what he did to them was good. In fact, in his mind they welcomed it.

Regardless of who is asked, the bottom line is the essence of the man was more than just disturbed. The truth in his mind was his reality. Whatever he believed was real, became real. He was evil combined with the attitude, that what he did was for the good of his victims. When you are finished with his story, which is really the story of his victims, I will leave it for you to decide who the man was known as Gerard John Schaefer. That is if you can.

CHAPTER THREE

THE HISTORY OF GERARD SCHAEFER

1946 - JUNE 1972

Gerard John Schaefer, Jr. was born in Wisconsin, to Gerard John Schaefer, Sr. and his wife Doris on March 25, 1946. He was the oldest of three children. His middle sibling a sister, named Sara and his younger brother Gary.

When Gerard was a small boy, Gerard, Sr. moved his family to Chamblee, Ga., which is a suburb of Atlanta, Ga. The elder Schaefer was a salesman for Kimberly –Clarke. He had been transferred to the south. Gerard spent the next few years in Chamblee.

The Schaefer's were devout Catholics. It was logical that Schaefer would attend parochial schools. When his family moved to Chamblee they enrolled their oldest son in Marist Academy. The time Schaefer spent at Marist Academy would help to influence his persona later in life.

Marist Academy now known as Marist School is an independent Roman Catholic college preparatory day school. It enrolls about 1,042 boys and girls in grades seven through twelve. The school is owned and operated by the Society of Mary, or the Marists. This is a religious congregation of priests and brothers, which was founded in France in 1836.

The first Marists took Mary the mother of Jesus as their inspiration. They had one mission. That mission was to bring to people an understanding of God's profound love as revealed through the Gospel.

In 1897, the Marists came to Atlanta. They came to serve the people. The name of their parish was the Sacred Heart. After arriving they found that the young men of Atlanta were in dire need of Catholic education at a much higher level. On October 2, 1901 the Marist College opened its doors. The school was located in a three-story schoolhouse on Ivy Street. The street name was later changed to Peachtree Center Ave. The first class consisted of thirty-two boys.

In 1962 the name was changed to Marist School and it was relocated to Ashford-Dunwoody Road in DeKalb County. During the 1960's and early 1970's they were considered a military school.

During the years Schaefer lived in Chamblee something happened. That something created the idea in a young boy's mind that his father did not love him. At least not as much as he thought his father loved his sister Sara. She was younger than her brother Gerard. No one knows if this idea was real or imagined. To Schaefer it didn't matter. In his mind it was real. This was just one of the many truths in Schaefer's mind which was part of his reality. He combined that supposed truth with another either real or imagined one, that being he was that he was "the illegitimate product of a forced marriage."

This statement leads one to believe maybe Gerard, Sr. and Doris had to get married. Maybe Schaefer felt his father resented the fact that he had to marry his mother. Not only was it expected during those years, the Catholic Church demanded it. For whatever reason Schaefer never felt he was loved at all by his father.

However, he saw the love of his father which should have been rightfully his given to his younger sister, Sara. But in later interviews while in prison Schaefer states a different reality. He tells the interviewer, he had a great childhood. He said he was on the football team, the golf team, the baseball team; he fished at Chastain Park in DeKalb County and his life as a child, was idyllic. But Gerard Schaefer led a secret life even as a pre-teen.

At the age of twelve, Gerard John Schaefer, Jr. began his descent into his own private hell. He discovered that if he wore women's underwear he could get sexual gratification as well as punish himself at the same time. It became his pain, punishment and pleasure.

Schaefer, at the tender age of twelve, when he should have been playing sandlot baseball, was in the woods with a hangman's noose and a tree. These became his first tools of the trade as he practiced autoerotic sex hanging. Autoerotic sex included Schaefer putting on a pair of women's underwear going to the woods and hanging himself until he received sexual gratification.

To add to his already twisted reality, in every game Schaefer played as a child he always got killed. The question that begs to be asked is this- Was Schaefer born this way, or did he become this way after his feelings of rejection either real or imagined.

Was the feeling of never being able to please his father the catalyst for his twisted personality or was he born with his brain already crossed? Or was there another underlying twist to his demented personality? Did something else happen in his life that set him on the path of destruction and murder? Was there an anger residue left from a traumatic experience he had suffered? Did he feel he had to purge certain things from his psychic? Was he angry at someone close to him? So angry that he spent his life taking it out on young women who he labeled as whores? The question one must ask is who did he really want to kill?

Schaefer always said his father was an abusive alcoholic and he was never home. Schaefer, Sr. was supposed to be away on business trips. However, Schaefer, Jr. felt his father used these trips to commit adultery. Did this also contribute to the disintegration of Schaefer? Or did he use this as an excuse for his behavior? Did he think of all women were independent as loose? Is this how he came to the conclusion they were whores if they did anything outside the scoop of his catholic teaching. Added to this litany of problems real or imagined Schaefer felt his mother stayed on his back to excel. Was Schaefer the child used as his parents excuse for their unhappiness? Did they blame him because they may have had to get married?

In 1960 Schaefer, Sr. moved his family of five once again. This time it was to Fort Lauderdale, Fl. Gerard was fourteen years old. He was going through the pains of growing which all boys go through when they reach the age of fourteen; their bodies are changing from small child to young man. The hormones take on a life of their own and unleash emotions, which until that time have been buried. Gerard Schaefer at the age of fourteen had been playing autoerotic sex games for two years.

Shortly after Gerard Schaefer moved into his

new environment, he met a young girl named Cindy who became his first girlfriend. They were an item until about 1964. That was also the year he graduated from St. Thomas Aquinas High School.

According to Schaefer, Cindy broke up with him because he refused to play the scripted scenario sex games with her. Schaefer stated Cindy could only have sex if he pretended to rape her and tear her clothes. The question will always remain unanswered, was it Cindy or was it Schaefer? Did Schaefer write the scripted sex games and she just got tired of them or was she part of his destruction? Did she wind up being a silent victim? Was she one of the ones who screamed silently? One who never reported the abuse? These are questions that died with Schaefer. During the time with Cindy, Schaefer appeared to have never engaged in his auto erotic bondage or orgasmic asphyxia.

One wonders if Schaefer played those two games with Cindy as well. Was he perfecting his ability to torture, rape and kill with Cindy as his testing ground?

With Cindy was no longer in his life, Schaefer returned to pain and pleasure of self-gratification. He returned to the woods of his youth with the tools of his trade, the women's underwear and the hangman's noose. He added another dimension to his twisted personality.

He began to spend many hours in the Everglades hunting. A family friend said Schaefer would hunt things which could not be eaten, like songbirds and land crabs. Was this the shades of things to come? Was Schaefer learning to hunt those things that could not fight back? Those things that was innocent and helpless. Did he know somewhere in the back of his mind he would one day use those stalking skills to claim the lives of young women who trusted his face? Or was Schaefer preparing the places of torture in his mind?

When the family moved to Fort Lauderdale, Schaefer attended St. Thomas Aquinas High School. This was yet another catholic school with strict moral codes and guilt ridden ideas. Schaefer was not the model student. He spent his time mostly as a loner, and was labeled as weird and out of it by his classmates. He never seemed to fit in anywhere. But he always seemed to be able to draw attention to himself.

There were two separate instances, which showed a side of Schaefer that would perpetuate itself later. In one, Schaefer debated with the teacher about religious issues. Debating religious issues in its self was not wrong. It was the intensity and the bitterness in which he debated these issues. Was he trying to quantify his actions of self-abuse? Did he in some dark place know what he was? Did he want to justify his actions? Did he really hate who he was becoming? Was his mother in his mind evil? Was his father evil? Did he feel his religious beliefs were contradictory to his lifestyle or did he feel his lifestyle was in some way very wrong? Was Schaefer conflicted in his soul? Did he feel if he argued the religious beliefs he had been taught he could justify his actions? Did his intelligence get in the way of his common sense, his sense of decency, his sense of what was right or wrong? Or the most important question ones must ask is Was Gerard John Schaefer just pure evil?

The second incident involving Schaefer and his teachers involved writing a long essay trying to scientifically challenge the virgin birth of Christ. He apparently didn't believe Christ was conceived by "immaculate conception." The question one must ask is did Schaefer think Mary was a whore? Did he think she used the "immaculate conception" idea to hide her adultery from her husband? Did he feel his mother was a whore and his conception of that created his twisted idea about the virgin birth? He couldn't accept that which in his mind couldn't be proven. However, he used this same scenario in his quest to rid the world of the "whores" he found. He believed any girl who was out on the street was a whore. He had no evidence to substantiate his assumption, but he believed it. Were these incidents added building blocks to his path of destruction?

After his break-up with Cindy, in the spring of 1964 Schaefer met another girl by the name of Sandra Steward. Schaefer had attended a high school dance. Sandra was there with another young man. He went up to this young woman and asked her if he knew her from someplace. Maybe she just ignored him or maybe she played the game most women play, the game of "chase." She wouldn't give him her phone number. This only served to make Schaefer pursue her all the more. He was not able to use his boyish charm to lure her to his side. This became a mission for Schaefer. He found another way to get her to succumb to his wiles. He went on a hunt for her number. Schaefer asked around until he found where she lived and her phone number. He contacted her. The reason she agreed to date him is not known. Maybe she was flattered that he would spend so much time looking for her. Maybe she thought he believed her to be special. The reasons while remaining a mystery, didn't affect the outcome. They dated until college started in the fall. While at Broward Community College his relationship with Sandy started that southern path.

Sandy may have heard and seen the arguments between Schaefer and his father, and she may have listened to his constant ranting about Cindy his former girlfriend. Eventually the relationship ended.

However, Sandra Steward would later play a bigger role in the reality that was Schaefer's.

Before his breakup with Sandy he allegedly used her as his therapist. He would talk to her at length about his urge to kill women, especially Leigh Hainline, as well as another unknown female who had the nerve to sunbath in her backyard in the nude. After the breakup he spent even more times in the Everglades. Was Schaefer perfecting his plan to kill? He was already obsessing about Hainline and the unknown nude sunbather.

Leigh was a neighbor of the Schaefer family. Schaefer and Leigh's brother were at one time friends. In interviews Schaefer said Leigh would undress in her room at night with the blinds up. He knew Hainline always got ready for bed at the same time. Schaefer would watch the clock and at 10:00PM he made it a point to be outside looking up at the second story window where her bedroom was located watching her undress. This type of behavior appeared to be conflicting to Schaefer's psychic. On the one hand it turned him on, but on the other it disgusted him.

Schaefer told his friends she was a loose woman and was asking for it. She went to a secular school and didn't have the same "moral values" as the good catholic girls. He bragged to them he could give "it" to her.

In an interview Schaefer told the interviewer that Leigh Hainline was not a nice Catholic girl. She was a very liberal free spirit. Schaefer in his mind was going to take care of the problem. He told the same interviewer he had walked up to her front door one day and told her she was asking for "it" and he could oblige her.

He said they went to her room and he really gave "it" to her. Did he abuse her? Did he play the scripted games he had played with Cindy? Did he treat he like the whore he felt she was? No one will ever know. Leigh Hainline disappeared.

After Schaefer graduated from high school and before he went to Broward Community College he decided he wanted to join the priesthood. The reason for this decision remains unclear. He was already at odds with the Catholic Church because of his disbelief in the virgin birth.

What did he hope to gain by becoming a priest? Did he think a priest garb would cloak his dark side? Did he believe he could use his priestly calling to justify ridding the world of the whores? Did he think his priestly robes would convey a feeling of trust on his part before he committed murder? Was he going to use the calling to expunge his guilty secret? Did he think if he hid behind the garb of priesthood he would lose the guilt of his sins? Whatever reasons he used to convince himself of his new "calling" he fully expected it to work.

He applied to St. John's Seminary located in W. Coral Gables, Fl. Once again, it was not to be. The Seminary told him that he didn't have the mindset to become a priest. They told him that he was not dedicated enough. Did they already know something no one else did? Did they see the darkness in Schaefer? Did they know he would spiral out of control?

He was rejected. This rejection sent Schaefer into a different orbit. He decided he had enough of what he called the "mind control" of the Catholic Church. So he denounced the church. He cut himself off from it altogether. This could have left a void in his psychic. He tossed off the last vestige of his moral upbringing like a pair of dirty socks. Now Gerard Schaefer had absolutely nothing standing in his path of destruction. The church had rejected him so he rejected the church. He was on his way down the road to hell full speed ahead and no looking back. He had cut the last tie to any conscience he might have.

At a loss with himself and not really knowing what to do Schaefer enrolled at Broward Community College. While at Broward he took a creative writing class. It was in this class that the reality of Schaefer's mind began to come to the forefront.

Schaefer approached his creative writing teacher and told him about his homicidal tendencies. The teacher referred Schaefer to the college counselor Dr. Neal Crispo. In his sessions with Dr. Crispo he allegedly revealed he wanted to join the Army because he liked to kill things. He talked about his urges to kill and that he would kill livestock beheading them before raping their carcasses. Had Schaefer already made these urges a reality? Had he already charted his course with the final destination, which was the senseless destruction of young women? Was he asking for someone to stop him then? Or was he already bringing his narcissistic personality to the spotlight? Was this the beginning of "catch me if you can."

Schaefer went back to Broward in the fall of 1965 but only completed one semester before he went on a singing tour with the group Sing- Out 66, a musical road troupe of the super Patriotic "Moral Rearmament" movement. It was on this tour he would meet his first wife to be Martha Fogg.

In September 1966 Gerard Schaefer returned to school at Broward Community College and graduated with an associate's degree in Business Administration in 1967. He became bored with his life and started Florida Atlantic University in January 1968.

Schaefer decided he wanted to be a teacher.

But once again he couldn't cut the mustard. Due to failing grades Schaefer was sent his draft notice in April of 1968.

He promptly fled and hid. When he was finally found he was referred to Dr. Raymond Killinger for emergency psychiatric testing. He used the ruse he was unstable and he was going to commit suicide. He was apprehended wearing women's underwear. After Dr. Killinger talked with him, his jacket was stamped unfit for military service. This was another clue into the darkness of Gerard Schaefer.

It would appear that Gerard Schaefer had begun to have a dark cloud continuously over his head. In May of 1968 Gerard Schaefer, Sr. lost his job with Kimberly- Clark, and his wife Doris filed for divorce. By July of 1968 Gerard Schaefer, Jr. who had been working on a construction quit his job and fled to Michigan. Were the events of the last several months too much for him? Or was there another event no one knew about except for his family the reason Schaefer fled? This too is another question that died with him. Several months later he returned to Fort Lauderdale with Martha Fogg in tow. In December of that same year they were married.

Upon returning to Florida and after marrying Martha Fogg, Gerard Schaefer decided he would return to school and become a teacher. In 1969 Schaefer returned to Florida Atlantic University to get his teaching degree. In that same year he was assigned as a student teacher at Plantation High School on February 27th. This job didn't last long. After a few weeks he was dismissed because of his inappropriate behavior. No one seems to know just what that inappropriate behavior was. However, it left Gerard Schaefer jobless for several months.

In September 1969 two more events occurred. Doris and Gerard Schaefer, Sr.'s divorce was final and Gerard decided to return to school. He went back to Florida Atlantic University. Once again he was given a job as a student teacher at Stranahan High School in Fort Lauderdale. His stay there only lasted a very short while. Richard Goodhart the school supervisor removed him from his position and told him never to come back to one of his schools. This poses the same question again, "What had he done to cause this supervisor to make that strong a statement"?

In March 1970 Schaefer petitioned Florida Atlantic University administrators to alter his records from the previous November to incomplete instead of withdrawal so he could return to school. By May 1970 his wife Martha Fogg had enough and filed for divorce. Schaefer decided he needed to get a way for a while so he fled to Europe and Africa for a month. No one knows what he did while he was overseas. However, his writings indicate he was a very busy person. He talked about killing women in a story setting.

After Schaefer returned from his sojourn in Europe he took a job as a security guard at Florida Power and Light in October of 1970. He needed money for tuition to return to school one more time. It was at Florida Power and Light that Gerard Schaefer met Teresa Dean who would become his second wife.

In August 1970, Gerard Schaefer married Teresa Dean and graduated from Florida Atlantic University with a Bachelor's Degree in geography. September 3rd Gerard Schaefer was hired by the Wilton Manor Police Department. He returned to Broward Community College to attend the Police Academy. December 17th Gerard Schaefer hit the streets for six months on probation as a Wilton Manor Cop. In March of 1972 Gerard Schaefer received a commendation for a drug arrest at Wilton Manor. Then he had an altercation with Chief Scott. The chief was going to fire him. Schaefer begged Scott to let him keep his job. In the meantime Schaefer applied at Broward County Sheriff's department. He was not hired. He failed his mandatory psychological exam. He was rejected again. In June of 1972 Gerard Schaefer applied with the Martin County Sheriff's department.

Chief Scott fired Schaefer when he was told that Schaefer had an interview with Martin County. Scott was stated as saying, "I fired him. I don't want him around." (Donovan, 1973)

He had a letter allegedly written by Chief Scott touting his outstanding work performance. The letter was a forgery. However, no one checked the validity of the letter. He was hired.

Gerard John Schaefer was with the Martin County Sheriff's department 28 days when his reign of terror began.

CHAPTER FOUR

THE BEGINNING OF THE END

JULY 22, 1972

Friday July 21, 1972, the air was humid and the sun was hot. Two young, girls aged 19 and 18 years old, found their way to South Florida for a few days of fun in the sun and water. They had hitchhiked from Michigan to the town of Stuart Florida located on the east coast also known as the treasure coast.

The next day Saturday July 22, 1972 was to be a day that each girl would remember for the rest of their life. It would always be imbedded in their memories. This day would be a new beginning after it had become a nightmare of an almost ending.

Nancy Ellen Trotter and Pamela Sue Wells were minding their own business as they hitchhiked to Jensen Beach on this particular day when a Martin County Deputy in his patrol car approached them. He asked the girls what they were doing and they told him they had hitchhiked from up north. After identifying himself, he offered to take them to where ever it was they were headed, and they went with him. They had no reason not to trust a law enforcement officer.

On the drive to their destination, Deputy Gerard John Schaefer expounded on the evils of hitchhiking and that it was against the law in Florida. However, at that time hitchhiking was not against the law in Florida.

Schaefer offered to meet the two girls the next day, which was Saturday to take them to the beach. His wife was in Fort Lauderdale some 80 miles to the south at a dentist appointment. He was footloose and fancy-free.

Saturday July 22, 1972 dawned hot and humid. As the sun rose in the clear pale blue of the Florida sky Gerard Schaefer met the two young girls and they went with him. He took them on a ride. A ride that would forever, change them and the lives of many people.

Deputy Schaefer told the young naïve women he was going to take them to the beach- but first he was going to show them an old Spanish fort. There are no Spanish Forts in Martin County. The old Spanish Fort turned out to be just an old barn. The barn was boarded up and falling down.

As Gerard Schaefer drove Nancy Ellen and Pamela Sue north on A1A to a remote area on Hutchinson Island, one wonders what went through their young minds.

This was two young girls who had come south from Michigan. They didn't know anyone in the area. They were hitchhiking and trusting. Schaefer was a cop. When Schaefer reached his destination it was not at an old fort. It was in a remote area filled with tangled undergrowth, mangroves, dead trees, mosquitoes, tiny black gnats and rot.

Hutchinson Island was a sparsely populated area in the 1970's. There were no condos; very few hotels and these were mostly family owned. A couple of bars and a two lane narrow blacktop road. There were no bike paths, no emergency lanes, and the growth of mangroves, palm trees; undergrowth, bushes and water were close to the road.

Mangroves are trees and bushes, which are native to the coastal regions of Florida. The Red Mangrove is a tree whose roots grow out of the ground. They are fed and watered by the salt water of the Atlantic and the fresh water of the Intercostal. The White Mangroves are bush like trees that grow further inland. However, they also are fed by both salt water and fresh water. Both of these trees grew in abundance on Hutchinson Island.

The Indian River flows on one side of A1A and the Atlantic Ocean rolls the tide in and out on the other. In the 1970's there were only two ways on and off the island. One was a bridge on the southern end, which crossed from the city of Stuart, located in Martin County. The other was a drawbridge located on the north end in Fort Pierce in St. Lucie County.

It was from the Stuart Bridge Gerard Schaefer took the two girls to Hutchinson Island. He had located a very isolated area on the west side of A1A near the Indian River. The area was known as Joe's Point, which had been in its heyday a bean farm. It was located on a peninsula, which jutted out into the Indian River. There was a dirt road, which led to the barn. The area was filled with mangroves, undergrowth and trees with large extended branches. It was an area that could not be seen from A1A.

This writer wonders if perhaps he had already researched this particular site. If he had planned all along that he would bring females here. It would seem logical. He knew it was isolated, it was close to the bridge and it was in Martin County. As a deputy for Martin County Schaefer could contain the girls at that location, leave them and come back as many times as he wanted to. His presence in that area would never be questioned. He could torture, rape, kill and bury the bodies. He felt they would never be found. However, he was wrong, so very wrong. He had not counted on the fact that one of the girls would escape after he left.

Deputy Schaefer ordered both girls from the

vehicle. He restrained each girl's hands with handcuffs, all the while telling them the dangers of hitchhiking. Once the girls were restrained, Schaefer tied one girl to a tree by a hangman's noose. They were made to precariously balance on an exposed mangrove root so they wouldn't hang themselves. Then while she watched he tied the other girl to a different tree. Then he gagged them. All the time he expounded on the evil men in the world and what could happen if the wrong person had picked up them up. He kept telling them about the white slave traders who could pick up hitchhikers and sell them overseas as prostitutes. He continued to expound about the dangers they faced being on the road without someone to protect them.

One wonders what thoughts of terror ran thru each girls mind as she was bound, gagged and noosed. Did they feel as if this dark forest would be their final place of life? Did they understand the danger they were in? Did they regret their trust in a person who was sworn to serve and protect? One can only imagine the thoughts of sheer terror, horror, disbelief, shock and nausea that ran through their minds like a runaway freight train.

Gerard Schaefer finally told the girls he would be back with slave traders to take them away. Then he got in his car and left. When I asked Sheriff Crowder why Schaefer left his contention was that

Schaefer had forgotten something he needed to complete his crime.

The two girls were left behind handcuffed, gagged and standing on a tree root with a noose around their necks. Their legs growing tired from balancing on the root waiting for an unknown fate. They had urinated on themselves from the fear. They were alone in a dark, damp forest hearing the strange sounds of the residences of the environment, the bellowing of the gators, the skittering of the land crabs, the flurry of the wings of birds. They felt the constant biting of the mosquitoes which left large welts on their exposed body, along with the small black gnats which would land on their sweaty faces, in their eyes, noses and mouths. They heard screeching of owls and saw the slow circling of the birds of prey. They heard the sounds of the boats on the river behind them.

What thoughts of horror, dread, apprehension and unspeakable fear ran through each girl's mind? Did they regret making the trip to the sunshine state? Did they regret hitchhiking and trusting a person who had been hired to serve and protect? Did they wonder what they might have done to be where they were? Did they believe they might die in the dark, damp, remote, and scary place?

Funny how the instinct of self-preservation will kick in when one is faced with such a situation.

It's funny how one will struggle against all odds just to survive. That is exactly what Nancy Ellen Trotter and Pamela Sue Wells did on that hot, humid, day in July.

Nancy Ellen Trotter with sweat running down her body in rivers managed to escape her noose. She carefully maneuvered her head around in the noose until it slipped out. She probably did a form of ballet as she struggled to keep from hanging herself with the noose as she struggled free.

Once free from the noose but still in handcuffs, she ran, fell and tripped her way through the mangroves, water and underbrush to a road. The road was A1A. She was seen running down A1A by a man driving on the road. He stopped for her. She took a chance, for all Nancy knew it could have been Gerard Schaefer coming back. One can only imagine what the stranger felt when he saw a wide eyed, frightened, cut, scratched, with hands still bound young girl emerging from a place she should have never been.

When Schaefer returned to the scene he did not like what he found. He found the girls gone. Panic must have become the emotion of the moment when Schaefer found his quarry no longer captured. He went back to his house in Stuart and called Sheriff Crowder with a story he just knew in his mind was truth. His reality! His justification for his actions!

Sheriff Robert Crowder, at age 26 years old had just been appointed Sheriff in May. He received the phone call that hot July day that not only changed his life, it also put Martin County and its county seat of Stuart on the map.

Schaefer told Sheriff Crowder, he had done a bad thing. He said he had tried to scare two young women who were hitchhiking and he had gone overboard. He admitted to taking Nancy Trotter and Pamela Wells to the remote area to give them a good scare.

Sheriff Crowder first reacted with disbelief, then anger then embarrassment. It was not only a smear on the small Sheriff's department it was Crowder's livelihood at stake. Here was a new officer who had kidnapped two girls and assaulted them by binding, gagging and hanging them. Crowder's job was also on the line.

He had hired Schaefer. He asked Schaefer what he had been thinking. Schaefer told Crowder that he was trying to teach the girls a lesson and it got out of hand. He said when he picked them up on Friday and tried to explain what could happen to them they laughed at him and made fun of him. Schaefer told Crowder he just wanted to show them what could happen. He was just going to leave Trotter and Wells tied up for a little while and then come back and get them.

Crowder told Schaefer to report to the duty Sergeant and hung up the phone. He got into his car and started toward Hutchinson Island to see if he could find the two girls. As he drove north on A1A he saw a car parked on the side of the road at Joe's Point. At about the same time he noticed a man waving his arms. Crowder pulled over and got out of his patrol car.

The man told Crowder that he had been driving on A1A when he saw Nancy Trotter running down the road still in handcuffs. Crowder, Nancy and the stranger all walked back into the mangroves when Nancy told them Pamela Wells was still back there. When they arrived at the place the girls had been tied up, they saw Pamela Trotter in the Indian River. She was still handcuffed. When she saw Crowder and the stranger and Trotter she came out of the water. Each girl was put in a separate car and taken to the Martin County Sheriff's office to give their statements. They even knew the name of their kidnapper.

After Schaefer was fired he was arrested and charged with two counts of aggravated assault and false imprisonment, fingerprinted, and booked. When Sheriff Crowder questioned Schaefer he was nonchalant as to what he had done. He appeared unconcerned as to the consequences. He figured he was smart enough to wiggle his way out of his predicament. He had no prior record and he had a college degree. Schaefer believed he was safe. Schaefer stayed in jail from July1972 until September 1972 when he was released on his own recognizance.

By allowing Gerard Schaefer to be released in this manner it set off a chain reaction that would haunt law enforcement for many years to come.

CHAPTER FIVE

THE ESCALATION BEGINS

SEPTEMBER 27, 1972

When Judge D.C. Smith with the 19th judicial circuit released Gerard Schaefer on his own recognizance, Schaefer went back to Fort Lauderdale, which was his comfort zone. The place he had grown up. The place his mother still lived.

His plan for Nancy Trotter and Pamela Wells had failed. He could no longer take his victims to that remote area close to Stuart. He had to find another place, one which would be more secure, and one which no one would find.

No one knows how long it took him to do that. No one knows how long he stayed in Stuart. All that's known are females started disappearing shortly after Schaefer was released from jail.

The first known victims were two young girls with their entire lives in front of them who left on September 27, 1972 from Fort Lauderdale with a male companion named Jerry Shepard. The two girls were Susan Place age 17, five feet four inches tall with blond hair and blue-green eyes and her friend

Georgia Jessup age 16. According to Susan's mother they were all going to the beach to play the guitar. They didn't say which beach.

How Georgia Jessup and Susan Place become acquainted with Gerard Schaefer aka Jerry Sheperd was never known. What is known is that Georgia had known Jerry Sheperd before her friend Susan.

Mrs. Place had misgivings about the person her daughter was leaving with. She felt he was too old for her young daughter. To her something didn't feel right. She followed her daughter outside and wrote down the tag number down. That was the last time Mr. and Mrs. Ira Place saw their daughter.

On October 1, 1972 Mrs. Place called Oakland Park Police Department to report her daughter missing. The officer arrived at the residence at 12:07 P.M. Mrs. Place told the officer her daughter was last seen on September 27,1972 in the company of her friend Georgia Jessup and Jessup's male friend Jerry. She told the officer that Georgia and Jerry had talked of going to Colorado or Mexico.

Susan had been allegedly seeing a young man who was currently residing at the Ocean Mist Motel, located at 1500 Ocean Dr. #16 Hollywood. However, Mrs. Place didn't know the young man's name.

Mrs. Place stated that her daughter Susan was an epileptic and had not taken any medications with her when she left home on September 27. She admitted in the missing person's report that Susan had mental problems was very unstable and had been using drugs, including heroin. She told the officer that Susan had been arrested several times for drugs and that she had been reported missing twice to the Fort Lauderdale Police Department.

The report showed that Susan had been arrested as early as September 21, 1972 in N. Palm Beach by a Sgt Poole for drugs and she had agreed to cooperate with Gene Sedberry of the Ft. Lauderdale Police Dept. as a drug informant. According to Mrs. Place, Susan never followed through with this. Susan had also dropped out of the Adult Vocational School three different times.

According to Mrs. Place Susan had problems fitting in with her peer group. She told the officer that Susan had the propensity to do anything to fit in. She also told the officer that Susan had not fought with her parents except for the usual confrontations, which were normal with a teenage girl. But Susan had stated many times that she was going to leave home.

The reporting officer noted in his missing person report that due to the nature of Susan's past behavior and the length of time it took the parents to report her missing, that he felt they expected that type of behavior from their daughter. On September

27, 1972 when Susan Place left home she was wearing a short sleeve white blouse, dark blue green bell-bottom pants and blue suede shoes. Even though Mrs. Place told the attending officer that her daughter had not left the house with any clothes, purse or jewelry it didn't mean she had not already packed her belongings leaving them in another location.

Being a young girl with a possible rebellious streak with a prior arrest record maybe Susan Place felt she had to hide her intentions. Those misplaced intentions cost her more than just leaving the security of her comfort zone. It cost her life. It left her screaming silently behind a gag in her mouth.

During this same time period two more young girls disappeared from the Fort Lauderdale area. On October 23, 1972 Mary Briscolina age 14 and Elsie Farmer age 14 were last seen hitchhiking to a local restaurant in Fort Lauderdale.

They were never seen again. The escalation of Gerard Schaefer's crime spree had begun.

CHAPTER SIX

DECEMBER 1972

THE VERDICT

Gerard John Schaefer, Jr. appeared before Circuit Judge D.C. Smith December 1972 and was sentenced to six months in the county jail for one charge of aggravated assault against Nancy Ellen Trotter and Pamela Sue Wells. The other charges of aggravated assault and false imprisonment were dropped. Schaefer was also placed on three years' probation.

The judge even allowed Schaefer to turn himself in on Jan 15, 1973 to start serving his sentence. Schaefer had told the judge he needed to get his wife Teresa settled in Fort Lauderdale with his mother. The delay also gave the county commissioners the opportunity to get the work release program up and running. These actions were afforded to Schaefer because he had been in law enforcement and up until that time had a spotless record. He had even received a commendation for a drug bust.

Before Schaefer was sentenced he played the

"throwing himself at the mercy of court card."

He told Judge Smith "When I met the people (Nancy Trotter and Pamela Sue Wells), they had no money and no place to stay. They were hitchhiking. I didn't want to see them out on the road. Most crimes have a motive. My motive was to get the girls off the street. I wanted to show them the dangers of hitchhiking. I would appreciate any leniency and mercy you could show. I'm trying to rebuild my life. I got a job with Wynn-Dixie and am training to become a manager."

The truth in Schaefer's mind appeared to be that if they had not gotten away, he would have killed them, but that his actions were justified. He not only wanted to show them what could happen, he wanted to be a part of it. However, when they escaped, Gerard Schaefer, found another way to justify his actions. He would become the hero the savior of wayward girls. He would be the one who would show them the error of their ways.

He was right, most if not all crimes have a motive. Schaefer's motive was to show Nancy and Pamela what could and did happen to whores and loose young women on the streets. In his mind they were bad so they should be punished. His motive was destruction of a human life but in his mind justified. Schaefer really believed that because his truth was real, he should be granted mercy from the court. The only thing he really felt he had done wrong was in his words "go too far." He maintained the "arrest" was a clean arrest. He had not done anything wrong in that aspect.

That is how he tried to justify his actions. But in fact, he felt he had not gone far enough.

Schaefer's attorney, Jerry Randolph of Stuart, Fl., helped to enable this defense by his remark to the court. "All he was trying to do was show the girls the dangers of being out on the road. He just overstepped his authority. I feel he is a good candidate for probation."

One can only surmise that Schaefer convinced his attorney that what he had done was in all innocence.

Schaefer took this as an opportunity to plead his case even more.

He implored the judge by saying; "I've never done anything wrong in my life before this. I implore your mercy to let me stay with my wife." (Fryer, 1972)

Judge Smith fired back with, "It is beyond this court's imagination to conceive how you were such a foolish and astronomic jackass as you were in this case. If I were to let you off scot-free before I walked in court this morning I may as well have let all these people go. We have unanimous opinion that you acted foolishly. I can't understand how a man of your background can do such a foolish thing. You can't be a fool as far as the court is concerned. The State Attorney's went the last mile in dropping the other charges. I am going the last mile in trying to put you on the work release program. I could have sent you to the State prison." (Fryer, 1972)

Before he was released from Martin County Jail after serving the six-month sentence for the aggravated assault charge, Chuck Hemp from the Oakland PD and his partner Pete Renje traveled to Martin County Jail to interview Schaefer. They wanted to know if he had anything to do with the disappearance of two girls in September of that same year. As they left the jail Hemp told his partner that he would make Schaefer his life's work. During the interview Schaefer had been arrogant, belligerent, and hostile as he tried to bait the officers.

The door to hell had been opened. The problem was no one yet knew that Schaefer had done a lot wrong, very wrong and had been doing it for a long, long time. The true Gerard John Schaefer would come to the forefront.

CHAPTER SEVEN

THE FIRST FIND

APRIL 1, 1973

MONDAY

On Sunday April 1, 1973 Jessie Joe Holley and his father, Calvin thought it would be just another lazy Sunday afternoon as they looked for cans on Hutchinson Island along State Highway A1A.

Highway A1A runs south from Jacksonville to Miami. It passes through Hutchinson Island in St. Lucie County. Blind Creek runs parallel with A1A and the Atlantic Ocean. Blind Creek was in a very remote area. There were no houses, no gas stations; no human life was located in this area. The only thing close was the St. Lucie Florida Power and Light power plant, which was just being built. Both sides of A1A were thick with Mangroves, palms and undergrowth. Blind Creek is about ten miles north of the Stuart Bridge on the east side of A1A. It was at Blind Creek that the lives of Jessie Joe Holley, his father and others were dramatically impacted. This particular day they found more than just aluminum cans. As the two men combed a remote area, off the beaten path a quarter of a mile north of the nuclear power plant located on the island, they came across a scene that woke up the residences of sleepy St. Lucie County.

Jessie and Calvin, in their search for aluminum cans, instead found several body parts and scattered clothing near a hole in the ground. The damp, dark, mosquito infested, perpetually dark, airless area held the final resting place of two bodies in pieces. They immediately left the area and went back to Stuart. When they arrived at Stuart they placed a call to Sheriff James D. Holt with the Martin County Sheriff's Office. After calling Sherriff Holt they went to the home of Jessie's brother-in-law Calvin Wiggins. Wiggins was the chief ambulance attendant for the City of Stuart.

Calvin Wiggins in turn called both the Martin County and St. Lucie County Sheriff's dept. Wiggins had both departments meet him at the dirt road off A1A leading to the bodies. From that moment on lives took different path. Parents grieved, families were torn apart and law enforcement as it had been known in South Florida grew in knowledge in the science of crime scenes and forensics.

The expertise known as forensic science as we now know it was unheard of. DNA was unknown.

The ability to identify decomposed bodies was primitive at best and guesswork at worst. Press, law enforcement and the curious onlookers often contaminated crime Scenes.

When law enforcement descended on Blind Creek about 1:30 in the afternoon, jurisdiction was established. The jurisdiction belonged with the St. Lucie County Sheriff's Department. The State Attorney's office of the 19th Judicial Circuit was notified and assigned Jack Sewell, one of the investigators, to the case.

Law Enforcement first found two upper torsos, parts of a pelvis, and a leg. Not far from the first find, a lower part of a body clad in blue jeans lay in the black murky soil. The blue jeans were covered with several patches. These patches were an owl, a half-moon, a Star of David and a roadrunner. These patches were very good evidence. They would later help to identify one of the bodies.

As deputies continued to work the crime scene, they found, two dresses and a black shoe next to the shallow grave. Lt. Pat Duvall who was the chief Investigator for the St. Lucie County Sheriff's Dept. at the scene also dug up from the shallow grave, a pink Shorty nightgown, and another woman's black shoe that matched the one found by the grave. He found human vertebrae in the grave.

But by the end of the first days search, the

heads were still missing and the identity of the decomposing bodies remained a mystery.

Blind Creek the final burial place of Georgia Jessup and Susan Place

CHAPTER EIGHT

THE IDENTIFICATION

APRIL 3, 1973

TUESDAY

On Tuesday April 3,1973 two teams which consisted of a combined total of twenty five Florida Law Enforcement agents headed up by Lt. Pat Duval, Captain Wayne Scambler and Chief Deputy Finn Parrish, had been working two shifts and finally uncovered more bones.

These law enforcement agents who had worked around the clock, survived the prior days on the job by eating sandwiches, drinking coke, water and fighting heat, mosquitoes and the ever popular gnats.

The teams had painstakingly worked over 2,800 square feet of massive tangled, undergrowth and rich black wet muck in the humid, airless mosquito ridden air that made up this Florida forest which always gave the illusion of night.

As they walked around in the water and black muck it stuck to their shoes like black glue; they functioned on little if not any sleep and lots of adrenaline.

Adding to the teams of searchers there was a helicopter hovering over the terrain. They were taking pictures of the crime scene in the air. Robert Crowder had lost his bid in the election for the Sheriff's job so he had taken a job with the Florida Power Plant as head of the security department. He was on the roof of the power plant the day the bodies were found. He watched as the helicopters snapped their overhead pictures. He wanted to be a part of that search.

As law enforcement officers combed the area they used four metal detectors, shovels, machetes and rakes. However, the biggest asset was a shifter, which Investigator Steve Williams created by taking a piece of screen and building a frame around it. This shifter proved to be a godsend. Williams hit pay dirt.

Buried in the dark recesses of black soil were teeth, some with fillings. To add to the mother lode of evidence was a scalp with longish brown hair, two three-inch pieces of a jawbone, a blonde scalp and other small pieces of bone.

Around 9:45 in the morning a valuable discovery was finally recovered. A skull had been found. It was immediately sent to the district medical examiner along with the rest of the discovered body parts for identification. However, still missing were the second skull and a hand.

Lt. Duval stated that the bodies had probably been at the crime scene between four to six months and that the bones appeared to be the size of someone 15 to 18 years old. He also stated that the legs from one of the bodies appeared to have been forcibly removed by a heavy knife, ax or hatchet. Duval said that dental records could probably determine identification that they would compare to all of the missing girls in their files.

A carving that was found on one of the trees that looked like either "CJ" or "GJ, as well as the patches on the blue jeans would help determine the identity of the remains.

The biggest determination would be the mother of one of the missing girls. Mrs. Ira Place the mother of a missing girl, by the name of Susan Place, had a story for law enforcement.

The last day she had seen her daughter alive was September 27, 1972. Her daughter along with her friend Georgia Jessup had gotten in to a car with a man who stated his name was Jerry Shepard. Mrs. Place with a mother's instinct felt very uncomfortable with this person. As the car with the two girls left, Mrs. Place walked outside and wrote down a tag number. The first two numbers she wrote were 24. She thought she had written down 42.

When her daughter didn't return home that evening, Mrs. Place took the tag number to the local police department so they could run a trace. Nothing showed up.

A tag number beginning with the numbers 24 was for St. Lucie County. The numbers 42 was for Martin County.

Mrs. Place and her husband continued to look for their daughter for several months with no luck. However, months later as they traveled north on US1 she noticed tags on the backs of cars.

These tags showed the first two numbers as 42. She told her husband she thought she might have transposed the numbers the day she wrote them down. Mr. and Mrs. Place went to the Martin County Sheriff's Department and explained to the desk sergeant what had happened.

The desk sergeant ran the tag using 42 as the beginning two numbers. When the tag came back he told them who it belonged to and that this person was already in jail for one count of aggravated assault on Trotter and Wells. He told Ms. Place the owner of the car was a Martin County Deputy Sheriff. When she was shown a lineup of pictures of men who all had similar features, she identified one, as the man who had picked up her daughter and her friend, the man was Gerard Schaefer aka Jerry Shepard.

She described the clothes her daughter was wearing the day of her disappearance. She told law enforcement her daughter had worn a pair of jeans with the very same patches found on the jeans at the crime scene.

With the validation of the tag number, the picture and the description of the clothing worn by Susan Place the day she disappeared, law enforcement scrambled to get a search warrant for the home of Gerard Schaefer and his mother Doris Schaefer. These two search warrants involved St. Lucie County, Martin County and Broward County.

The results of that search and seizure would create a firestorm that South Florida had never before encountered.

CHAPTER NINE

THE SEARCH WARRANTS

APRIL 7, 1973

SATURDAY

Saturday April 7, 1973 should have been just another humid day, families at the beach, spring break in full swing and visions of tourists for the summer. However, this day was not a walk in the park for the St. Lucie County Sheriff's Department, the Broward County Sheriff's Department and the Martin County Sheriff's Department.

Henry Dean, police officer and brother of Teresa Schaefer, called Lt Yurchuck saying, "Dave, I need to meet with you. I have something for you. It is a small purse that my brother in law Gerard gave my sister Teresa."

The two men met at the Lake Worth turnpike exit near the Holiday Inn. Lt. Yurchuck took the purse and called Mrs. Jessup in to identify it.

She brought in her younger daughter and her mother all three stated the purse was Georgia's. Using this purse and the other charges against

Schaefer for Trotter and Wells, Law Enforcement was able to get a search warrant for Mrs. Schaefer's house based on the Williams Rule.

The "Williams Rule" is based on the holding in the Florida State case of Williams v. State of Florida, 110 So. 2d 654 (Fla., 1959) in which relevant evidence of collateral crimes is admissible at jury trial when it does not go to prove the "bad character" or "criminal propensity" of the defendant but is used to show motive, intent, knowledge, modus operandi, or lack of mistake.

When law enforcement presented the affidavit to the Judge to sign he granted the warrant based on the purse, and Mrs. Place stating the blue green Datsun was the car her daughter and Georgia Jessup got into on Sept 27, 1972 and the fact that he was already serving time for Trotter and Wells.

Due to the fact the bodies were found in St. Lucie County, the search warrant affidavit was issued from that county for both Schaefer's residence in Stuart and his mother's residence at Riverland Rd in Fort Lauderdale.

Martin County Law Enforcement served the search warrant to Teresa Dean Schaefer, Gerard's wife at the residence in Stuart. Once the warrant was served, they backed off while Broward and St. Lucie County Law Enforcement searched the apartment. There apparently was no evidence seized at that residence.

However, this was not the case at the residence of Doris Schaefer, Gerard's mother. Trophies were found, evidence that would help to convict Gerard John Schaefer of two counts of murder and speculation of many others. This evidence was found in a steamer type trunk in a locked bedroom that Ms. Schaefer said belonged to her son

Among the evidence found at Mrs. Schaefer's residence were two gold crowned teeth, human bones, photographs of a nude male body, rope, a rifle, and a hunting knife.

Lt Yurchuck was part of the search team. He sat in the living room with Mrs. Schaefer while the evidence was being brought out of the bedroom. As each piece was placed in his hand for him to inventory, he would ask Mrs. Schaefer if she knew who the girls in the pictures were, if she had seen the jewelry before, if the gold jewelry box was familiar. Every time her answer was the same. "No." Part of the evidence, some teeth, were later identified as belonging to Collette Goodenough. But no one had reported her missing.

When all of the evidence was seized, they would find evidence, which opened a Pandora's Box of unsolved crimes. Among the evidence seized were hundreds of photographs that showed presumably dead females, views of crime scenes, as well as a photograph of a man tied up and dressed in women's underwear.

One of the most damming pieces of evidence was the photograph of a man in the nude suspended from a tree by a rope. The picture was an 8x10 photograph. At first the photograph appeared to be a woman in nylon stockings. The photograph appeared to show only the torso and the buttocks with a y- shaped scar on one cheek. The photo had been taken using a mirror to photograph the buttocks. So it looked like the picture was three-dimensional. Schaefer had such a scar on the same place.

There were two gold crowned teeth found in Schaefer's mother's house. Those teeth belonged to another missing female. There was jewelry taken into evidence that belong to even another missing female. There was a suede purse, driver's license, passports, and a journal found in Schaefer's room at the residence of his mother. There was a manuscript with hundreds of pages of handwritten and typewritten stories as well as hand drawn pictures of women hung and bound.

This manuscript described killings of a girl in Broward County. It also described "How to kill a woman in order to remain un-apprehended." Part of the manuscript detailed the hanging and sexual abuse of women. The pages were like a journal of

Schaefer's "good deeds" his imprint of leaving behind the good as opposed to the bad.

Anyone who has ever studied the criminal mind or profiled serial killers, know this type of behavior is typical of serial killers. They keep trophies. It is part of their narcissistic behavior. They use these trophies to relive their crime, to feel the excitement and gratification of the kill. The fantasy has become real and they have the trophy to prove it. They never believe they will be caught. It becomes a game of catch me if you can. When they tire of not being caught they do things to drive law enforcement to them. They want to share this newfound freedom. The new found game.

This thrill of having something that someone else is looking for. They truly believe they are smarter than the cop. They truly believe they have it all under control and that the rest of the world is stupid. Sometime this is the very thing that gets them caught. In Schaefer's case he pretended innocence. When that didn't work he pretended insanity, mental illness and selective memory loss. He tried the "evil twin" did it.

The revelation of this evidence sent a firestorm of phone calls from all over the country by law enforcement. The calls became so many that Lt. Yurchuck had to report daily to his supervisor.

Lt. Dave Yurchuck with the Broward County

Sheriff's Office made an appointment to visit Schaefer at Martin County Jail. The media went nuts. They all converged on the Martin County jail to write the story. Schaefer's lawyer went in first to tell Schaefer that Yurchuck was coming. When Yurchuck arrived he was told that the attorney had left and when he left he was extremely white faced. Shortly after that he dismissed himself as Schaefer's attorney. Schaefer refused to speak with Lt. Yurchuck.

CHAPTER TEN

GERARD JOHN SCHAEFER TRIES TO FIND A WAY OUT

Gerard Schaefer was granted a public defender after the evidence was taken from his room at his mother's house in Fort Lauderdale, and after Mrs. Place identified Schaefer as the man who took her daughter Susan Place to the beach. Added to the evidence was the tag that had been traced back to Schaefer.

Once Schaefer was added to the investigation for the death of Susan Place and Georgia Jessup, the possibility of being part of the work release program was no longer an option. From that moment Gerard Schaefer had control of his case. He called the shots. Schaefer immediately had his public defender Elton Schwarz find a psychiatrist to examine him. The reasoning behind this thought process was Schaefer's claim of being psychotic with suicidal tendencies. That psychiatrist was Dr. Robert C. Eaton.

Not only did Schaefer ask for the exam he asked to be "civilly committed."

His reasoning was if he could be found insane,

he could not be charged criminally. To add fuel to this fire, Schaefer's mother and wife got in on the act.

They filed a request that Schaefer be civilly committed. Maybe they thought there was strength in numbers. If the request were to be granted Schaefer would be committed for a minimum of six months. This was just another ploy on Schaefer's part to keep him from being charged with murder.

Robert Stone, the State Attorney for the 19th Judicial Circuit appeared before Circuit Court Judge C. Pfeiffer Trowbridge and requested that another psychiatrist examine Schaefer. Judge Trowbridge granted the request. The psychiatrist was Dr. Mordecai Haper of Fort Pierce. Dr. Haper made the determination that Schaefer was dangerous and in need of more evaluation. This was the deciding factor for sending Schaefer to the State Mental Hospital Chattahoochee in North Florida.

All of the players were in place to keep Schaefer from being charged with the murder of Susan Place and Georgia Jessup and there were players in place to keep that from happening.

Gerard John Schaefer knew that in 1971 the "Baker Act" was developed in Florida.

The Baker Act came into existence to prohibit the indiscriminate admission of persons to state institutions or the retention of persons without just cause. The Baker Act mandated court-appointed attorneys to represent each person for whom involuntary placement was sought and provided for independent reviews every six months for all involuntary placements. The new law established a patients' bill of rights to communicate with whomever they wished to receive and send unopened mail, to use their own possessions and to vote, among other rights. The law also prohibited the placement of persons with mental illnesses in jails, unless they had committed criminal acts. (Unknown, 2002)

Schaefer was going to use the last part of the Baker Act to keep him from being charged with the deaths of Susan Place and Georgia Jessup. If he could be proven mentally ill he would be committed under a civil act and he would not be charged for the murders. Added to the request to be admitted to the institution for evaluation was a form that asked if he had ever been hospitalized for a mental disorder, and his answer was no.

However, on a separate sheet of paper were the names of five psychiatrists in Broward County that Schaefer had seen since 1967. The list noted group therapy at Florida Atlantic University in 1968 and 1969. There was also reference to a "suicide note" in F.A.U. medical records in 1968. The last piece to the puzzle was a psychiatric test by the Broward County

Sheriff's Department in 1972. It is this writer's opinion that he may have felt that with all this evidence, he was a slam-dunk for being admitted to the state mental institution.

Elton Schwarz the public defender for the 19th Judicial Circuit played into Schaefer's plans with the ability of a home run hitter in a World Series game. When the local paper interviewed Schwarz he told the interviewer, that Schaefer's suicidal tendencies were not as strong as they had been. He said there was reason to believe that Schaefer would soon be going to Chattahoochee (the State Mental Hospital located near Tallahassee). Schwarz also said that Schaefer didn't have any conscious knowledge of committing the crimes. He said that all of the media attention concerning the murders had aggravated Schaefer's conditions.

Schwarz was quoted as saying, "Anyone locked up in jail, hearing that he is being investigated in connection with so gruesome a happening would be a candidate for the funny farm whether they actually did it or not."

Schaefer played the locked up in jail card very well. He used Elton Schwarz, his attorney, as his unsuspecting pawn, in this game of "catch me if you can". Schwarz was quoted as saying that he felt Schaefer could not get a fair trial anywhere on the east coast of Florida because of all of the publicity he had already received and he had not even been charged. He also stated that Schaefer needed to get into a mental institution before he had a "mental breakdown". Schwarz continued by saying that he had noticed a marked change in Schaefer's attitude. Schwarz said Schaefer had become extremely distrustful of everyone. That he was apprehensive and he appeared pale from the lack of sun.

Schwarz appeared to imply that Schaefer had been trying to receive "help" since May 1968. He referred to some psychological testing which had been done on Schaefer during that time. He was going to use this testing as a basis to have Schaefer committed for evaluation.

Schwarz stated that the evaluation in 1968 read in part…" This is indicative of decreased ego control and of impairment in reality testing, which is often found among psychotics or in pathology…. It is suggested that the nature of his reported alteration of consciousness be further investigated through additional psychiatric and neurological evaluation."

Schwarz also stated that Schaefer had tried to get the help he needed but could not afford continuing treatment. He added that a Dr. C.W. Long had reported to the selective service administration that Schaefer was "emotionally unstable" and that "even with weekly treatments, he would make a poor risk for any division of military service...that even with minimal stress he would suffer a complete mental breakdown." Elton Schwarz and Gerard Schaefer had laid the groundwork for Schaefer's commitment to Chattahoochee when the other shoe dropped.

State Attorney Robert Stone had been busy doing his homework. On May 18, 1973, he dropped the other shoe. Stone assembled the grand jury, which was still in session and presented them with enough evidence to bring the charges of two counts of first-degree murder against Gerard Schaefer. Then he and his team worked through most of the night to put the charges together before the appearance in court the following morning. They knew if Schaefer got to Chattahoochee before he was charged they couldn't touch him for at least six months.

He went into court and announced that Gerard John Schaefer was being charged with the first-degree murder of Susan Place and Georgia Jessup. This announcement stunned Schaefer and his attorney Elton Schwarz. They were under the impression that Schaefer was working on a civil voluntary commitment to a mental institution. State Attorney Stone killed that action by the charges he had filed.

The language of the charges as they were read to the court –"Gerard John Schaefer did unlawfully and feloniously from a premeditated design to effect the death of Susan Carol Place, a human being, did kill and murder her, the said Susan Carol Place, by inflicting wounds and injuries in a manner, means or by an instrumentally unknown to the state attorney, from which said wounds and injuries the said Susan Carol Place did languish and die…" The second count against Schaefer was worded the same as the first count the only difference was that Georgia Jessup was named as the victim. (Fryer, Accused Double Murderer Will Fly to Chattahoochee, 1973)

Gerard Schaefer would not be going to Chattahoochee under a civil commitment. He would be going under a criminal commitment to see if it could be determined that he was not insane and that he was competent to stand trial for the senseless murders of Susan Place and Georgia Jessup of Fort Lauderdale, Fl.

CHAPTER ELEVEN

THE MENTAL HEALTH TWO STEP

When State Attorney Robert Stone threw the curve ball in court on May 18, 1973 and openly formally charged Gerard Schaefer with two counts of First Degree Murder, he threw Schaefer and company into a two left feet dance. Schaefer was all set to be admitted voluntarily for at least six months under a civil action. He would have to perform a different style of dance. He could no longer waltz. He had to learn how to two-step.

Schaefer stated that he had no involvement with the Blind Creek Murders. But he alluded to the crime by telling the court that he wanted "help and treatment for the mental problems that he knows he has." Schaefer's attorney Elton Schwarz followed Schaefer's lead by saying that Schaefer's goal was to reach the day "when he can return to our society as a useful member." (Quina, Lawyer: Schaefer Desires, Needs Mental Health Care, 1973) (Unknown, 2002)

Attorney Schwarz made the statement that he didn't believe his client was guilty, but he did think that Schaefer was in need of mental health treatment. Schwarz backed up that statement by saying he had examined some of the evidence and talked with psychiatrists and based on what he had read and heard, he felt Schaefer was not guilty, but he was mentally sick.

Schaefer again led the dance. Schwarz when interviewed by the local paper stated that Schaefer was better than he had been. He was no longer considering suicide.

Schwarz was quoted as saying; He (Schaefer) seems to have much more control of himself now than he did when we took him to Dr. Eaton. However, I think the slightest little emotional disturbance could reverse the entire situation." (Quina, Lawyer: Schaefer Desires, Needs Mental Health Care, 1973)

Schwarz continued with his defense of Schaefer, "If he had been involved, or consciously been involved, in any of these murders. I don't think he would have been able to maintain his composure as well as has." (Quina, Lawyer: Schaefer Desires, Needs Mental Health Care, 1973) (Chattahoochee)

Judge Trowbridge joined the mental health dance when he ordered Schaefer to Chattahoochee. State Attorney Stone also joined the dance when he told the judge that the order had been under a civil action and since Schaefer had been charged with two charges of First Degree Murder he should be assigned three psychiatrists to examine Schaefer.

Elton Schwarz, Schaefer's attorney, took the lead. He told the court that the 30-day evaluation Judge Trowbridge had ordered had nothing to do with the two murder charges. He went on to tell the Judge that Chattahoochee had room for Schaefer now. Judge Trowbridge took the final lead in this dance of mental health "Two step." He told Schwarz that Schaefer would go to Chattahoochee, however, in thirty days he would be returned to the Martin County jail where he was still serving time for the aggravated assault on Nancy Trotter and Susan Wells.

State Attorney Phil Shailer, who had been assigned to assist Stone, stepped up and started a new dance. He told the court that if Schaefer were transferred to Chattahoochee, the state would have a problem unless Schaefer first had a "rights hearing" within 24 hours of the murder charges being filed.

Shailer's argument was struck down when Judge Trowbridge took over the lead of the new dance of "Tango" when he stated he had not determined the man to be insane. Trowbridge went on to say the question of insanity was a matter to be taken up in criminal proceedings. The order for the commitment was to have Schaefer examined for mental illness. Judge Trowbridge stated the state was willing to help get the evaluation and he could not think of any better way to prepare for questions about his mental condition than for those observations and tests to be performed.

Judge Trowbridge called a 20-minute recess. It was time to take a break and re-group.

When all the players returned to court, Gerard Schaefer told Judge Trowbridge, that Elton Schwarz was his attorney for this case. His reason was he had no money for a lawyer. Apparently Schaefer believed that Schwarz knew how to lead this dance of "Two step."

Schwarz, immediately started a new dance routine, one this writer would call the "Bob and Weave." He requested bail for Schaefer on the basis that murder charges were not a capital offense, since the death penalty was not in effect in the State of Florida at the time it was believed the two young women were killed.

Judge Trowbridge bobbed when Schwarz wanted him to weave.

He told Schwarz, it would be inconsistent to set bond. But he told Schwarz that he could ask for bond when Schaefer returned from his 30-day evaluation.

The dance of words, and motions were finally over. On May 21, 1973, Gerard Schaefer left for a command performance at Chattahoochee the State of Florida's Mental Health Facility. He would only be there 30 days for evaluation and treatment.

CHAPTER TWELVE

SCHAEFER GOES FROM DANCING TO SINGING

Before Schaefer left for Chattahoochee his lawyer Elton Schwarz told the Tribune the rumors allegedly perpetrated by State Attorney Bob Stone were not true. The rumor being that Schaefer was hiring F. Lee Bailey to represent him. Stone had stated that he had a letter from Schaefer to his mother asking for Bailey. The question is was that yet another ploy by Schaefer for media attention? Did he think that Bailey would be retained free? He had already been assigned a public defender because he was indigent. Did he think because he had been a cop that Bailey a renowned high profile criminal lawyer from California would really come to South Florida and represent him? Was his ego that inflated? Did he really believe he was that important? Or was all of this part of his media hype to help inflate his guise of innocence?

On May 21, 1973, Gerard Schaefer boarded a small plane to be flown up to North Florida near the Georgia border. He was being admitted to the Chattahoochee Mental Facility that was located in the town of Chattahoochee in the panhandle of Northwest Florida.

The State Hospital is located on the site of an old civil war arsenal built in 1834 just below the junction of the Flint and Chattahoochee River. It was built to command the shipping on the Apalachicola River. The U.S. Army built the arsenal to be used as an arms depot during the second Seminole Indian War. Between 1865 and 1868 it was the State's first penitentiary. In 1861 the first action of the Civil War in Florida took place at this location when a militia unit from Quincy took the arsenal from it garrison of soldiers. Later the confederates used the arsenal for a training camp. Only two of the original buildings still stand. The Officer's Quarters which is now the Florida State Hospital Administration Building and a Powder Magazine, which is being restored to be used as a museum and conference center. Until 1947 Chattahoochee was the only state mental hospital in the state of Florida and today it is still the largest. (Chattahoochee)

Schaefer had thirty days to be evaluated to determine what exactly might be wrong with him. The dance wasn't working so Schaefer and company decided to try singing.

As Schaefer was waiting to boards the plane he was allowed to speak with reporters. He used this spotlight to begin his begin his career in oratory remarks to plead his case of innocence. As he was waiting, he smiled at reporters and answered their questions. He appeared to be charming, and affable. He carried in his handcuffed hands a black book. When he was asked what it was he stated it was a book called "Run Baby Run." This book was by the same author who had written "The Cross and the Switchblade." He made it a point to tell the reporter a minister had given him the book.

Schaefer begin his singing to the press with a song of how good he had been treated in jail. His second verse was how ready he was to go to Chattahoochee. The chorus was, "they can get to the bottom of this thing, if there is a bottom to it." He changed tunes saying if the reporter wanted to say anything about him (Schaefer) to say that he was innocent of all the charges. Schaefer added the tune of poor me when he talked of being in jail and how being falsely accused was very stressful. He included the second verse of how hard it was on his wife. Schaefer went to the third verse with she appeared to be holding up all right. Schaefer then sang the chorus of this pitiful me song, his decline of physical health when he told the reporter he had caught a cold in jail. As he started to board he changed his tune to a more upbeat verse of how much better he would be once he got to

Chattahoochee. He knew they would take good care of him.

CHAPTER THIRTEEN

MAY 21- JUNE 21, 1973

SCHAEFER'S SOJOURN AT CHATTAHOOCHEE

Gerard Schaefer arrived at Chattahoochee for the court appointed evaluation. Twenty-seven days later, Schaefer was again allowed to use the news media as his stage to expound his words of innocence and injustice of the judicial system.

Pat Quina, with the News Tribune, went to Chattahoochee to see Schaefer. She had previously interviewed him at the Martin County Jail. He played this interview for all he thought it was worth. He met with Quina in the visiting wing of the forensic ward on Wednesday June 13, 1973. Sitting with Schaefer were his lawyer Elton Schwarz and Dr. Hector Gianni.

When asked if he remembered Ms. Quina he was quick to reply he remembered her well. This opened the door for him to use his craft of cunning, charm and lies to win over Ms. Quina and to spin a web of victimization and pity. Schaefer began his monologue with the statement of how she had scared him the first time he spoke to her at the Martin County Jail. He emphasized she really scared him.

This statement was a prelude of things to come during the interview. Schaefer had a captive audience and he played to it well.

Here was a person who knew how to manipulate people and who knew how to play mind games. Schaefer knew which emotional buttons to push in order to gain the sympathy of his audience. He set the stage for his act of "being the victim". He added charm to his statement when he appeared to innocently explain why Ms. Quina had frightened him so badly. She was the big bad wolf to his Little Red Riding Hood.

Schaefer's cell at Martin County Jail had consisted of solid concrete block walls with openings into the cells covered with solid metal doors. Quina had to interview Schaefer by speaking through a small circular window in the door. He used this confinement to add to his belief of his victimization. It was the perfect stage for his alleged fear.

Schaefer wove his explanations of his fear of Ms. Quina for his audience. He began by saying when she came to visit him the first time at Martin County jail he hadn't understood how she was able to gain access to visit. She was a stranger. Schaefer stated in the interview that he had not seen many visitors. He told all in the room that he might not have jumped when he saw Ms. Quina if he had seen the guard come back. Apparently he had not understood why he was being left alone with this strange woman.

He compared himself to an animal in that his fear was from animal instinct. Schaefer went on to state the animal instinct came from being locked up and having to look through a hole in the door. He punctuated his statement by adding that having no contact with the outside world created that feeling. Then he went one step further after this statement with one that was even more outlandish and absurd because he had been allowed visitors while in jail. His wife Teresa and his mother Doris had visited him every day. His attorney also had unlimited access to him. Schaefer continued with "When you don't have any human contact after being used to having a lot of human contact, it breaks you down so that your more basic nature becomes apparent." (Quina, 1973)Schaefer had only spent from July until September behind bars at the Martin County jail. He played that card well.

Schaefer finished his performance with a statement completely out of left field. One that not only bordered on absurd it reeked of obsession. He explained the reason he was scared of Quina. The day of that interview he thought she was a spy for Robert Stone, the State Attorney. Schaefer had fixated on Robert Stone as his nemesis. Stone was quickly becoming the reason Schaefer was "the victim." The premise which Schaefer based his belief of Ms. Quina as Stone's spy was the fact he had looked out of the window and had seen her run to her car after her interview with him. He assumed she had been sent there to get a confession. He ended this performance by telling Ms. Quina she had appeared very happy with herself after her interview with him. In his mind this only quantified his belief that she was Robert Stone's minion.

Schaefer changed gears. He went from the "I was so afraid to I'm happy to be here card." The being "here" was Chattahoochee. He went from the caged animal to the free bird performance. He explained about the simple joy of being able to not only see his wife but to visit with her without the restrictions of bars between them. He elaborated about how he was able to hold his wife Teresa's hand, and "you know talk, love words." (Quina, 1973)

Schaefer put such a spin on his poor pitiful me routine he had Pat Quina eating out of his hand. In her newspaper article she stated that it didn't take long in talking with Schaefer to realize he was an intelligent, reflective man. She expanded this line of thought by saying that even though Schaefer was facing two charges of murder, he still had the capability to laugh and much of his conversation included philosophical, religion, law enforcement, prison reform and last but not least man's inhumanity to man. He continued to spin his web of lies and deceit when he told all in the interview that he had a serious mental problem. However, he was quick to add that his mental problem was never apparent when he was being interviewed. Ms. Quina played into that spin full force. She stated in her article, the whole time she was interviewing Schaefer he never exhibited even the slightest hint of mental problems. However, Ms. Quina pointedly stated there one thing which stayed with her long after the interview. During the interview with Schaefer his gaze remained fixed. It never wavered or changed. She went on to explain, when Schaefer was asking or answering a question he had a very intense stare. However, Ms. Quina was quick to point out she saw nothing beyond that intense gaze. It was just his eyes. She said, "Only the eyes, the gaze, leave you asking questions." (Quina, 1973)

It was as if Schaefer was the puppet master and Ms. Quina his puppet. One minute she saw the polite, charming, charismatic man. Later she saw glimpses of the evil that lurked just beneath the surface. She couldn't quite reach that person. For the most part Schaefer kept that person well hidden. He had an agenda. That agenda was to use Ms. Quina and the newspaper to his advantage. He wanted to appear the injured party. He needed the sympathy of the public, especially women to win his case.

Gerard Schaefer began to spin his web of pity and self-analysis when the interview started. He appeared to have already decided what his problem was and why it had not been taken care of. He said he knew he had problems and that his problems started when he was twelve years old. He followed that statement by saying he knew he was different from other people. He had "certain ways". (Quina, 1973)

Schaefer continued with his self- analysis by admitting to all in the room, he was not a gregarious person, nor was he not a joiner. He went on to say his remark sounded very depreciating. Schaefer added to the ambiance of the intimate setting by speaking softly as he appeared almost shyly talking about himself. He played the "well, I am a loner, and I don't think along the status lines of social conformity" card. He also threw in the "I have trouble with fitting into organized religion" chip. As if to add credence to the self-analysis of himself, he added a statement, which was supposedly stated by another patient. He said, "One guy in my ward says I'm a heretic and should be burned at the stake. I am a Catholic. I'm not a devout Roman Catholic. I'm a nominal Catholic." He explained he tried to take the best part of all religions in the world and incorporate them into his own philosophy- which in his mind meant "Love God above all things and your fellow man as you love yourself." He tried to explain to all in the room he was an altruist.

He wanted to help people. Schaefer said he originally wanted to be a teacher. However, he blamed "the people" for not letting him teach. He said they didn't feel he would make a good teacher.

Schaefer told all his second choice was to become a law enforcement officer. He said he wanted to "gain a deeper knowledge of law from the law enforcement side. In his "reality" he had aspirations of becoming a lawyer. He showed he had delusions of grandeur. He said he was "blessed with a reasonable amount of intelligence." (Quina, 1973) If that statement were true, this writer wonders why he chose to kill and mutilate females. He did have a very high IQ.

Schaefer's reality and his truth came through in his next statement. "You can be disconnected mentally or emotionally, and still be intelligent. I am able to sit down and read a good book by Plato, or Aristotle or Dante or St. Thomas Aquinas and enjoy it while at the same time I see a doctor for a problem that exists in my personality, which I have no control over." Then he begins to back- peddle and says, "Well, I guess I should delete that and say that I don't know that I have any control over it the problem." (Quina, 1973)

Schaefer attempted to cover up a layer of himself, which he had let slide out with his revelation that he might have multiple personalities. He said that everybody was schizoid, but that some people were more than others.

He continued to work damage control by saying he wanted to get rid of his problem. He tried to justify himself by adding it was a bit unusual however, he didn't feel it was all that bad.

Schaefer decided it was time to play doctor to the maximum mid-way through the interview. He began to give further details about his "problem". Explaining the "problem", when it manifested itself in physical, anti-social forms, could then be bad. However, he justified it by saying that as long as stayed on a fantasy level it served a useful purpose. That useful purpose prevented a person from becoming overtly hostile in society. (Quina, 1973)

He continued, "You know if you can fantasize something away and can play games with yourself, this takes away the necessity to play games with other people, and if the games happen to be hostile or against society's grain, then you're better off playing in your own sandbox than going off and playing in theirs."

Continuing, Schaefer said, " There's an element of society that thinks I'm some sort of a maniac, or something- that I've gone around and murdered, or am responsible for the disappearances of some people. Anyway, this element of society prevents me from being as open and frank as I'd like to be with you because I have to worry about them. If they have an opportunity to put a shaft to me so to speak, they're going to do it."

Ending this monologue Schaefer told Ms. Quina, "Once all of this is cleared up, then I will really give you a good story- Pat Quina exclusive one on one." (Quina, Schaefer Denies Guilt, Admits Problems, 1973)

During the interview Schaefer was asked what he thought his reaction might be if he were found guilty of the murder charges and then given a life in prison sentence. Schaefer's response appeared to be conflicting.

He said, "Considering the fact that I didn't do this thing, I don't expect to be convicted. But if I was sentenced to life in prison, I would probably cop out. I would probably kill myself, frankly, I would."

Then he continued with "If I would be going to a mental hospital where I could be receiving treatment, or where my mind could be improved, or where I could receive some sort of a positive treatment toward recovery, I could see that. But as to just stagnating the rest of your life away in a little cubicle somewhere, it's not worth it. I 'd go along with my chance that there is a hereafter, and that it's better than here." (Quina, Schaefer Denies Guilt, Admits Problems, 1973)

Schaefer implied that he would not object to being confined to a mental institution. He was building his case for empathy with his statement of "killing himself." He wanted to be committed. He knew he would be out in due time. He knew if he were committed he would eventually be a free man.

He pled his case of wanting to be committed further when he said, "I'm sure that there would be some sort of a useful thing that I could do in a place like this hospital. I have a certain degree of medical training. I am licensed to teach in the State of Florida and there are a lot of things I could do. I could teach people to read and write. I could do something useful."

Schaefer made it quite plain that he didn't want to go to Raiford Prison. He explains this by saying "Being confined in an institution like this (meaning Chattahoochee) would not nearly be as bad as being confined in an institution such as Raiford where you're treated as less than human."

He continued with his plea, "I've never been

there, but this is an observation based on what I've heard from people who've come from there- that Raiford is the end of the world. Jail is nothing more than a torture chamber or a den of iniquity, or a hell on earth" (Quina, Schaefer Denies Guilt, Admits Problems, 1973) Somewhere along the line Gerard Schaefer appeared to forget that he had produced a torture chamber in the mangroves, and underbrush on Hutchinson Island. He appeared to forget he had already made a hell on earth for Susan Place and Georgia Jessup.

Schaefer added his advice on things which could be done with society misfits by saying, "There's a lot that can be done with society misfits, if only society will realize that these are not people you put away and lock up in dungeons. They are human beings who have feelings, who should be re-introduced into society as well as they're capable of being."

Did Schaefer really believe he was a misfit instead of a cold-bloodied killer? Did he in his twisted mind think that he was not all to blame for the deaths of Georgia Jessup and Susan Place or the many other missing and dead girls?

Gerard Schaefer used one last opportunity to show the injustice of the judicial system and his non-accountability for his actions. He ended the interview on a blame the judge note.

He said, "At my own sentencing last December for the aggravated assault charge, the judge said something about what I did was crazy, or maybe he said 'what you've done is insane.' I think it would have been a much more intelligent decision on his behalf to sentence me to psychiatric treatment, on an out-patient basis and have me on a work release program, where I could be under the supervision of the probation and parole commission, rather than letting me sit in jail for six months, serving absolutely no purpose at all, except to be a drain on society."

What Judge Smith actually stated to Schaefer was in fact not that at all. He said, "It is beyond this court's imagination to conceive how you were such a foolish and automatic jackass as you were in this case…. We (meaning the judicial system) reached a unanimous opinion that you acted foolishly. I can't understand how a man of your background can do such a foolish thing. You can't be a fool as far as the court is concerned. The state attorney went the last mile in dropping the other charges. I am going the last mile in trying to put you on the work release program. I could have sent you to state prison." (Fryer, Former Deputy Sentenced for Stringing up Teenage Girls, 1972)

Gerard Schaefer somehow forgot that conversation on December 24, 1972 when Judge

Smith sentenced him to six months in the county jail and three years of probation. He twisted the Judge's words and changed them to make him "the victim". Schaefer conveniently forgot that three other charges against him had been dropped and that two of those charges were for kidnapping. He was given a very light sentence compared to what he could have served. However, Schaefer never saw that he only saw what he wanted to see and heard what he wanted to hear.

The question that remained to be answered that hot, humid day in June was whether or not Gerard John Schaefer was sane or insane.

Pat Quina left Chattahoochee after the interview with Schaefer with conflicted feelings and thoughts about Gerard John Schaefer and his innocence or guilt. In some of her last statements in her article dated Sunday June 17,1973 for the News Tribune, Ms. Quina had this to say, " I come away from Schaefer interviews, convinced that the field of psychiatry has let him down simply because he couldn't afford his problems, as he told me this week. I keep wondering what would or would not have happened during the past five years if Schaefer had been admitted to a mental hospital back in 1968 when he told a psychiatrist that he was having grave problems with some of his sexual-related fantasies." (Quina, Schaefer Says News Tribune Reporter

Scared Him in First Meeting, 1973)

She closed with this thought, "People ask me constantly if I feel Schaefer is guilty of any of the alleged murders. All I can reply is not the man who talks to you philosophically. Not that Schaefer. And the other Schaefer? He is so sick, which Schaefer readily admits. The question I always ask is this one, "What exactly happened to produce the mixed up confused, mentally ill world of fantasy about which Gerard John Schaefer is so confused. What happened to him, way back long ago? I think a lot of parents, journalists, attorneys, and psychiatrists would like that question answered." (Quina, Schaefer Says News Tribune Reporter Scared Him in First Meeting, 1973)

Schaefer had succeeded in the game of manipulation, charm and the twisting of statements to raise doubt in her mind. If she doubted then the public would most defiantly doubt that he was guilty.

CHAPTER FOURTEEN

THE BATTLE OF THE LAWYERS

Those left in St. Lucie County set the wheels in motion for several legal venues. First Judge C. Pfeiffer Trowbridge was named to sit the bench for the trial. Apparently Judge D. C. Smith, the chief justice of the circuit had requested Judge Trowbridge be the presiding judge.

Elton Schwarz made a "Demand for Discovery". He wanted to be provided with all the names and addresses of all persons known to the prosecutor who would have information that might be relevant to the offense charged. He also wanted any written or recorded statement, which was made by the accused and known to the state, with the name and address of each witness to the statement. He asked for any tangible papers or objects that were obtained from or belonged to the accused. Schwarz continued with his requests by asking for any material or information, which has been provided by a confidential informant. He wanted any electronic surveillance including wiretapping on the premises of the accused or the conversations to which the accused was a party. Schwarz asked if there had been any search or seizure on any documents relating to the crime.

Finally he asked for reports of statements of experts made in connection with the particular case, including results of physical or mental examinations and of scientific tests, experiments or comparisons.

Elton Schwarz added to the circus that was Schaefer. The defense team which consisted of Elton Schwarz, Bruce Colton along with the State Attorney Robert Stone and Philip Shailer spent many hours in Fort Lauderdale taking depositions for trial.

Elton Schwarz carried a county checkbook and when he got to Fort Lauderdale, he went into a camera shop and spent about a $1000.00 for camera equipment. He bought a camera, and a tripod to hold the camera on to photograph from the table. He wanted pictures of all the witnesses including the police involved in the investigation. This didn't bode well with law enforcement. Elton's reasoning was he wanted a face to go with the depositions.

Robert Stone, the State Attorney did his part. He told a reporter due to the wide spread media coverage he didn't feel that acceptable jurors would be found. He felt that maybe the trial could be held in Okeechobee County. He told the local Kiwanis Club because of the media attention a fair trial would be impossible.

Elton Schwarz quickly jumped on the bandwagon. He accused Stone of grandstanding. He said Stone was using the case to promote the re-instatement of the death penalty. The mud- slinging had begun.

Judge Trowbridge set a court date of June 22, 1973 for the hearing of Schaefer's competency to stand trial. Dr. Hector Gianni had been subpoenaed to the hearing to testify about Schaefer's mental condition. Dr. Gianni had been Schaefer's doctor of record at Chattahoochee.

However, Dr. Gianni indicated to Pat Quina, a reporter for The News Tribune he needed another thirty days to evaluate his patient. He told her he had learned quite a bit, however he felt in order to render a valid opinion he needed more time.

Dr. Gianni continued that he felt Schaefer wanted help; however, he had not received the manuscripts Schaefer had allegedly written until a week before he was supposed to testify. This tactic may be been used to keep Schaefer in Chattahoochee for a while longer.

On June 22, 1973 the hearing became a three-ring circus. Judge Trowbridge denied Schaefer the extra thirty-day confinement at Chattahoochee.

He said sending him there in the first place might have been a mistake. The standard operating procedure was to have the prisoner examined at the county jail or in a doctor's office. The judge continued by stating three psychiatrists and that had already examined Schaefer was more than sufficient to determine his sanity. He stated he had been more than lenient in allowing Schaefer to be committed in the first place.

Schaefer had been calm and collected up until that point. He was dressed in blue jeans and a blue and yellow striped T-shirt. He wore his wedding band on the second finger of his left hand. During most of the hearing he sat with his chin in his hand, almost as if he were not interested in the proceedings. He and Teresa his wife exchanged warm smiles throughout the hearing. She sat next to Schaefer's grey haired mother Doris. That day Doris was wearing a blue and white polka dot blouse, white mini-skirt and white knee- length boots. Schaefer had been smiling and very placid until the decision by the judge sent him to take the floor with an act of extreme anger. When he heard the Judge's decision he clenched both his fists, shook them and shot quiet angry words at his lawyer, Elton Schwarz.

Schaefer was so enraged he called Robert Stone a name as he (Stone) walked back to the prosecutor's table after making a motion to the judge. The name-calling was so loud it was heard several rows back in the spectators section.

When Stone called Schwarz to task for failing

to keep his client under control, Schaefer said, "You're dammed right I called you a name. And I'll call you another one too." (Quina, Schaefer Warned after Outburst, 1973)

This outburst led Judge Trowbridge to warn Schaefer if he had another one he would be removed from the courtroom. Even though Schaefer remained quite the rest of the hearing he was nonetheless very grim. However, he played to the crowd by nodding to his wife Teresa from time to time.

Not to be outdone in this media frenzy, Assistant State Attorney Richard Purdy, from Broward County, had to get into the act. He pushed for a motion to Judge Trowbridge to allow the state to enter into evidence a deposition from Fort Lauderdale News Reporter Yvette Cordozo. She had interviewed Schaefer at Chattahoochee.

Judge Trowbridge exploded. He said, "Are you trying to tell me that a newspaper reporter is going to inform me if the doctors need more time?"

Purdy taking his life in his hands replied, "Yes. The reading of her deposition will make it obvious that there is no further need for evaluation. The reading of the deposition makes it painfully obvious."

Trowbridge replied, "Miss Cordozo is an expert in her field of endeavor, but I think I'll not accept her opinion".

The longhaired Purdy pushed the Judge's button even more when he balked. This caused the Judge to blast out at him.

He said, "Don't argue with my ruling, or you'll be evicted from the courtroom." (Quina, Schaefer Denied Further Testing, 1973)

Dr. Mordecai Habor a forensic psychiatrist was not left out of the Judge's stinging wrath. When Dr. Habor was on the witness stand, he was instructed not to tell the court his opinion about Schaefer competency to stand trial. Dr. Habor decided not to heed the judge's stern warning.

He opened with "Based on my opinion, the man's mentally competent." (Quina, Schaefer Denied Further Testing, 1973)

Judge Trowbridge ordered his statement stricken from the record. To add insult to injury he gave the state ten days to amend the information filed against Schaefer.

The state had charged Schaefer with the slayings of Susan Place age 17 and Georgia Jessup, 16. The hang up on the information were the dates the state alleged the crimes took place. If the information stated they were killed after December 8, 1972 then a grand jury would have to convene and return an indictment against Schaefer since first-degree murder became punishable by death after December 4, 1972.

Prior to December 4, 1972 the United States Supreme Court had ruled the death penalty unconstitutional. The two young women had disappeared from their home on September 27, 1972 and were not seen again until their bodies were discovered April 1, 1973. The state had alleged that the girls were murdered between Sept 27, 1972 and Jan 15, 1973.

The final act of this judicial circus came when court was dismissed for the day. Before Schaefer was led away by the deputies he was allowed to kiss both his mother and his wife.

CHAPTER FIFTEEN

THE LEGAL WAR BEGINS

With every capital crime there is a dance in the legal world of lawyers, defendants, and evidence or lack of evidence. The State files the charges. They say they have all the evidence they need for a conviction. The defense demands discovery. They look at all the evidence the state has gathered.

The State of Florida has very liberal discovery rules. The State must turn over any and all evidence, statements, etc. good or bad for the defendant or for the State's case. In other words there can be no ambush by either party. The defendant has to turn over witness lists, witness statements, etc. to the state. Federal Courts on the other hand are more conservative.

Then the defense file motions for dismissal on the grounds there is not enough to convict. The state stands its ground. The defense files more motions for dismissal changing the language of the motion. This dance was played out in the Month of May 1973.

Once Schaefer appeared in front of Judge Trowbridge, and stated he was indigent, Judge

Trowbridge assigned Elton Schwarz as his public defender.

Mr. Schwarz had only previously represented Schaefer when it was believed that he would be going to the state mental institution as a civil matter. Once Mr. Schwarz was assigned as the public defender for Schaefer, he filed five motions for dismissal.

The first motion for dismissal was "The allegations of the information do not charge the defendant with a violation of any law of the State of Florida. The information is so vague, indefinite and uncertain that the defendant is not apprised of what he is called on to defend against at the trial of this cause. The second motion read as follows "The information fails to meet and comply with the legal requirements of the Florida Constitution and the fifth, sixth, and 14th Amendments of the United States Constitution. The third motion stated "The prosecution for the offenses charged therein fails to comply with the provisions of Rule 3.140(a) Fla. Criminal P.R. Rules, in that; if the offense is alleged to have occurred subsequent to Dec 12, 1973 prosecution thereof must be by indictment rather than information. The fourth motion was "Misjoiner of unrelated offenses in several counts of the information. Finally the last motion was listed as "The motion for a statement of particulars asks that the state attorney be required to "specify the place, date and all other material facts of the crime charged as are within the knowledge of the state and with such particularity as may be necessary in order to properly prepare a defense to the charges set forth therein. Including but not limited to, the time and date of death of the individuals referred to therein, the cause of death, and the means or instrumentality by which such death was affected or caused."

Three of these motions were considered "routine grounds" to preserve the record. The fifth motion was filed because Schwarz believed there was no indication that the two deaths were related or had occurred at the same time. The fourth motion was made because Schwarz felt that Schaefer should have been brought before a grand jury. All motions were struck down.

The reason Gerard Schaefer had not been brought before the grand jury was the death penalty had been ruled unconstitutional therefore a person charged with first degree murder did not have to appear in front of the grand jury. However, Schwarz's argument was the death penalty had been re-instated December 1972, hence the need to appear in front of the grand jury.

The last two motions appeared to be almost an oxymoron- First Schwarz files a motion that the state must prove the deaths happened, how they happened and where they happened. Then he files the motion that in order for Schaefer to be charged, he should have appeared in front of the grand jury because the death penalty was re-instated Dec. 1972 a full two months after the murders occurred. (Unknown, 1973)

The last stand was that Schwarz demanded all the evidence the state had collected. The state had until June 2, 1973 to comply.

State Attorney Robert Stone began to gather the list of Witnesses he planned to call at the trial. This included 97 people who had information that might be relevant to the state's case against Gerard John Schaefer.

Included in this list of names was Pat Quina. She had interviewed Schaefer while he was at Martin County Jail when the charges of murder were first filed. She also interviewed him during his stay at Chattahoochee. Stone added Bob Fryer, a reporter for the Stuart News, and Michael Tschudi of the Palm Beach Post. Stone included former Martin County Sheriff Robert Crowder, Martin County Sheriff James Holt, Sgt. William Scott, Sheriff's department, William H. Holly, Calvin Wiggins, Jesse Joe Holly, Detective Gene Hinton, sheriff's department, Sgt. H.O. Thompson, sheriff's department, Sgt. Bart Kanuff, sheriff's department, James F. Littman, Esq., Carol Deal, and Bruce

Colton, Assistant Public Defender.

Stone also put on his list Ben Mallard, Lt. Pat Duval, Sgt. Rick Browning, Chief Deputy Fenn Parrish, Lt. Al Test, Det. Sgt. Aaron Richardson, Deputy James Carter, Sgt. George H. Miller, Sheriff Lanie Norvell, Capt. Wayne Scambler, Deputy Steve Williams, Deputy Anderson and Sgt. Bill Boyd all of these witnesses were with the St. Lucie County Sheriff's Department.

From the Mental Health Clinic Attorney Stone had listed Kenneth Conrad and Dr. R.C. Eaton.

Nancy Ellen Trotter and Pamela Sue Wells would be the State's star witnesses. They would tell of the horror the day they were abducted. Robert Stone added insult to injury when he added Teresa Dean Schaefer, who was the current wife of Schaefer and also his ex-wife Martha Fogg Schaefer Mara. (Quina, Stone Lists 97 Witnesses in Case Against Schaefer, 1973) The Chief Investigator Jack Sewell was left off the witness list. The reason being he was seated at the prosecution table coordinating the evidence and witnesses and any other matters that needed to be handled when the attorneys couldn't leave the court room due to the trial.

State Attorney Stone wanted to leave no stone unturned in the state's quest to convict Gerard John Schaefer for the horrific murders of Susan Place and Georgia Jessup two young women whose lives were snuffed out before they had time to live.

CHAPTER SIXTEEN

THE FIRST ACT

All of the pre-trial legal wrangling had been presented. The witnesses were in place, the motions filed and denied. The charges amended. Schaefer had been sent to Chattahoochee for the asked for thirty days. Now it was time for the first act.

Gerard Schaefer was returned to the St. Lucie Jail Hospital cell. Judge Trowbridge ruled he would not go back to Chattahoochee for further testing. He told the attorneys Schaefer had been given sufficient testing by the doctor at Chattahoochee. Schaefer had appeared before Trowbridge several days earlier and three psychiatrists had testified as to the need or lack of need for further testing.

Since Judge Trowbridge refused to allow Schaefer to return to Chattahoochee, the assistant Public Defender, Bruce M. Wilkinson got into the act. He filed a writ of habeas corpus.

His writ was filed in the Fourth District Court of Appeals in West Palm Beach. The writ stated Gerard Schaefer had been "illegally detained" in the St. Lucie County Jail in "derogation of his rights under the Baker Act."

Assistant Public Defender Wilkinson argued that Schaefer had voluntarily asked to" receive treatment for a mental disorder." But, Wilkinson argued, Judge Trowbridge denied his request. However, Trowbridge had ordered Schaefer to undergo a 30-day examination. Wilkinson's argument under the writ of habeas corpus stated that the order from Trowbridge "improperly attempts to combine involuntary hospitalization with an order for evaluation." He went on to say this was outside of Trowbridge's jurisdiction.

In the meantime, Judge Trowbridge set the sanity date for July 9, 1973.

The Competency Trial was to determine if Gerard Schaefer had the ability to help prepare his own defense of if he was "insane" and had no idea what the charges against him were or why he was on trial.

Sheriff Norvell had custody of Schaefer at the St. Lucie County jail, which created a problem. Schaefer was not allowed with the general population. Sheriff

Norvell felt Schaefer's life would be in danger if he were allowed to be housed with the general population. So Schaefer was put in a single cell.

CHAPTER SEVENTEEN

SCHAEFER'S SANITY OR INSANITY

On June 22, 1973 there was a hearing in Judge Trowbridge's court it was a sanity hearing for Gerard John Schaefer. Trowbridge said Schaefer would not be returned to Chattahoochee. He also ruled that on July 9.1973 there would be a hearing to determine if Schaefer was competent to stand trial.

Dr. Hector Gianni, who had been Schaefer's psychiatrist at Chattahoochee, told Judge Trowbridge he needed another 60 days to evaluate Schaefer and in order to arrive at a conclusion as to whether or not he was legally sane. He continued by saying he had not received the copies of Schaefer's writings or other information about Schaefer until almost three weeks after Schaefer had been sent to Chattahoochee. Added to this Dr. Gianni, told the Judge he had only talked to Schaefer five or six times for short periods.

He concluded by telling the court that he had over sixty patients and he had been too busy to spend much time with Schaefer. He felt that due to the complexity of the case he needed additional time with Schaefer to reach a good conclusion.

Dr. Reginald C. Eaton, a psychiatrist and director for the Indian River Mental Health Center, told the court he could probably reach a decision on Schaefer's ability to stand trial in a shorter time than Dr. Gianni.

He said, "If I had the results of the tests conducted at Chattahoochee, plus two or three interviews, I could determine his ability to stand trial." (Fryer, No Decision made on Schaefer's Sanity, 1973)

Dick Purdy, the Assistant State Attorney from Fort Lauderdale, got into the act. He called Dr. Mordicai Haber of Ft. Myers as a witness for the state. Dr. Haber had previously examined Schaefer to determine if he should be sent to a mental institution for study. He told Judge Trowbridge he could give an opinion about Schaefer's sanity without any further testing. He added that he would be able to do that if he were provided with the results of the tests that had been conducted at Chattahoochee. Dr. Haber stated he had already seen some of the writings that had been attributed to Schaefer.

Judge Trowbridge denied the motion to have Schaefer re-admitted to Chattahoochee. He told the attorney for Schaefer, Elton Schwarz he felt the state had not done their part when he sent Schaefer to Chattahoochee the first time. He said in his opinion the state did not feel the urgency of the situation in completing the thirty day examination on time.

CHAPTER EIGHTEEN

SCHAEFER CHANGES THE SONG AGAIN

On July 6, 1973 Gerard Schaefer had his attorney, Elton Schwarz change his plea from insanity to not guilty on the two first degree murder charges in the deaths of Susan Place and Georgia Jessup.

Schwarz went several steps further. He filed six motions in addition to filing the change of plea. He filed a demand that his client Gerard John Schaefer be tried on the charges of murder within sixty days. He also wanted a reasonable bond set. If the courts didn't grant bond, Schwarz wanted Schaefer released on his own recognizance.

Once released he stated Schaefer would admit himself to a mental institution. The voluntary admittance would give credence to the insanity Schaefer was trying to portray. Then attorney Schwarz stated in yet another motion that Schaefer was being denied his right to treatment of mental illness by being in the St. Lucie County Jail. He had filed a writ of Habeas Corpus. The writ maintained the detention of Schaefer in the jail was illegal and that his competency to stand trial or insanity had nothing to do with his right to receive treatment under the Baker Act.

Schwarz also filed a motion requesting Schaefer be tried separately on the two murder charges. He kicked the song up a notch when he filed the motion requesting the murder charges be dismissed or to a have preliminary hearing to establish probable cause to believe an offense of murder had been committed. The language in the motion read, "There are facts which, even if true, would not constitute the offense charged in the amended information." (Fryer, Insanity Motion Withdrawn By Accused Double Killer, 1973)

Schwarz added fuel to the motion fire by filing a motion to suppress evidence seized in an alleged unlawful search. He then added another motion, which stated he wanted any evidence that had been seized at Schaefer's apartment. He also wanted anything his wife Teresa had turned over to lawmen. Schwarz filed a motion to suppress anything that Teresa may have said to State Attorney Robert Stone when she was called to his office to be questioned under oath.

Schwarz was not yet done with his motions. He filed one to have Roger Poitras, the Clerk of the Circuit Court in St. Lucie County declared in contempt of court. Schwarz's motion stated that

Poitras refused to make payment to witnesses who gave depositions to Schwarz and refused to pay the court reporter at the depositions.

The final motion was an order to keep all of Schaefer's mental examinations from being used in his criminal trial unless the insanity defense was used as a defense.

Schwarz final act was to name the witnesses for the defense. Included in those were Teresa Dean Schaefer, Martha Mara, Schaefer's first wife, Sara Jane Lane, Schaefer's sister, Gary Schaefer, Schaefer's brother, his father Gerard Schaefer, Sr., several friends, seven psychiatrists, six women who were said to have been missing and were publicly connected with Schaefer and last but not least the Fort Pierce Water Dept. Superintendent.

To add insult to injury, the Florida Supreme Court denied Schaefer's return to Chattahoochee. They not only denied the return they made the decision without comment. That being they didn't give an opinion for their denial.

On Tuesday, July 31, 1973 Gerard Schaefer talked with Stuart News reporter Bob Fryer. He told Mr. Fryer he feared for his life. He believed there were people on the outside who wanted to kill him if he posted the $200,000.00 bond that was the topic of the hearing, which was going to happen that day. He said a deputy had told him this life was in danger.

He told Mr. Fryer, he had no money and he was indigent.

Bob Fryer asked Schaefer if he was ready for the trial to get underway. Schaefer told him he was more than ready. He said he was being kept from his wife, and he had a job waiting on him when it was done. When Fryer asked him what kind of job, Schaefer told him it was in construction. That story was different from the one he told Trowbridge when he was arrested and convicted for the assault on Trotter and Wells. He told Judge Trowbridge in that hearing he had a job as a manager at Winn-Dixie waiting on him.

Schaefer continued with his comments to Bob Fryer. He told Fryer he felt the press coverage of his case was unfair. He also wanted to be able to present his side of the case. That wish was going to come true sooner than he anticipated.

CHAPTER NINETEEN

JULY 31, 1973

TUESDAY

On Tuesday July 31, 1973 all the players in this drama assembled in Judge Trowbridge's courtroom. The first player Gerard John Schaefer added another layer to his reality. He was now paranoid.

Next there was Elton Schwarz, the defense attorney, and his assistant Bruce Colton who had just graduated from law school. The public defender's office right had just hired Colton before Schaefer was charged. The defense team added another player. His name was Attorney James Brecher, a research lawyer. He worked for the Public Defender Lou Frost from the Jacksonville office. He was put on the team to put a different spin on the case.

On the other side of the platform was Robert E. Stone, State Attorney, from the 19th Circuit, Assistant State Attorney, Richard Purdy from Fort Lauderdale, Lem Brumbley the chief investigator and Jack Sewell Investigator and Executive Director for the 19th Judicial Circuit. There were reporters from different papers, and last but not least Judge Trowbridge. The players were set, the scene was in place, and the drama began to unfold.

The morning crackled with electricity. Each side wanted to get their arguments on the table and they all wanted to win this first battle of legal wits. Even though this was just a bond hearing, this was a pivotal point in what was yet to come.

The morning started on the wrong foot for the defense. Judge Trowbridge had stated to Attorney Schwarz that in his opinion it was up to the State to show burden of proof why Schaefer should not be granted bond. However, State Attorney, Robert E. Stone, had shown up for the hearing prepared to argue that it was not on the State to show burden of proof.

Stone's argument was based on a legal opinion which stated it required the accused to carry the burden of proof that he can have bail set. He followed this opinion up by stating it was a matter of law that bail not be set for crimes punishable by life imprisonment "if presumption is great or proof is evident." (Fryer, Schaefer Fears Assassination, 1973)

Judge Trowbridge reviewed the law, which Stone had cited. Score one for the State. Trowbridge had to rule in favor of the motion.

Defense Attorney Schwarz immediately went on the attack. He countered with "This is the first time in 20 years before the court that I've learned that merely the filing of information by the state attorney completely does away with the presumption of innocence" (Fryer, Schaefer Fears Assassination, 1973)

Schwarz took things one step further. He asked the court for a recess. He needed to regroup. What Schwarz decided to do shocked, even Schaefer. Schwarz made the decision to put Schaefer on the stand in his own defense.

Stone's questions began.

First Stone asked if Schaefer was at the crime scene.

Schaefer's response "It's possible that I could have been there, but I don't remember being there."

Stone- "Do you know whether for sure, you didn't kill those two girls?"

Schaefer- "I killed no one. No, I didn't kill anyone."

Stone handed Schaefer a statement, which had been filed by Schwarz, which stated a defense of insanity, might be used at the time of trial for the alleged crimes.

Stone "Do you know this says you are suffering from paranoid schizophrenia and that you might have killed them without ever knowing it?"

Schwarz raised an objection to that line of questioning. Schaefer didn't answer.

Stone continued –"Are you suffering from a mental disorder?"

Schaefer- "Yes."

Stone- "And does this mental disorder mean you sometimes don't know what you do?"

Schaefer – "Yes, I am sometimes confused."

Stone- "Does it mean you can't sometimes separate fact from fantasy?"

Schaefer- "Yes, I would have to say that."

Stone continued with his questioning. He asked Schaefer where he was on September 27, 1972. Schaefer replied that he would need a calendar to recall where he was on that day.

Stone- "Is it your testimony that you've never seen these two girls in your life?'

Schaefer- "I've never seen them."

Stone asked Schaefer if he has visited a friend in Oakland Park around September 27, 1973.

Schaefer's reply was "I have very few friends. If you can tell me who the person was, I might remember." (Fryer, Schaefer Fears Assassination, 1973)

During this bond hearing all of the motions were heard. Among those heard were some of the ones that Defense Attorney Elton Schwarz and his team had filed and the few, which State Attorney

Robert E. Stone and his team filed.

One of the motions heard and ruled on was the one of change of venue, filed by Schwarz. The language of the motion read, “the open hostility toward the defendant throughout the entire Southeast section of Florida has been and is now such as to render it impossible for this attorney to have any reasonable belief that a fair and impartial jury could, under any circumstances be selected to try the charges pending herein and that any attempt to select a jury would be futile and excessively costly to St. Lucie County or any other county wherein the venue might be changed in the South Florida area.” (Fryer, Schaefer's Notions are Heard, 1973)

Schwarz added to this motion an affidavit which was signed by Schaefer, stating “Not withstanding defendant’s assertion of innocence for many months, newspaper articles, circulated throughout the St. Lucie County area have been such as to continuously assert the guilt of the defendant and such of the articles as have been read by the defendant clearly reflect that opinion of the news media is that the defendant is guilty before ever being brought to trial and that such a situation likewise renders a fair and impartial trial within the entire Southeast section of Florida impossible.” (Fryer, Schaefer's Notions are Heard, 1973)

Schwarz included ten affidavits of St. Lucie County residents to the motion. The residents stated in their affidavit they didn't believe Schaefer could receive a fair trial in their county.

The affidavit that Schaefer had signed boiled down to the opinion he had already been tried and found guilty by way of the news media.

With Schwarz's filing of a change of venue, Robert Stone decided to add his own motion for change of venue. He wanted the trial to go to the town of Okeechobee, which was about thirty minutes from Fort Pierce and still part of the 19th Judicial Circuit.

Judge Trowbridge who was not to be out done in his courtroom let it be known he would be the one to decide if or where there would be or not be a change of venue. During one discussion about this very same motion on the day before in the courtroom, Judge Trowbridge stated that it had been suggested the trial be held at Disney World. This statement could have been taken to mean the trial even though it had not yet started was becoming a circus. Trowbridge said he would set the place for the trial later in the week and at the same time set the date. That motion was tabled.

To add to the flavor of the circus was the motion filed stating that Schaefer would possibly use the defense of insanity as part of his defense.

The motion stated he was suffering from an acute form of paranoid schizophrenia. This form of illness would render one incompetent and not conscious of what he had been doing or even if the act was wrong. Schwarz added, "If it could be proven that any such act was, in fact, committed by him." (Fryer, Schaefer's Notions are Heard, 1973)

Not to be outdone Robert E. Stone inserted his input into this motion. After he had examined the statement he said, "Does this mean he's relying on an insanity defense at the time of the alleged crime or "insanity at the time of the trial? I want a clarification." (Fryer, Schaefer's Notions are Heard, 1973)

Next on the agenda the newest team member of the defense stood to add his input. James Brecher, a research lawyer from the Public Defender's office in Jacksonville stood up and gave his argument regarding the legality of the search warrants and the seizure of the evidence.

Brecher argued the searches at the home of Schaefer's mother and his apartment violated the Fourth and 14th amendments of the US Constitution. His arguments were based on three points.

The first point maintained there was no probable cause for issuing the search warrants. The second point said the description of the items to be seized were outside the scope of the search warrants.

The last point stated the description of the items to be seized were not specific enough to meet legal requirements.

Attorney Brecher argued, “A search warrant is not to be used to discover evidence but to seize evidence already known to exist. Merely because a subject is a suspect does not give an officer probable cause for a search warrant. A search warrant is not a license for unlimited search and seizure and general exploratory, searches are illegal.” (Fryer, Schaefer's Notions are Heard, 1973)

Stone’s rebuttal was the search warrants were specific enough to meet legal requirements “It’s one of the better warrants I’ve seen.” Stone stated. (Fryer, Schaefer's Notions are Heard, 1973)

Judge Trowbridge agreed with Stone and denied the motion to suppress evidence. He stated, “Frankly, I think the specificity is very good. It was not possible and practical for the officers to know a detailed description of the items to be seized.” (Fryer, Schaefer's Notions are Heard, 1973)

But Judge Trowbridge followed up that statement with, “This ruling does not mean the items will automatically be admitted into evidence at the time of trial.” (Fryer, Schaefer's Notions are Heard, 1973)

Assistant Defense Attorney Bruce Colton had to add his motions to the mix. He wanted to present a motion to have statements Teresa Dean Schaefer made to Attorney Stone suppressed. There statements were made prior to May 18, 1973 the day Schaefer was charged.

His argument was the confidential privilege for communications between a husband and a wife, and no waiver was obtained to allow Teresa Schaefer to make statements.

This statement sent Assistant State Attorney Richard Purdy to his feet. He said, "This matter should come up at the time of trial, not now."

Judge Trowbridge shot down Colton's motion, by saying; he was" making a mountain out of a molehill." Then he added insult to injury by saying "There is nothing illegal about taking testimony before a trial. I will deny the motion, but will sustain objections to disclose confidential communication s at the time of the trial" (Fryer, Schaefer's Notions are Heard, 1973).

At the same time Trowbridge also denied the motion to strike a report from Dr. Mordicai Haber, the forensic psychiatrist who had examined Schaefer before he was charged. Schaefer's attorney argued the examination involved "privileged information."

Schwarz then played the motion card to have the availability to have anyone specified by Schaefer to have free accesses to talk to Schaefer while he was in the St. Lucie County jail.

Judge Trowbridge reserved the ruling. “I will not rule on this motion. If you have a specific instance of a specific denial of access, you can raise the matter again for a ruling.” (Fryer, Schaefer's Notions are Heard, 1973)

Schwarz played his last motion. He wanted to prohibit the censoring of mail, the suppressing of mail and to return mail that had been received.

Trowbridge again shot down that motion when he said, “I’m not running the jail.” (Fryer, Schaefer's Notions are Heard, 1973)

Schwarz tried one last time to argue a motion to have a transcript made of all hearings in Martin County relating to Schaefer’s sanity.

Trowbridge said, “This is just an expense item and the case is going to cost enough as it is. I am not going to issue a blank check to transcribe all those proceedings.” (Fryer, Schaefer's Notions are Heard, 1973)

Schwarz complained that all the evidence had not yet been returned to St. Lucie County and he wanted it returned as soon as possible. Judge Trowbridge agreed it was a problem.

Stone made the last motion of the day when he stated that he wanted to strike a motion Schwarz had made asking for a speedy trial.

He said, “If you file a motion for a dismissal at the same time you file a motion for a speedy trial that indicates you are not ready for trial. This is what happened in this case."

Trowbridge agreed with Stone and granted the motion to strike the demand for a speedy trial.

The day in court of what was supposed to be just a bail hearing turned into a day of who could one up who with motions.

As Schaefer left the courtroom he commented to Bob Fryer, "Personally, I think the constitutional issues that were raised were ignored. I was a policeman, so I know what the law on search and seizure is."

That statement by Schaefer brought the close to a day that was just shades of things to come in Judge Trowbridge's court and the case of "The State of Florida vs. Gerard John Schaefer."

CHAPTER TWENTY

SIDE BARS OF THE PRESS,

INTERVIEW WITH MRS. DORIS SCHAEFER AND SCHAEFER'S INTERVIEW WITH PAT QUINA

Pat Quina interviewed Gerard Schaefer while he was a Chattahoochee. In this interview he talked about his wife Teresa, the girls he had dated and the crime of assault against Ellen Trotter and Pamela Wells.

When Gerard Schaefer was arrested and questioned by Law Enforcement Officer's for the assault of Nancy Trotter and Pamela Wells, he couldn't tell them why he had committed that act. However, he claimed total recall during his interview with Pat Quina. He claimed the two girls had laughed at him.

When he was asked why he had tied up the two girls his reply was, "This is a question that's gone through my mind and it's part of the reason I'm here at the hospital. I'm not sure what was on my mind. My thought was to show them the dangers for young girls in hitchhiking.

I stopped them the day before and told them not to hitchhike. I was on duty. I stopped them the next day, when I was off duty, and picked them up. One thing led to another and it ended up as it ended up.

It was mainly because they were laughing at me and I was trying to convey the seriousness of it (hitchhiking). You know people are disappearing all the time. Look how many murders and disappearances we've had. People are still disappearing even now." (Quina, Girls He Tied up Laughed at Him, Schaefer Says, 1973)

At this point in the interview Schaefer began to proclaim his innocence. "I'm not doing this. Someone else is out there doing it. Not, me. It all hasn't stopped you know. I'm thinking the police are trying to clear their blotter by using me as a scape (sic). I'll tell you this, if I had read what has been written about me, I would have formed an opinion and my opinion would probably be unfavorable based on what I read in the newspapers." (Quina, Girls He Tied up Laughed at Him, Schaefer Says, 1973) It would appear Schaefer even at that time was alluding to the fact there were others.

Schaefer changed gears and began to talk about his marriages. He said his first one to Martha Fogg was a disaster however; he got along "famously" with his second wife Teresa.

"I love my wife very much. She of course, does not believe I'm capable of committing any of these alleged acts." (Quina, Girls He Tied up Laughed at Him, Schaefer Says, 1973) Did he really believe his wife didn't think he was capable of committing the acts nor had he fooled himself into believing it? That question died with Schaefer.

When he was asked how Teresa felt about the manuscripts that had been confiscated his reply was "She recognizes that people have personalities that are subject to fantasy. That happens to be one of my fantasies. I enjoy writing and was an "A" student in creative writing in college. It's an endeavor I enjoy. I have an active imagination." (Quina, Girls He Tied up Laughed at Him, Schaefer Says, 1973) Schaefer's fantasy became reality, however in his mind it was still fantasy.

While Schaefer was playing to the media through Ms. Pat Quina who was with the Fort Pierce Tribune, and Bob Fryer with the Stuart News, his mother added her rhetoric to the mix. She decided it would add to the drama of the circus, which was Schaefer by talking to Pat Quina.

Ms. Quina met with Doris Schaefer at her home in Fort Lauderdale during the last week of June in 1973. She sat down with Doris so she could explain her side of the debacle, which was the life of her son Gerard John Schaefer.

The interview had the flavor that her life and those of her children- was as police lingo goes “10-4”. Doris had three grown healthy children and two small grandchildren. Gary the youngest son had a new girl in his life. Her daughter Sara was married and had two children. She told Ms. Quina that even though her son Gerard had been divorced, the young girl he had just recently married was a gentle young girl named Teresa Dean.

Doris told Ms. Quina some of the problems were due to the fact she and her husband had divorced. However, she felt that as long as she had her children and they were happy life was good. Good that is until, last July 1972. That was the day Doris Schaefer’s oldest son Gerard Schaefer kidnapped two young girls and tied them to trees with hangman’s nooses on Hutchinson Island.

As Doris Schaefer sat on her living room floor by the coffee table she talked about her oldest son Gerard John Schaefer, she called John.

Doris said, “My brother and others said they could see John doing that, but they can’t see him going any further than that. From the accounts they had in the paper, it sounded terrible, I wouldn’t want it to happen to me.” (Quina, Schaefer's Mom: He's Not a Monster, 1973)

She went on with her dialogue. “Since April 1,

it's been a nightmare, really. I worry about him. I worry about Teresa. I just can't believe that John has done these things that they say he's done because he's not that kind of person. They're making him out to be a monster, and he's not." (Quina, Schaefer's Mom: He's Not a Monster, 1973)

Mrs. Schaefer told Ms. Quina she had been in Miami when she got the news. The entire family had been called there. Her father was sick and the doctors felt he was going to die.

Ms. Quina in her interview reported that Ms. Schaefer's father had survived just as Ms. Schaefer had. However, she stated the strain of the past six months was showing on the petite attractive woman's face. Mrs. Schaefer added the worst times were going to see her son in jail, worrying about his young wife, running from photographers and trying to avoid hostile phone calls.

She was quick to say that one such call had been made to her parent's house. The caller asked if Doris's mother who was 86 years old knew if her grandson had killed twenty-six women. She went on to say that she had no idea who that person was and her mom didn't know either.

She continued with "I can't allow myself to give in to this situation because I have to work."

Doris went on to talk about how happy she had been when John (Gerard) had married Teresa. She said she was happy because someone had finally brought her son some happiness.

She said, "I hate the possibility of John not being able to come back and be with Teresa and pick up his life. That's all he was living for June 15th." (Quina, Schaefer's Mom: He's Not a Monster, 1973)

June 15th was the day Gerard was to be released from Martin County Jail for the assault conviction.

Doris continued with her soliloquy, "All he talked about was June 15th and that he could be back with Teresa and they could start over. I just cannot believe that any of this stuff is true that they are saying about him, because he was so completely in love with Teresa and there would be no reason for him to have any problems.

He just beamed all the time, like when they would walk in the back door for the weekend, or come over with their friends. They'd have a good time.

From what John says in his interview with you, (Ms. Quina) he obviously know he has some problems and that he's had one for many years." (Quina, Schaefer's Mom: He's Not a Monster, 1973)

As the interview continued Ms. Schaefer stated she knew her son had a problem. She had taken him to a psychiatrist; however it cost her twenty-five dollars every session. She also told Ms.

Quina the psychiatrist would not tell her what was wrong with her son. She said he told her if he did she would always be looking for things. She explained the doctor also told her if he told her what was wrong with Gerard "it might do more harm than good." (Quina, Schaefer's Mom: He's Not a Monster, 1973)

This revelation by Ms. Schaefer leads one to believe the problems were very deep seeded and probably started from a very young age. However, the question remains why didn't the psychiatrist tell Ms. Schaefer what the problem was?

The interview concluded by Mrs. Schaefer saying she didn't believe her son had committed the crimes. She said he was not that kind of person, and there was no way anyone could make her believe he was.

She wanted him to be found not guilty so he could go back and live his life with Teresa and they could all be happy again.

Pat Quina asked Mrs. Schaefer if she had thought about the fact Gerard could be found guilty and sentenced to life in prison or committed to a mental facility for a very long period of time.

Mrs. Schaefer replied, "Well, my god, after all reality is reality and you have to face it. You have to live with it no matter how much it hurts. Of course if he needs help, then I think he should receive it. I know that's what he wants. I think that John has the intelligence to go ahead and get it, too." (Quina, Schaefer's Mom: He's Not a Monster, 1973)

At times Mrs. Schaefer appeared to tear up during the interview. She told Ms. Quina she could talk to her son; she couldn't talk about him.

CHAPTER TWENTY-ONE

THE SECOND ACT BEGINS

Thursday, August 2, two days after Judge Trowbridge set a $200,000 bond for Gerard Schaefer, he called all the parties back into court and reversed his ruling. He revoked the bond.

Trowbridge stated the reason for the revocation was due to the fact a psychiatrist had testified the prior Thursday that Gerard Schaefer had a "Character Disorder, which is manifest by sexual deviation and erotic sadism." (Fryer, Schaefer's Bond Revoked, 1973)

On Tuesday July 31, Judge Trowbridge had told the state they had not presented enough evidence to show guilt on Schaefer's part. Therefore, he had no choice but to grant bond. However, Robert Stone, the state attorney, filed a motion to vacate the order. Stone presented a witness to support his argument that Schaefer would be a danger to society if he were allowed to be released from jail. That witness was Dr. Mordicai Haber, a Fort Myers Forensic Psychiatrist. Dr. Haber had been one of the doctors who had examined Schaefer on April 12.

Dr. Haber was sworn in on the witness stand.

He repeated a statement he had written in his report about Schaefer after his examination of him. He stated Schaefer "is dangerous, less to himself than others."

Defense Attorney, Schwarz on his cross-examination asked, "Do you consider him (Schaefer) to be mentally ill?"

Dr. Haber, "I do not."

Schwarz "Do you consider him to be psychotic?"

Haber, "I do not. Schaefer is an anti-social personality, which is manifested by sexual deviation and erotic sadism. He has a character disorder, a personality disorder…."

He continued by saying there was no disturbance of Schaefer's mental process.

Dr. Haber, "His thinking process is very clear. Because of the nature of his character traits, he can be dangerous. He has difficulty in more than one area of his life."

Schwarz, - "Can you speculate how long this has been so?"

Dr. Haber, "Yes, since childhood on…. Very chronic, deep, and abiding."

The defense presented their expert witness Dr. Charles Long, a psychiatrist who said he had treated Schaefer off and on from 1968 to May 1971.

Schwarz "Did you arrive at an opinion concerning his (Schaefer) mental condition?"

Dr. Long, "Yes"

Schwarz, "Is he dangerous to other people?

Dr. Long, "He is potentially dangerous. He has a propensity to sexually molest people."

Schwarz, "Is he insane?"

Dr. Long, No."

Schwarz, "Is he competent to stand trial?"

Dr. Long, "Yes."

The doctor also added that he felt Schaefer's propensity to sexually molest people had been a "lifelong problem."

Schwarz "Is he dangerous to himself as well as others?"

Dr. Long, "Yes."

Schwarz, "When you examined him did you believe he is suicidal?"

Dr. Long, "I felt he was suicidal."

Dr. Long also added that he felt Schaefer's danger to others was directly related to a propensity to commit sex offenses. (Fryer, Schaefer's Bond Revoked, 1973)

Schwarz at that time presented his argument to the court that probable cause existed to believe that Schaefer was a mentally disturbed sex offender. He asked Trowbridge to certify Schaefer as such and turn him over to the custody of the Division of

Mental Health. Schwarz indicated he knew that by turning Schaefer over to the Mental Health Division there would be a delay in the trial. However, he made it clear he wanted the case to be tried within the 180-day limit of a state, speedy trial rule.

State Attorney Robert Stone offered nothing else He allowed his arguments to stand as presented.

Judge Trowbridge offered up this statement in regard to Schwarz's request. "We are only taking things one step at a time. The hearing at this time is on a motion to vacate the bond. The sole question the court is going to determine is whether the defendant is likely to injure himself or others." (Fryer, Schaefer's Bond Revoked, 1973)

With that statement made Judge Trowbridge ordered the bond vacated. Then he set another date for a court hearing. This one was to rule on the motion for change of venue. Judge Trowbridge told the lawyers he was not going to make an immediate ruling on the change of venue the day of the hearing. He was going "to take the matter under advisement." (Fryer, Schaefer's Bond Revoked, 1973)

From May 1973to August 2, 1973 Gerard Schaefer had been in court at least four different times and still had not been tried. The court appearances had been a media feeding frenzy a as well as a three-ring circus with an act in each ring at the same time. The ringmaster was Judge Trowbridge and the papers were having a field day.

Gerard John Schaefer was the front-page headline and his every move, motion and voiced thought was spotlighted. Schaefer played this game well. He used it to his advantage at every opportunity.

CHAPTER TWENTY-TWO

SCHWARZ FILES MORE MOTIONS

August 10, 1973 all of the players were back in Judge Trowbidge's court yet again. The defense filed another of the never-ending motions. This motion again asked that Gerard Schaefer be handed over to the Division of Mental Health.

The defense filed the motion using the statute, which related to mentally disordered sex offenders. The application sought the commitment using five points.

That Gerard Schaefer was not insane at the time and was competent to stand trial.

That he had a mental disorder which according to three psychiatrists had rendered him dangerous to others because of a propensity to commit sex offenses.

He was charged with a non-capital crime and had previously been convicted of a crime. (The reason the murders were considered non- capital was there was no death penalty in the state of Florida.)

By virtue of the testimony of C.W. Long, M.D. which was given to the court on August 2, 1973 there was probable cause to believe the defendant was a mentally disordered sex offender.

The condition had existed for more than four months immediately last past.

Schwarz also told the court he knew the commitment of Schaefer to the mental facility might waive his right to a speedy trial. He told Judge Trowbridge he didn't want Schaefer committed permanently. He was just trying to get Schaefer to a hospital before his mental condition deteriorated. Schwarz tried the sympathy routine by saying that Schaefer being in jail was beginning to be more than he could take.

Schwarz told the court that Schaefer was in extremely bad condition. He had just found out his grandfather had died. He continued by saying that Schaefer had spent a lot of time with his grandfather.

"He's also been under tremendous strain the past week and it is just beginning to show. If we don't get him in a hospital and this case isn't tried in two months, I don't think he'll be competent to stand trial. We are ready to go to trail anytime." Schwarz argued in his bid to get Schaefer committed. (Fryer, Schaefer Asking to Be Committed, 1973)

To add to the drama, Schwarz told the court that Schaefer was extremely nervous and tense. He added fuel to the argument by saying that Schaefer continued to talk about suicide.

As a snide remark Schwarz said, "The only reason he hasn't tried it by now, I think, is he doesn't want to do Bob Stone any favors."

At this hearing Judge Trowbridge heard motions and arguments as to why the defense felt the trial should be moved. Schwarz subpoenaed newspaper reporters to appear in court with copies of stories written in connection with Schaefer. The stories went back to July 15, 1972. That was the time he was arrested for the abduction of Nancy Trotter and Pamela Wells.

He also called two investigators to the stand. They testified they had conducted interviews with certain people in St. Lucie County about the chances Schaefer getting a fair trial. One investigator, Ronnie Hayes stated he interviewed thirty people and ten had stated Schaefer couldn't receive a fair trial in St. Lucie County. The second investigator, Allen Hayes testified he had interviewed fifty people and the majority stated they felt Schaefer wouldn't get a fair trial. Several of those same people stated they felt Schaefer was guilty.

Robert Stone argued there were 2,705 prospective jurors in St. Lucie County and all the court needed was six.

The drama of the commitment continued. This

time there was a discussion about the date of the hearing to determine if Schaefer would go back to a mental hospital. Robert Stone told Judge Trowbridge he wasn't given enough notice and therefore he didn't have sufficient to notify his witnesses. Trowbridge told him the defense witnesses had traveled from out of town and they would be heard at that time. Stone was given a continuance until August 21, so his witness could be heard.

The defense witnesses were Dr. Benjamin Augburn, and Dr. Hector Gianni, psychiatrists from Chattahoochee, and Dr. C.W. Long, a Bartow psychiatrist. All three were in agreement that the incident in which Schaefer had tied Trotter and Wells to trees on Hutchinson Island in July of 1972 was indeed sexually related.

Dr. Augburn's testimony stated he felt Schaefer believed most women who hitchhiked were loose, immoral girls and felt they should be punished. He also stated that Schaefer had the propensity to dress in women's clothing most particularly undergarments. He stated dressing in women's undergarments gave Schaefer a sense of sexual release. Dr. Augburn testified that Schaefer admitted to having intercourse with animals and the doctor diagnosed Schaefer as a "schizophrenic, paranoid type", with sadomasochistic tendencies.

(Fryer, Motion to Move Schaefer's Trial Continues, 1973)

Dr. Gianni added to the defense testimony with his statement. He told the court Schaefer had admitted to him that he had started masturbating at twelve and from age 14 to 17 he had regular intercourse with a steady girl. (That girl was Cindy. The one he said he dumped because he refused to play her sex games.) Dr. Gianni added more about Schaefer and his so called uncontrollable urges. He stated that when Schaefer saw a prostitute he had an urge to destroy her. To control that urge he would tie himself to a tree and by doing so received sexual fulfillment.

Dr. Long who had interviewed Schaefer right before court, testified that Schaefer had told him during one of the examinations, his feelings when he had picked up the Trotter and Wells. Dr. Lang stated Schaefer told him the two girls were loose girls who should be punished. He said Schaefer had a lot of fantasies surrounding the punishment he would inflict on them.

Schaefer told Dr. Lang he would like to hang them, and then kill them. They would suffer before for a while before he committed all kinds of sexual intercourse with them after they were dead. Dr. Long continued with his testimony, by stating Schaefer had told him that he had fantasized about taking girls into the woods, hanging them, and then having sexual intercourse with them until they were almost completely rotten. (Fryer, Motion to Move Schaefer's Trial Continues, 1973)

Long testified he told Schaefer to write down his fantasies. He went on to explain Schaefer never told him that he had acted out his fantasies. However, he did tell Dr. Long that he had thought about it.

When the testimony ended both the defense and the state agreed the trial should not be delayed no matter how Judge Trowbridge ruled on the commitment of Schaefer. They both agreed that Schaefer could not be admitted as a mentally disordered sex offender if he was not determined to be sane and competent for trial.

August 15, 1973 Judge Trowbridge again had all the players in his courtroom. He denied the change of venue. He said it didn't matter where the trial was held the news media coverage would follow the trial wherever it was. He also stated that since the charges were considered a non-capital crime, there would only be six jurors plus one alternate. Judge Trowbridge finally set the date for the murder trial of Gerard John Schaefer to begin. That date was September 17, 1973.

CHAPTER TWENTY-THREE

SEPTEMBER 23, 1973

LET THE GAMES BEGIN

On August 21, 1973 Judge Trowbridge called a conference to lay the ground rules for the trial of Gerard John Schaefer, which would begin on September 17, 1973. He told the two attorneys he would allow each of them twenty preemptory challenges when the jury was picked.

Defense Attorney Schwarz had a couple of things he put on the table. He told the Judge he felt it would take three days to select the jury and he intended to continue to seek change of venue if they couldn't seat a jury in thirty days. He also wanted the jury sequestered during the trial.

Trowbridge countered by saying he would take the request to sequester under advisement until after the jury was selected. He also said that due to a conflict in the court calendar the beginning of the trial might start in a smaller courtroom, which would limit the spectators.

Trowbridge stated there would be no recording

devices in the courtroom. He also would not allow cameras.

Schwarz complained he had not received any lab tests on the evidence, which had been conducted by the state lab. He needed the reports in order to make a decision as to whether or not he needed to order his own testing. Judge Trowbridge ordered all tests had to be completed by Sept 1 and all results furnished to the defense team by Sept 5. Stone not to be outdone by the defense asked for handwriting and blood samples. Trowbridge granted the request.

Schwarz again asked that Schaefer be committed to keep him from "going insane in the middle of the trial." (Fryer, Ground Rules Laid for Schaefer Trial, 1973) State Attorney Stone called his witnesses to the stand.

The first witness was Dr. Michael Gilbert psychiatrist from Miami. Dr. Gilbert testified that he didn't believe Schaefer was a mentally disturbed sex offender. He also testified that when Schaefer tied the two girls to the trees last July that being Nancy Trotter and Pamela Wells, it was not an overtly sexual in nature. It may have been an unconscious sexual manifestation on Schaefer's part.

During the cross examination by Schwarz Dr. Gilbert stated that Schaefer had the propensity to commit sexual offenses, however there had been no such sexual offenses related to him during Dr.

Gilbert's previous examinations. He continued by testifying that if Schaefer were to be committed to a mental hospital for treatment before the trial it would be of little use to him.

He said it would take long-term intensive individual therapy… (Fryer, Ground Rules Laid for Schaefer Trial, 1973)

Stone brought up the question to Dr. Gilbert about the authorship of the writings. Dr. Gilbert testified Schaefer had admitted to writing the manuscripts. Schwarz objected. He said the discussion Dr. Gilbert had with Schaefer was privileged. He also objected on the grounds that the press should not be allowed to report on the alleged authorship of the manuscripts. (Fryer, Ground Rules Laid for Schaefer Trial, 1973)

Judge Trowbridge overruled Schwarz objections stating he could not restrict freedom of the press.

Next was Dr. Mordecai Haber of Fort Myers. He testified about some of the evidence, which had been seized at Doris Schaefer's house. He told the court he had seen drawings and magazine pictures of nude women whose breast and genital areas were mutilated by a pencil or pen. (Fryer, Ground Rules Laid for Schaefer Trial, 1973)

On cross Schwarz asked if the incident on July 1972 with Wells and Trotter were the result of a sexual disorder.

Dr. Haber, "Hardly" (Fryer, Ground Rules Laid for Schaefer Trial, 1973)

He went on to explain that the incident was an act of aggression a manifestation of Schaefer's desire to hurt or destroy. He continued saying he didn't believe Schaefer fit the definition of a mentally disordered sex offender. Dr. Haber continued by saying that at one time Schaefer had wanted to become a priest, but when he was rejected he retaliated by rejecting the church by sexual deviant behavior.

Dr. Haber testified that Schaefer had the birds and bees talk with his father after he had intercourse with a girl. He told the courts Schaefer's first wife left him because of sexual incompatibility. Schaefer's reasoning to Dr. Haber had been that "he was a product of the city and was liberal in thinking while his first wife believed that sex was only for the purpose of procreation." (Fryer, Ground Rules Laid for Schaefer Trial, 1973)

Dr. Haber stated that Schaefer had said he had heard a voice talking to him since 1966. This voice told him to destroy evil. Finally Dr. Haber testified that Schaefer knew all along what he did and was accountable for it.

Monday August 27, 1973 Judge Trowbridge again called all the parties back to court. This time he gave his ruling regarding whether or not to send Schaefer over to the Division of Mental Health. His decision was Schaefer would stay in jail. The reason for his ruling was that Schaefer had been determined competent to stand trial, the hospital had been lax in treating him during his first thirty day stay and that the hearing would go on regardless of whether he was in jail or a mental facility. Lastly, Schaefer had said he would be present for all of the trial. Trial was set for September 17, 1973.

Finally all the legal motions had been heard and ruled on. The decision of the admittance to a mental facility had been settled. It was time to hear the evidence. It was time to try the case.

However, Schwarz had another card to play before Sept 17. On August 31, 1973 Schwarz filed yet another motion. He filed a motion to have all charges of murder dropped against Schaefer.

The reason for the motion for dismissal of charges was based on Schwarz's allegations that Schaefer's Fourth and fourteenth amendment rights had been violated when Judge Trowbridge had denied a demand for a preliminary hearing.

In a surprise move, Schwarz filed a motion to allow Schaefer to take lawmen to locations in South Florida that were described in writings as places where criminal activities supposedly took place. Lawmen would sweep the scene to see if indeed any crimes had taken place. Schwarz filed another motion stating he did not want the state to introduce into evidence any similar writings that described criminal acts of Schaefer unless Schaefer was allowed to disclose the exact location of the area in the writings. This was to prove that no crime had actually taken happened in the location in the writings.

Lawmen along with Schwarz, a Broward County lawman, two officers of the St. Lucie County Sheriff's department, officers of the Fish and Game Commission, and Jack Sewell from the State Attorney's office took the field trip with Schaefer to Fort Lauderdale to the place of the alleged writings. The place was Powerline Rd.

Powerline Rd was known to be the place where Schaefer and others who were into erotic asphyxia were known to perform their sexual release games of hanging themselves until they reached sexual climax. This field trip was one more of Schaefer's tactics. He was "cooperating" with law enforcement. There was no evidence found. Schwarz was quoted as saying that his client "didn't lead anyone on a wild goose chase. No wild goose was found…."

Schwarz continued to file motions to have the trial moved. He told the court the stress Schaefer was feeling was getting greater as the trial got closer. He didn't know if Schaefer would hold up. He stated that was why he wanted Schaefer committed in a hospital until the trial.

CHAPTER TWENTY-FOUR

SEPTEMBER 17, 1973

THE TRIAL BEGINS

Monday, September 17, 1973 at 9:30A.M, courtroom B located on the third floor of the courthouse, the trial of Gerard John Schaefer officially started. All the motions had been filed and ruled on. All the players were in place. The first day was filled with anticipation as six jurors and one alternate were chosen by the defense and the state to hear the evidence and the witnesses to decide the fate of the man accused of kidnapping, raping, killing and mutilating Susan Place age 17 years old and Georgia Jessup age 16 years old. These two girls were last seen in Broward County, Florida September 27, 1972.

Schaefer arrived for the appointed time dressed in a tie and white dress shirt. He was clean-shaven and appeared to be very calm. He arrived in the courtroom around 9:40A.M.

The courtroom was packed. The press had two bench rows set aside for their use. Three hundred jurors had been summoned for jury duty. Schaefer's mother Mrs. Doris Schaefer and Schaefer's wife Teresa Dean Schaefer were among the spectators.

At the defense table sat Elton Schwarz, Gerard Schaefer and the rest of the defense team. Sitting at the Prosecutions table was Robert E. Stone, State Attorney, 19th Judicial Circuit, Philip Shailer, who was the State Attorney from Fort Lauderdale, Broward County and Jack Sewell, Stone's investigator. Sitting behind the State's table was St. Lucie County Sheriff Lanie Norvell.

Judge Trowbridge addressing the 300 prospective jurors told them that none of them were to important not to serve as jurors. He explained it could take several weeks for the trial to come to a conclusion however they all were there to perform a very important service.

The first six prospective jurors were called in court to come forward. They were Miami Redling, Barbara C. Lanzer, Dorothy M. Miller, Julian R. Arten, Francis S. Colbeck and Betty P. Hawe. State Attorney Stone told them this was a very serious case.

"We're here to select six people who are fair, impartial, and objective to sit here and hear the evidence." Stone stated. (Quina, Prospective Schaefer Jurors Quizzed, 1973)

Stone continued by introducing the defendant by saying "This is Gerard John Schaefer, also known as Jerry Shepard." (Quina, Prospective Schaefer Jurors Quizzed, 1973)

Schwarz was not happy with this statement he sent Stone a hard glare when Stone called Schaefer by Jerry Shepard.

The paring of the jury lasted until noon. By that time a jury had still not been seated. One of the prospective jurors, Miss Judith A. McCarthy said she had looked at articles concerning the case. She also told the court her father had been concerned about her being selected because a man had accosted her before with a stocking pulled over his face. She had escaped. However, she felt she could handle being on the jury.

State Attorney Philip Shailer asked if she had ever hitchhiked. She replied she had although she always had a friend with her. She stated a man who said he was a cop had picked her up a one time. He was in an unmarked car and took her to West Palm Beach. Neither attorney objected to Miss. McCarthy being seated.

The next prospective juror was Mrs. Betty J. Haugh. When she was asked if she could be impartial, she told the court she didn't like gory incidents. She said it was a very grave responsibility she was faced with and that she really didn't want to be in court, however she would stay if she were needed.

John H. Hallows another prospective juror told the court he had closely followed the newspaper accounts of Schaefer in the newspapers.

"I watched things from day to day and decided he was guilty." Hallows said. (Quina, Schaefer Jury List Pared, 1973)

Paula Fusco told the court she just didn't want to sit on the jury. Stone was not happy with her remark and he told her he had twenty instances where he could excuse and he was letting her go.

John Morales told the courts he didn't read too much about crime. The day continued with the jury still not set. Stone stated it would probably be Wednesday before they would have six jurors picked.

At the end of the first day, Schaefer played to the media once again. He showed them the red splotches on his left hand that he said was poison ivy. He also told his audience he had it on his feet as well.

CHAPTER TWENTY-FIVE

THE FIRST AND SECOND DAYOF TESTIMONY

Once the jury was finally seated the trial got under way with a flourish. On Wednesday September 19, 1973 the small courtroom was seated to capacity with standing room only. The defense table and the prosecution table were side by side within inches of each other and about three feet from the Judge's bench. The press was allowed several seats at the front behind the lawyer's tables. The six-man jury was seated to left of the judge's bench.

The air crackled with the electricity that comes from a high profile criminal case. Everyone wanted to be able to say, "I was there, and I saw and heard the case in person."

The heat of bodies in the small courtroom was comparable to the heat and humidity of a South Florida day in September.

All eyes were on Judge Trowbridge's court. Everyone knew this was big and it was history in the making.

State Attorney Robert Stone was ready. He was

up first to give his opening statement. He was well prepared and powerful.

He included in his opening statement the fact that he would show the body parts found at the scene on Hutchinson Island belonged to Susan Place and Georgia Jessup. He made it very clear he was going to prove that Gerard Schaefer killed the two young women.

Stone stated, "The last day Susan Place was seen by her mother was on September 27. That was when the defendant, alias Jerry Shepherd, went to Mrs. Place's home and actually had a conversation with Mrs. Place.

She talked with the defendant about her daughter leaving home. She said she was concerned, but they said they were going to the beach to play the guitar. The mother became so concerned she went outside and looked at the car her daughter drove away in. She became so concerned that she wrote down the car's license tag number. That tag number and car belonged to Gerard John Schaefer. She'll be able to identify him for you.

The girl's bodies were sent to the Dade Medical examiner. Because they had been dead for a long time, the examiner can't give you the exact date of death. But mutilation was consistent as the cause of death. Death by natural causes has been ruled out. It was deaths by a violent act of murder.

Among the evidence you will see, will be a small purse that belonged to Georgia Jessup. I have people who can identify that purse. The purse was taken by Hank Dean, Schaefer's brother–in-law and given to a detective in Broward County. Teresa Schaefer got the purse from her husband. This man had a scheme and a mode of murder- he put it into effect and operation. Between Sept. 27 and Dec. 8 he murdered these two girls on Hutchinson Island in St. Lucie County." (Quina, Some Jurors Pale at Schaefer's Trial, 1973)

Elton Schwarz the defense attorney waived his opening statements. He would give his opening and closing at the same time. So the State began to present its case.

The state presented its first witness Jesse Joe Holley from Stuart who testified that he was with his father and they had been looking for aluminum cans on Hutchinson Island. They were about a quarter of a mile from the nuclear plant when his father called him to the site of the bodies.

When he arrived at the location where his father was standing he saw four body parts near a hole in the ground. Joe and his father went back to Stuart and called Sheriff James D. Holt. Then they went to the home of Calvin Wiggins who was Holly's brother in law.

When Mr. Holley had finished testifying,

Calvin Wiggins was put on the stand. Calvin was the chief ambulance attendant for the Stuart Police Dept. He testified that when Holley and his father came to his house, he in turn called both the Martin County and St. Lucie County sheriff's depts.

Mr. Wiggins told the court and the jury that he and Mr. Holley and Mr. Holly's father went back to the crime scene and waited for the two Sheriff's Dept. to arrive. He said that he had found three parts of the bodies about 15 to 20 feet from the shallow grave.

Lt. Duvall, the chief investigator for the St. Lucie County Sheriff's Dept. was next on the stand. He described the crime scene. He stated the bodies were found about 1,000 feet in a heavily wooded area. Then he testified the bodies were found about sixty feet from the dirt road that ran east from A1A toward the beach.

The State Attorney's office brought into the courtroom two large tree limbs and a section of a tree root and introduced them into evidence. The sections of the tree limbs were approximately five feet in length with rope burns on them. Lt. Duvall pointed out the rope burns to the jury. The jury had already been visibly shaken when the limbs were introduced. Robert Stone brought into evidence the tree limb, which had been used to hang the two girls. He walked into the courtroom with the limb held up above his head by his hands. When the rope burns were pointed out the jury turned pale.

Lt. Duval testified that he believed the two girls were hung from the two limbs by a rope and had struggled violently to free themselves unsuccessfully as they tried to deflect the deathblows of the killer.

When the tree root was introduced there was testimony showing the hack marks in the roots as well as pieces of material. The material was from the nightgown found at the scene buried in the shallow grave. Lt. Duval continued with his testimony. He said also found were shoes, a dress, portions of human vertebrae, upper body torso, part of a pelvis, a leg and another torso.

Even more damming evidence came from Lt. Duval when he testified a pair of blue jeans had been found about 30 feet west of the grave. In that pair of jeans was a lower torso. He said the waist had deteriorated but the patches on the jeans were still recognizable. The patches consisted of a half-moon, Star of David, and the Road Runner character.

Lt. Duvall was not yet finished. He told the jury that south of that body section i.e. the jean clad torso he found an arm. He continued by testifying that due to the sifting screen, which St. Steve Williams had made, teeth had been found. There were thirteen teeth scattered close to a Palmetto bush about 25 feet away from the open grave. He testified parts of two jawbones were found. One jawbone still had teeth intact.

"Also, a reddish hair scalp was found near the teeth. We continued to search the whole area, but we had to take our machetes and clear the area so that we could see. It was like a jungle down there. Nine to ten feet north of the grave there was a rubber tree or banyan tree. On the tree were the initials "G.J." The initials hadn't been carved there too long.

At the bottom of the tree there was a root extending out with chop marks in it and inside the marks there was some cloth it looked like part of the clothing that was found in the grave. There were rope burns on the tree limbs. We took a chain saw and cut off the limbs and the root section. Also, the section that had the initials carved in it.

I continued to search almost daily on April 16 we found another scalp. The blonde scalp, but at that time the bodies had been identified. We also found two pillowcases one was black and blue stripped and the other was white. It appeared the grave had been dug then dug again." (Quina, Some Jurors Pale at Schaefer's Trial, 1973)

Mrs. Lucille Place the mother of Susan Place was next to testify. As Mrs. Place looked at a picture of her daughter, she wept. When she was asked to identify the man who Susan had left with on September 27, 1972 she stood up in the witness box and pointed to Schaefer.

Mrs. Place stated that her daughter introduced Schaefer as Jerry Shephard. She told the jury on the night her daughter left home they had a conversation about Susan moving to Colorado. Her mother had not wanted her to go.

“Susan, if you go, then I’ll probably never see you again.” Mrs. Place said.

She continued, “Then Mr. Shepherd said, “We were just going to the beach and play guitar.”

Mrs. Place testified that she noticed the guitar was still in the house when her daughter and the man she had been introduced to as Jerry Shepherd and Georgia Jessup had left the house.

In her earlier testimony she said, “Something made me go outside, I don’t know what, maybe it was intuition or something and I copied down the name of the car, the license tag number and the color of the car.”

The testimony referred to the car that was traced back to Gerard Schaefer. She had also identified the piece of paper, which had been introduced in evidence as the paper she had written the vehicle information on.

When it was the defense’s turn to cross-examine the witness, Elton Schwarz turned to his assistant Bruce Colton and told him to do the cross. This request was unexpected; Colton had no prepared questions and had to rely on his wit and quick thinking to question the witness. He did ask her if was true that her daughter had run away from home and if she was a drug user. Mrs. Place admitted her daughter had run away from home on several different occasions and that he daughter had taken heroin.

Next to testify Ira Place, Susan's father. He told the court he was positive when he identified Schaefer as the man who came to his house and had been introduced to him by his daughter as Jerry Shepherd

At the home of Schaefer's mother in Ft. Lauderdale, the search warrants had produced manuscripts explaining how to commit the perfect crime and get away with it. Included in those manuscripts were the instructions to use pillowcases, dig a grave and return to the dead bodies again and again.

As Gerard Schaefer heard the opening statements by State Attorney Robert Stone and the testimony of the state's witnesses, he sat calmly and shrugged his shoulders at the press when the tree sections were introduced.

Thursday September 22, 1973 Court resumed. The state called Lt. Dave Yurchuck, with the

Broward County Sheriff's Office to the stand. Lt. Yurchuck testified that several items were found in Mrs. Schaefer's house the day the search warrants were served and carried out. Among the items found were several gold filled teeth, a jewelry box, passport, driver license, poem book and journal. Lt. Yurchuck testified that when he had been given the jewelry box at the Schaefer home, Mrs. Doris Schaefer was asked about the jewelry box she stated she had never seen it before.

A suede leather purse was introduced into evidence. This purse had been given to Lt. Yurchuck by Henry Dean, Teresa Dean Schaefer's brother. Lt. Yurchuck testified to how and when he got the purse.

Once again Elton Schwarz told Bruce Colton to cross-examine the witness. Lt. Yurchuck had received medals and awards for his work on the case. His testimony for the state was impeccable. Schwarz knew it could not be shaken.

The state called Mrs. Shirley Ann Jessup to the stand. As she walked into the courtroom she was visibly upset. She had dark curly hair and she was dressed in a brown and white pants suit. When she was sworn in and given a picture of her daughter she wept.

When she was asked if the picture was her daughter Georgia Jessup, she whispered "yes."

As she was asked other questions she could barely answer due to the pain she felt. State Attorney Robert Stone showed Mrs. Jessup the purse and asked her if she could identify it. She said it belonged to her daughter Georgia.

The next person to identify the picture of Georgia was her 12-year-old sister Cheryl Lynn. She was also asked to identify the purse. She testified it was her sister's.

The next door neighbor Joyce Froggot age 16 went to the witness stand and also testified that the brown suede leather purse belong to Georgia.

Georgia's father came next. He identified the picture of his daughter. He also testified that he had met Schaefer about a week before the two girls disappeared.

After they disappeared Schaefer came back to Mr. Jessup's home and asked for "Crystal." Crystal was Georgia's nickname.

Mr. Jessup testified, "He told me his name was Jerry Shepherd and he kept saying it was important that he see her. I kept telling him I didn't know where she was, but that her mother was worried and if he saw her, to have her call her mother."

Then the State called Mrs. Ann Chapman. She was the grandmother to Georgia Jessup. She testified that Georgia was indeed her granddaughter. She identified the jewelry box as one she had given

Georgia for her birthday. She said Georgia had wanted the jewelry box to keep some jewelry in so she gave it to her.

Dr. Richard Souviron was called to testify as an expert witness. He was a forensic dentist. The jury did not get to hear all of the doctor's testimony. He testified that some of the teeth found belonged to Carmen Mae Hallock, age 22 who had disappeared Dec 18, 1969.

Philip Shailer, the State Attorney from Broward County, Florida, carried the teeth, which had been found in Mrs. Schaefer house, in Gerard's bedroom, to court in a small vial.

When asked by the State if there had been any good reason for the teeth to be extracted, Dr. Souviron stated there had been no good reason for the teeth to be extracted by a dentist.

He said, "These teeth are in excellent condition. I suppose the person could be alive without them, but there's no reason to remove them whatsoever."

He told Schwarz, "Mr. Schwarz, you told me those were the teeth of Mr. Schaefer and I told you to furnish me with Mr. Schaefer's x-rays. You didn't. I'll be glad to take a look at his mouth now and tell you if there're his teeth."

Defense Attorney Elton Schwarz declined the offer.

Out of earshot of the jury Dr. Souviron told the court the teeth belonging to Carman Hallock had been forcibly removed. He went on to say if a dentist had removed them it would have been a dentist with a heavy hand. He was allowed to testify to the jury that he had found a .22 caliber bullet hole in one of the jawbones sections found at the Blind Creek Crime Scene.

Sgt. William Scott was put on the stand as well. He testified that he was given a picture of Susan Place and he took it to the Martin County Jail. When he got to the jail and in front of Schaefer he showed Schaefer the picture.

When Sgt. Scott was asked about Schaefer's response to the picture he testified, "He said he hadn't seen her and didn't know anything about her. He stated she was a nice looking girl." (Quina, Girl's Relatives Testify at Trial of Schaefer, 1973).

CHAPTER TWENTY-SIX

THE SUEDE LEATHER BROWN PURSE

At some point in the day Teresa Dean Schaefer had been put on the stand. She testified that she had given the brown suede leather purse to her brother Henry Dean to take to her Mother in Law, Doris Schaefer's house in Fort Lauderdale. Schaefer had stated he had bought the purse for his wife on an overseas trip. Schaefer had testified to buying the purse several years ago but had waited until last November to present it to his wife.

When Teresa Schaefer was on the stand State Attorney Philip Shailer, Broward County asked her, why she gave the purse to her brother in April just a few days after the bodies had been discovered at Blind Creek.

She started to answer the question by saying, "John (Schaefer) had asked…"

However, she was prevented from finishing the answer because Elton Schwarz jumped up and yelled, "I object."

Schwarz told the court any conversation his client had with his wife was confidential. Judge Trowbridge sustained the objection. She was not allowed to finish her sentence.

When Henry Dean received the purse from his sister, he testified that he found a .22 caliber pistol and a paper sack, which contained .22 caliber shells, some were spent and some were not in that purse. Dean took the purse, the sack and shells and turned it over to Lt. Yurchuck.

Dean testified," I took the items, and told her (Teresa), that I was taking them to Ft. Lauderdale to Lt. David Yurchuck. I knew Dave was connected to this case and he was an old friend of mine."

When Dean was on the witness stand he told the jury he had been in law enforcement with the Broward County Sheriff's Department. He stated he had worked with Lt. Yurchuck.

He testified, "I thought maybe if I gave this purse to Dave it could clear up matters." (Fryer, Schaefer Trial Grind to Halt As Witness Flies in from Nairobi, 1973)

Dean continued with his testimony. He said he had a good relationship with Schaefer. He indicated that he and Schaefer had gone hunting on at least one occasion and that Schaefer was a good shot. He testified that he had seen Schaefer with a small .22-caliber pistol on several occasions. Dean said the pistol was a "Saturday Night Special.

Henry Dean then dropped the bombshell. He said he had gone to visit Schaefer in jail at Martin

County on the day Schaefer was charged with the two counts of first-degree murder. Schaefer had been going over the newspaper accounts of the charges and murders. Dean said that he believed Schaefer felt like Dean was interrogating him.

Dean stated that he told Schaefer that law enforcement had found teeth and bones and that the teeth were from the deceased Susan Place and Georgia Jessup. Dean said that Schaefer's response was no skulls or heads had been found.

Dean said Schaefer asked him "What do you want me to do, confess to you?"

State Attorney Shailer asked Dean if while he was visiting Schaefer at Martin County Jail if Schaefer mentioned selling a story about the murders.

Deans' response was "John advised us that he had been offered a sum of money for the story. He asked Teresa if she wanted him to sell the story and make her some money." (Quina, Two Tied -Up Girls on Stand Monday, 1973)

Defense Attorney Schwarz asked Dean if he felt that question had been asked in a sarcastic tone. Dean replied that he did not hear one. Elton Schwarz accused Dean of working with law enforcement to piece together the Blind Creek murder case.

Dean said, "I assured him my concern was my

sister and her being brought into this thing." (Fryer, Schaefer Trial Grind to Halt As Witness Flies in from Nairobi, 1973)

He continued by saying that the reason he spoke to Schaefer in the first place was because he wanted the truth. He said he wasn't out to "hang" John.

Schaefer told Dean he also wanted to know the truth.

The Blue Suede shoes Susan Place was last seen wearing the day she disappeared with Gerard Schaefer and Georgia Jessup. They were found at the crime scene April 1, 1973 at Blind Creek. (Courtesy of the 19th Judicial Circuit Florida)

Susan Place date unknown (courtesy 19th Judicial Circuit)

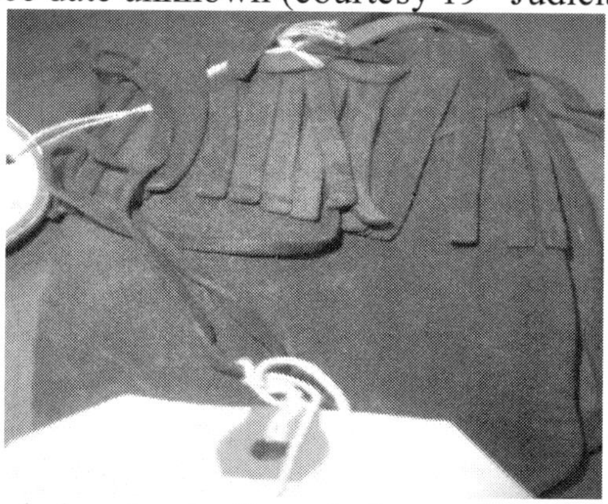

The suede purse belonging to Georgia Jessup which Schaefer gave to his wife

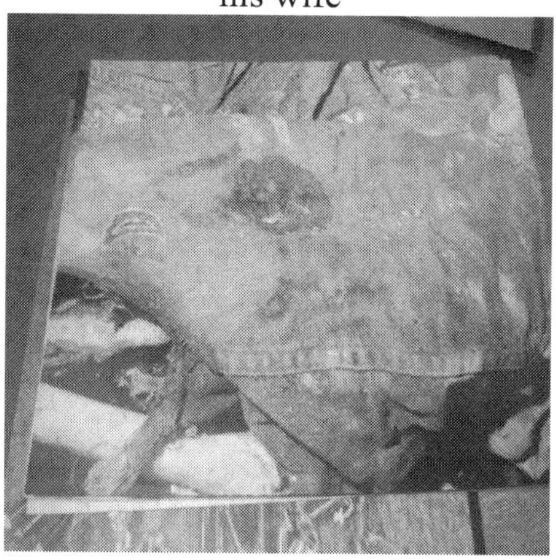

The blue jeans Susan Place was last seen wearing the night she disappeared with Gerard Schaefer and Georgia Jessup. When the crime scene was uncovered the torso was still in the jeans (courtesy of the 19th Judicial Circuit)

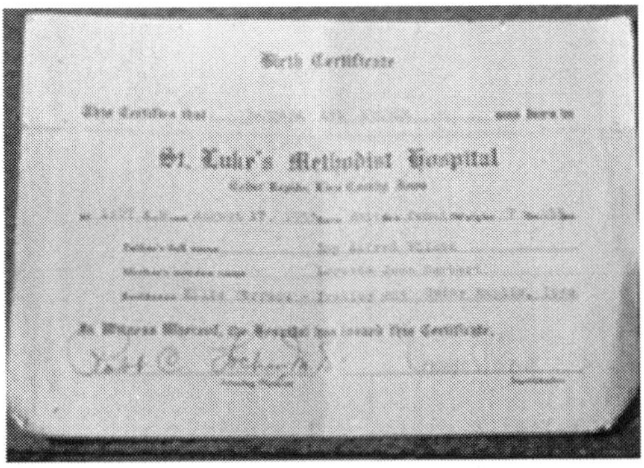
Birth Certificate

St. Luke's Methodist Hospital

Birth Certificate of Barbara Ann Wilcox found during search of Doris Schaefer's house. (Courtesy of 19th Judicial Circuit Florida)

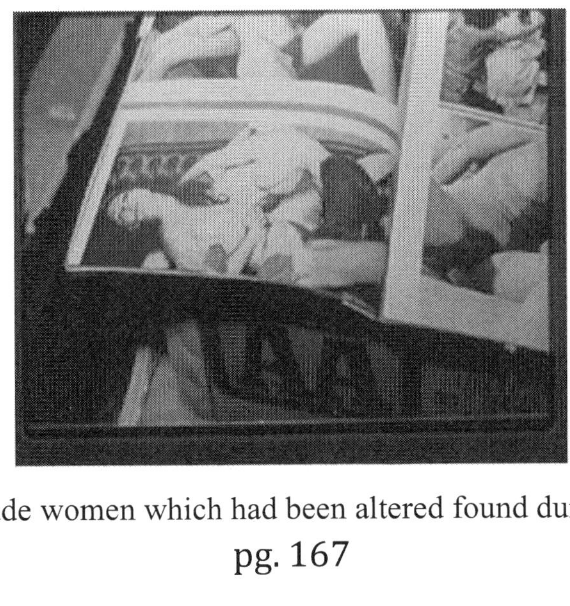

Photos of nude women which had been altered found during search of

Doris Schaefer's house. (Courtesy of 19th Judicial Circuit Florida)

Drawings by Schaefer found during search at Doris Schaefer's house. (Courtesy 19th Judicial Circuit Florida)

The Gold Jewelry Box which belonged to Georgia Jessup seized during search at Doris Schaefer's house (courtesy 19th Judicial Circuit Florida)

The arm of one of the victims still bound found at Blind creek crime scene (courtesy of 19th Judicial Circuit)

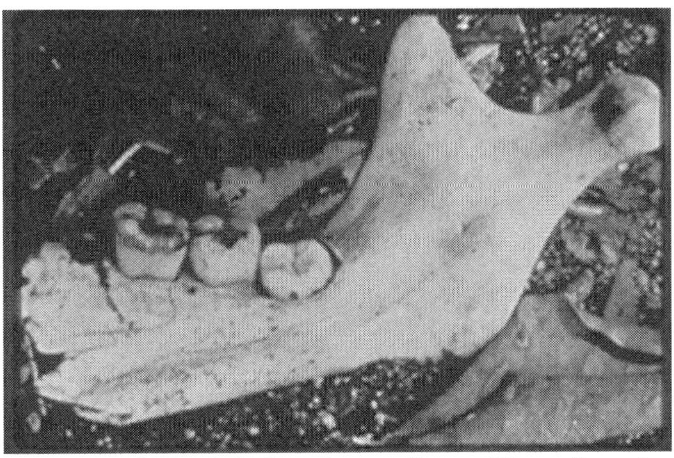

The Jaw Bone and Teeth belonging to Susan Place found at Blind Creek the Crime Scene (courtesy of the 19th Judicial Circuit)

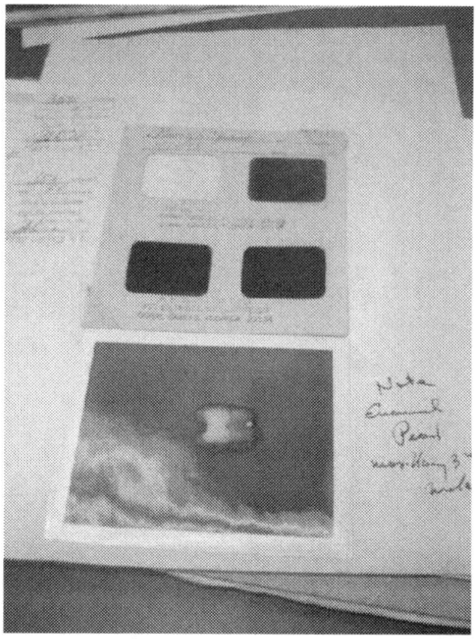

The tooth which was used to identify Georgia Jessup found at the crime scene at Blind Creek (courtesy of the 19th Judicial Circuit)

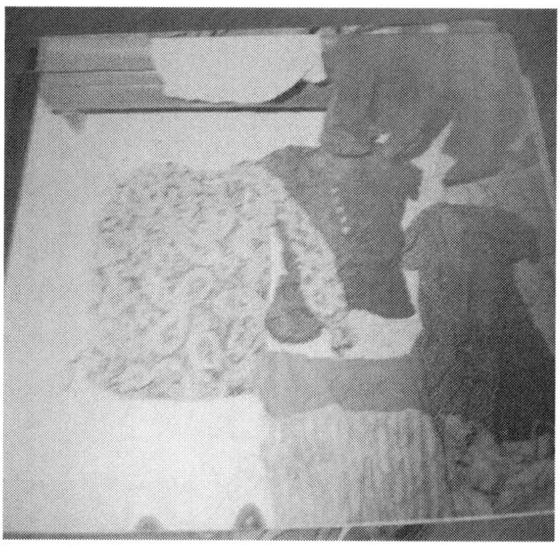

Clothes of Georgia Jessup and Susan Place found at Blind Creek (courtesy 19th Judicial Circuit)

The final resting place of Georgia Jessup and Susan Place at Blind Creek on Hutchinson Island (Courtesy of the 19th Judicial Circuit)

Nancy Ellen Trotter at the re-enactment

Pamela Sue Wells at re-enactment

CHAPTER TWENTY-SEVEN

THE STATE ADDS FUEL TO THE FIRE TESTIMONY THIRD DAY

SEPTEMBER 24, 1973

Monday September 24, the state had a whole new set of witnesses to add to the drama in the courtroom. Dr. Joseph Davis, the Dade County Medical Examiner was the first to testify. Dr. Davis had been out of the country in Nairobi Africa testifying in another case and was not able to be in the courthouse prior to Friday September 21.

Dr. Davis testified about the results of the autopsies he had performed on the two girls. He testified the girls didn't die by natural causes and the deaths were not self-inflicted.

Dr. Davis testified that the girl's bodies were so mutilated and decomposed so much that they were difficult to determine which part of the body belonged to which body. He told the jury the bones had been delivered to him in two black plastic bags.

"The degree of deterioration was such that the bodies had to be handled with care, I was delivered four major parts." Dr. Davis said to the jury.

"There were two upper halves of bodies and two lower halves of bodies. The heads in both cases were missing. The neck bones were partially missing. Body no.1, identified as that of Susan Place had been cut at the fourth vertebrae with some very sharp instrument – like a heavy – bladed knife, not a blunt instrument. Body no.1 had a separation through the backbone, or lower portion of the spine. The angle of the cutting was from the rear. There was another cut at the left shoulder joint, separating the arm bone into two sections. I found no blunt injuries, or simple injuries. No bullets.

Body no. 2 was identified as that of Georgia Jessup. Missing was the head and upper part of the vertebrae. Also both lower extremities were cut from the torso with a sharp- bladed instrument. There were chop marks and another partial cut, just above the knees." (Quina, Girls Tell of Schaefer Tying Them to Trees, 1973)

When Dr. Davis was asked if wild animals could have carried off the skulls, he answer was no.

Next up were the two girls who helped to bring Gerard Schaefer to his knees when they escaped their restraints in July 1972 and told Martin County Sheriff's Office they had been kidnapped by Gerard Schaefer.

Nancy Ellen Trotter age 18 and Pamela Sue

Wells age 18 both pointed Schaefer out to the jury as the man who had bound, gagged and put nooses around their necks. When they were asked if they had been harmed any other way, Nancy Trotter said, “He pinched me on my ass.”

Both girls testified that they had arrived in Stuart two days before the incident. They met Schaefer who was wearing a Martin County deputy uniform. When they met him the next day he was in plain clothes. He drove them to Hutchinson Island. They testified he was taking them to see and old Spanish Fort. This fort was supposed to be on a dirt road west of A1A.

Trotter and Wells said he stopped the car and handcuffed them, bound them and put nooses around their necks.

Nancy Trotter testified that Schaefer tied the other end of the hangman’s noose to a tree limb. She told the jury she had to hold her head up while she got her hands loose so she would not be strangled. She freed herself while Schaefer was occupied with Pamela Wells.

Pam was bound in a similar fashion; however she didn’t yet have the noose around the tree limb.

The two young women were asked if they had been sexually assaulted by Schaefer to which they replied no. Defense Attorney Elton Schwarz asked both girls if his client could have hurt them in any other way. They both said yes.

The testimony of Nancy Trotter and Pamela Wells set the stage for the video that the girls made with the help of law enforcement. The State called St. Lucie County Sheriff's Sgt. George Miller to the stand with the video of the re-enactment. Sgt. Miller and Jack Sewell investigator for the State Attorney's office had taken Nancy Wells and Pamela Trotter back to the place they had been tied, gagged and hung. They filmed a re-enactment of the crime with the girls once again bound, gagged and standing on a tree root with a noose loosely around their necks. They were terrified. They had to once again live the terror of silently screaming. They had to once again feel the tightening of the handcuffs on their hands, the rope around their neck, the feel of the cloth gag as it was wrapped once more around their mouths. They had to endure the feeling of the silent scream ringing in their head one more time. The feeling of total and utter helplessness that they had already endured. They didn't want to testify against Schaefer. They still had nightmares of the crime.

Once the video was shown it set the stage for the introduction of the manuscripts which had been seized at the home of Mrs. Doris Schaefer. The ability to introduce the manuscript into evidence was a slippery slope. The state had to prove that the manuscript was similar to the crime that had been committed. This case included a lot of legal maneuvering in uncharted waters.

The body of the manuscripts was "How to go un-apprehended in the perpetration of an execution style murder. The jury had been given the manuscript in a diluted version.

The manuscript gave a detailed method for carrying out the perfect "execution-style" murder without getting caught.

The manuscript read "In order to remain un-apprehended the perpetrator of an execution style murder such as I have planned must take precautions. One must think out, well in advance a crime of this nature in order for it to work. We will need an isolated area assessable by car and a short hike away from any police patrols or parking lovers. The execution site must be carefully arranged for a speedy execution once the victim has arrived.

Ideally would be two saw horses with a 2x4 between them. A noose attached to the overhanging limb of a tree and another rope to pull away the 2x4 preferably by car. A grave away from the place of execution. The victim could be anyone of the many women who flock to Miami and Ft. Lauderdale during the winter months. Even two victims would not be difficult to dispose of since women are less wary when traveling in pairs.

In case, it may be more preferable to bind and

gag the victims before transporting them to the place of execution. Then again, depending on what torture or defilement is planned for them, other items may be used."

The manuscript jumped to ways to prepare a woman before her execution, by "degrading her" and making her strip to at least her underwear. A white pillowcase should be placed over her head and her mouth gagged. The manuscript also suggested hanging the woman; revive her before death so that she would be subjected to even more indecencies. Continuing, "After death has occurred the corpse should be violated, if not violated already. The body should then be mutilated and carried to the grave and buried. All identity papers should be destroyed and the place of execution dismantled.

As the jurors read the manuscript, they were once more visibly shaken. They had already seen the tree limb used to hold the rope, which hung Georgia Jessup and Susan Place.

CHAPTER TWENTY-EIGHT

SEPTEMBER 25, 1973

THE FOURTH DAY OF TESTIMONY

CIRCLING THE WAGONS

On the fourth day of the trial of Gerard John Schaefer the defense presented its case to the jury and the court. They started with the sister of Schaefer, Sara Jane Schaefer Lane. She was shown the gold embroidered jewelry box, which had been seized in the search warrant. She testified it was indeed Grandpa Schaefer's jewelry box.

She identified a picture of her brother, which had been presented to her by Defense Attorney Schwarz. She told the court that the picture had been taken September 31, 1972. In the picture Schaefer had a mustache, short well-trimmed hair and fever blisters all over his mouth.

She told the jury that she had taken the picture at her home the last weekend in September.

When State Attorney Philip Shailer questioned her on cross-examination, she ended up in tears.

"The picture was taken on Sept 31?" Shailer

asked studiously

"Yes." Ms. Lane answered

"That's interesting because there are only 30 days in September." Shailer countered.

When Ms. Lane was dismissed from the witness stand she went out into the hallway and collapsed on a bench. She was seen crying and being comforted by her mother in law Doris Schaefer and her brother Gary. She told the local paper that Shailer "the dark-headed man," confused her.

Teresa Schaefer was put on the stand by the defense team. She testified that Schaefer had visited Dr. Davis in the middle of September 1972. He had gone to see the doctor for a high fever and he had blisters on his mouth for about two weeks.

She also told the jury under oath that her husband couldn't have possible been in Fort Lauderdale the night of Sept 27, 1972. Teresa stated that if her husband had been out that night she would have been with him. She said she was always with him if he went out at night.

She said, "He was home that night. If he ever got home after dark, I would have known about it. I would have remembered it."

At the end of her testimony she stated, "I want to help John."

When she was asked if she loved her husband

she stated, “Yes.” (Butsh, 1973)

Gary Schaefer, Gerard’s brother took the stand. He testified that he and Schaefer hunted together a lot. He also told the jury he knew about certain material that was located in the north bedroom. The north bedroom was Gerard Schaefer’s.

He also talked about the Suede Leather Brown purse. He swore that the purse had been purchased by his brother in Morocco when he had traveled over seas a couple of years earlier. Gary told the jury his brother used the purse to carry shells in when he went target practicing.

This testimony came after testimony saying Schaefer had bought the purse for his wife Teresa and had just given it to her a year later.

During the day of defense testimony there continued to be conflicting statements. Mrs. Doris Schaefer, who appeared nervous and at times close to tears, had testified that her son Gerard had a “horrible virus” the last week in September. She said he had at times run a high fever. She told the jury she had asked him not to go hunting in Iowa in October because she was afraid he would get pneumonia. She also testified that the jewelry box which had been seized with the search warrant as being the one she gave John after she had divorced his father. She said the small gold embroidered jewelry box had belonged to Schaefer’s grandfather.

Defense Attorney Elton Schwarz asked her if she had ever disposed of anything in her house between the time law enforcement first went to her house and the time they returned with a warrant. She testified she hadn't.

Schwarz asked Mrs. Schaefer if would ever lie for her son.

Her response was, "No, I wouldn't lie because I have no reason to lie. I couldn't anyway."

She was also asked if her son Schaefer had ever worn a long sleeve sports shirt in the last ten years. She denied it. That testimony conflicted with the testimony by

Mrs. Place who had stated Gerard Schaefer had been to her house on Sept 27, 1972 dressed in a long sleeve sports shirt. The shirt was plaid. She had also previously testified that same night Schaefer had worn a tan hat with a narrow brim. Mrs. Schaefer denied on the stand that her son even own such a hat. When Schaefer's sister and brother were on the stand earlier for the defense they also stated their bother did not own a long sleeve shirt or a tan hat with a narrow brim.

The defense had asked a question to Mrs. Schaefer, Sara and Gary as well as a family friend David Rogers regarding the license tag. That question involved an emblem that was supposedly on Schaefer's tag. The defense had produced one similar as evidence to the court. Gary, Schaefer's brother said he has seen the emblem on the car tag when Schaefer had worked for the Wilton Manor PD. Mrs. Schaefer testified she had seen the emblem on her son's car as late as Christmas of 1972. The testimony conflicted with Mrs. Place's testimony when she said she had not noticed any emblem on Schaefer's tag.

The victim's mothers also filled the day with much emotion. Mrs. Shirley Jessup had to be led from the courtroom in tears as she pointed to Gerard Schaefer and said, "That's the man who chopped up my Georgia."

CHAPTER TWENTY-NINE

SEPTEMBER 26, 1973

THE LAST DAY OF THE DEFENSE WITNESSES

September 26, 1973 was the last day the case of The State of Florida vs. Gerard John Schaefer was tried. The next step would be the conviction of guilty or not guilty. However, the defense was not finished. They had to try again to prove reasonable doubt that their client was not guilty of the charges of first-degree murder. So they put yet more character witnesses on the stand.

The first witness was Edmund J. Ferris from Fort Lauderdale. Mr. Farris stated he had been a friend of Schaefer's for about 14 years. He told the court he had gone to Mrs. Doris Schaefer's home on Sept. 27 and had spoken Schaefer.

"I took him a gun I had repaired for him and he gave me $20 or $25, but I told him it cost more than that- about $47." Ferris stated under oath. (Quina, Prosecution, Defense Rest Cases in Trial of Schaefer, 1973)

He continued by telling the court that Teresa wasn't home, but he was at Schaefer's mother's house from five in the afternoon until seven o'clock. He said when he left it was not yet dark. Teresa Schaefer had previously testified that she was always with her husband if he was out at night.

However, Mrs. Place had previously testified that Schaefer, along with her daughter and Georgia Jessup had left her house around 8:30 PM. Teresa Schaefer had previously testified that her husband was home with her the night of Sept 27.

Ferris continued with his testimony by telling the courts he and Schaefer had gone on a hunting trip to South Dakota October 1972. He said on the way back they had stopped in Iowa where Schaefer had called his wife Teresa.

When the search warrant had been issued for Mrs. Schaefer's house identification papers belonging to two Iowa girls was seized. The girls were last seen alive shortly before Schaefer began serving his six-month sentence for the aggravated assault of Trotter and Wells.

In a surprise move the Prosecution brought Lt. David Yurchuck back to the stand by State Attorney Philip Shailer. He gave some very eye opening testimony regarding the ownership of the jewelry box. Yurchuck's testimony blew apart Mrs. Schaefer's testimony of the ownership of the jewelry box.

While the search warrant was being executed at the home of Mrs. Doris Schaefer, Lt. Yurchuck and Mrs. Schaefer were seated in the living room where Lt. Yurchuck cataloged the items of evidence as they were brought to him by law enforcement. Mrs. Schaefer watched him as he did this.

Lt. Yurchuck- “Mrs. Schaefer was sitting there with me and she was very interested in what was coming out of that room. There were certain items that I would not let her read or see because of the nature of the items - drawings and photographs. The jewelry box was brought out of the bedroom and given to me. Mrs. Schaefer said she had never seen it before. There was girl’s jewelry inside the box- pins, broaches, and a charm bracelet. I asked her if she had ever seen any of the jewelry and she said she didn’t recognize any of it.” (Quina, Prosecution, Defense Rest Cases in Trial of Schaefer, 1973)

After the State and the Defense both rested their cases, Assistant Public Defender Bruce Colton asked the court again for a directed verdict of acquittal.

“We have shown more than a reasonable hypothesis of innocence and the law says that circumstantial evidence isn’t enough. This case should not go to the jury.” Colton continued.

“It’s a case for the jury to determine. “ State

Attorney Robert Stone countered.

"The evidence is so weak. It should not go the jury." Colton shot back.

Judge Trowbridge denied the motion and told both sides that the legal wheels would move forward.

CHAPTER THIRTY

SEPTEMBER 27, 1973

CLOSING ARGUMENTS

September 27, 1973 both sides pulled out all the stops with their closing arguments. Both the State Attorney's office and the Public Defender's office knew this would be the last time they would be able to present their case to the jury. Philip Shailer and Robert Stone knew that evidence alone was indeed just circumstantial; however, the evidence as well as the testimony combined made the totality of facts enough to close the noose.

The state felt the jury was convinced after Lt. Yurchuck's rebuttal of Mrs. Doris Schaefer's testimony concerning the jewelry box. State Attorney Shailer said he really needed no notes for his closing, all he had were bullet points the rest was committed to memory.

He had spent many nights playing his closing argument over and over in his head. He had lived with the circus that was Gerard Schaefer since the search warrant in April. He had seen the jewelry when it had been seized.

He had heard the testimony from both the defense and the prosecution. He had viewed the pictures from the crime scene more than once. He probably heard the silent screams of Georgia Jessup and Susan Place.

State Attorney Philip Shailer had put up with Schaefer leaning over to him during the trial and stating, "I had a picnic with your wife and children when I was at Wilton Manor."

Shailer had immediately bolted out of his chair and asked the judge to keep Schaefer from ever speaking to him again.

He was ready to give one of the best closing arguments of his career. He knew the jury would convict. It was time to take down the circus tent, pack up the clowns and close the show.

In an astounding legal argument Shailer told the court why Schaefer should be found guilty of two counts of first-degree murder in the horrific deaths and torture of Georgia Jessup and Susan Place between September 27, 1972 and December 8, 1972.

He opened his argument by saying, "It's rather fitting perhaps ironic, that one year ago today, September 27, 1972 was the last day Susan Place and Georgia Jessup were seen alive. One year ago today, they were last seen alive with that man sitting over there in that sweater." As Shailer made this last statement he pointed to Schaefer sitting at the defense table.

"Susan and Georgia left the Place home in Ft. Lauderdale with that man. Mrs. Place, Susan's mother, was so concerned that she wrote down the license tag number and auto description of Mr. Schaefer's car." (Quina, Schaefer Prosecutor Pulls out the Stops, 1973)

Shailer then went through the evidence that had been presented to the jury during testimony.

"What kind of evidence do we have?" Well, we have the license plate number copied down by Mrs. Place on the night of Sept 27. Mrs. Place said Schaefer was introduced to her as Jerry Shepherd and we have a manila envelope found in Schaefer's bedroom addressed as Jerry Shepherd.

Mrs. Teresa Schaefer, Schaefer's wife said her husband was at home with her the night of Sept 27. But Schaefer's own barber, who was called here to testify on Schaefer's behalf, told us that he talked with Schaefer in Fort Lauderdale, at Schaefer's mother's home, about 7PM. Teresa said he was always out with her husband if he was out at night. The barber said he didn't see Mrs. Schaefer. Where was Teresa, who wants you to believe her husband was never out of her sight after 9P.M.? That's ludicrous. Ridiculous.

Then we have this picture of Susan Place that

was shown to Schaefer at the Martin County jail. Schaefer said he didn't know her. What did you expect him to say? You think he'd start digging his own grave?

"The evidence we've presented here is overwhelming that Schaefer left the Place home one year ago tonight with those two girls." Shailer made this statement with emphasis.

Shailer brought up the small suede leather brown purse. Shailer told the jury that the purse allegedly belonged to Georgia Jessup and the defense alleged the purse was a gift Schaefer had bought several years earlier and gave to his wife Teresa in November 1972.

"We're told it's an ammunitions pouch. Shells were kept in it, his buddy says. If he used the pouch so much, isn't it strange that Teresa Schaefer told you she had never seen it before he gave it to her as a gift. And ask yourself this question: Why would a person decide suddenly to give his wife an old smelly ammunition pouch last November? That's kind of strange isn't it?

Shailer picked up the embroidered jewelry case. "This jewelry case has been positively identified as belonging to Georgia Jessup, but then we hear another story from the Schaefer team. Schaefer's sister said the last time she saw it was five years ago. She recognized it right away without even opening it to look inside.

Mama, brother and sister, the Schaefer team all remembered the jewelry box. Mrs. Doris Schaefer, Schaefer's mother leaned into that microphone yesterday and tears welled up in her eyes and she said, "Oh, yes, that was Grandpa Schaefer's. I don't know Grandpa Schaefer, but if he's alive today he must have had a heart attack when he heard that or, if he's dead, he must have rolled over in his grave.

Remember the old expression, "Circle the wagons- the Indians are coming? They did. The Schaefer family members circled the wagon- that was Grandpa's jewelry box.

But Lt. Dave Yurchuck, who is absolutely unimpeachable- all cop- told you yesterday that they were so busy circling those wagons on the jewelry box that they forgot when Yurchuck handed the jewelry box to Mrs. Doris Schaefer, she said, "I've never seen it before. It doesn't belong to anyone in this family. They circled so hard and so fast they just didn't see the forest for the trees. They got caught. Yes, they got caught."

Shailer then brought up a manuscript, which the jury had read earlier that week. The manuscript was written by Schaefer and described how to commit the perfect execution style murder.

Shailer continued, "Take this manuscript and see how many things you find in this case that coincide with the manuscript. The manuscript says find an isolated area accessible by car, put a noose over a tree, prepare a grave, bind and gag your victims, bring along a pillow case, nylon stockings, the bodies should be mutilated, all identification papers destroyed, dismantle the place of execution. – all of which happened at Hutchinson Island."

Shailer continued by saying, "This writing came from the mind, the thoughts and the pen of that defendant", as he pointed to Schaefer.

Shailer stopped talking and turned to the defense table where Schaefer had been whispering to his attorney and said, "Excuse me, am I interrupting you, sir?" (Quina, Schaefer Prosecutor Pulls Out the Stops, 1973).

Shailer continued with "When this defendant walked into this courtroom for this trial he was cloaked with the presumption of innocence. This trial is over now and that presumption is over and he doesn't sit there anymore with that presumption- he sits there for the murders of those two girls. But, our judicial system does provide the presumption of innocence.

Susan and Georgia didn't have any such rights did they? For them justice was prosecutor, judge and executioner all wrapped into one… all carried out by one. I'm confident you'll find the defendant guilty as charged."

State Åttorney Robert Stone closed the states closing arguments with a very profound statement.

He said, "I wonder what Susan Place and Georgia Jessup would say if they could be here? Jerry Shepherd, you hung me by a tree until-I died and then you mutilated my body. Is that what they would say?"

When Shailer and Stone had finished the states closing it was Public Defender Elton Schwarz's turn. He showed up for court dressed in a shocking red sports coat. Schwarz got up from his chair adjusted his jacket and addressed the jury which was made up of four women and two men.

This would be his last chance to convince the jury his client was not guilty of first-degree murder.

"The State's case was one of circumstantial evidence, but circumstantial evidence must be proved beyond and to the exclusion of every reasonable doubt. The decision you make here tomorrow will probably be the biggest decision you'll ever make in your life.

Mrs. Place has tried to tell you how concerned she was for her daughter. Well, her daughter left home September 27 and she didn't even report it until Oct 1. If that were my daughter, I would have found out a lot more than a license tag number. I would have found out his last name and when they'd be back. I'd have called the police department that night, at least by 1 or 2 a, not four days later. I don't know how Mrs. Place got that license tag number, but I don't think she got it off the car that night. Maybe she drove to Martin County to get it.

Isn't it unique that it was John Schaefer who went to the Place house, using a different name, but driving up in his own car? That's not consistent with what a person would do who was trying to hide his identity.

Now about the small leather pouch which John gave Teresa. Mr. Schaefer wasn't working at the time. He didn't have any money. It's not the cost of a gift, though, but the fact that he remembered his wife's birthday.

Schwarz brought up Blind Creek murder site. He talked about how it was not a pleasant site; however, he felt the state had not presented any evidence that proved Schaefer was in St. Lucie County the day of the murders.

Schwarz continued, "The state hasn't even proven that the murders occurred in St. Lucie County. The only evidence they have to prove a crime occurred here is that parts of bodies were found here, but nothing to indicate that death occurred at that scene."

Schwarz brought up the manuscripts, "If you are going to convict a man for what he has written, why is Alfred Hitchcock still walking around? Or

Earl Stanley Gardner?"

Schwarz told the jury there were too many unanswered questions – to many facts that never meshed together. He brought up the jewelry box that had been identified as belonging to Georgia Jessup. He tried to tell the jury the jewelry box was never tied to Georgia Jessup. He stated there was nothing to put Schaefer in St. Lucie County the day of the murders.

Schwarz tried to sway the jury by closing with this "Ladies and Gentlemen they've got the wrong man. Somebody did this but I don't believe it was Gerard John Schaefer."

His last statement to the six-person jury was they had to find Schaefer not guilty because there was too much reasonable doubt. The one thing that stood out in the trial was Schaefer never took the witness stand.

CHAPTER THIRTY-ONE

SEPTEMBER 27, 1973

THE SIDE SHOW OF THE DAY

As the last day of the trial wound down a sideshow of drama reared its ugly head. The sideshow came in the form of an anonymous phone call to the courts. The call was made on September 26. Public Defender Elton Schwarz brought the results of the phone call to the court's attention.

There was a separate hearing at 1:30 PM on Wednesday September 26; the jury had been dismissed from the courtroom for this hearing. Included in that hearing were Defense Attorney Elton Schwarz, Judge C. Pfeiffer Trowbridge, State Attorney Robert Stone and three witnesses who had been subpoenaed by the courts. Those witnesses were Ernie Davis, Clyde Hissong, and Janie Riley.

At this hearing Schwarz told the court he had received a phone call from a man the previous Thursday. The man made accusations to Schwarz about a juror by the name of William Forbes aged 30 from Fort Pierce. However, the caller would not give Schwarz his name.

He was supposed to call Schwarz again two days later on a Friday.

When the caller called Schwarz back on Friday he recorded the conversation. In the taped conversation the caller stated he was with other people while Mr. Forbes told about receiving a jury subpoena. The unknown caller quoted Forbes. "I think it is. I hope it is the Schaefer trial."

This same unidentified caller told Schwarz that William Forbes had stated he had known Schaefer when he was a deputy. He also said Forbes made the statement he didn't like some of Schaefer's tactics. The caller stated Forbes said to him that he would do all he could to have a conviction. Toward the end of the tape the caller told Schwarz that Forbes wanted to stay on the jury.

Schwarz found out why the caller wanted to remain unknown. The caller was a former convict and he didn't want to lose the ability of having his rights restored. Schwarz said he had made arrangements to meet the unknown caller at the St. Lucie County Courthouse the following Monday, however, the caller never showed up.

Schwarz told the court he didn't want to retry the case; however he did have a few suggestions.

He said, "The mere suggestion is sufficient to at least ask Mr. Forbes to step down and be replaced by an alternate juror or to declare a mistrial." (Fryer,

Caller Accuses Juror of Wanting to Hang Schaefer, 1973)

Judge Trowbridge's response was he felt there would be no reason for a mistrial. But, he took his ire out on the unknown caller. He said, "The juror is accused by a nameless faceless, cowardly, person who will not come forward and tell his story under oath." (Fryer, Caller Accuses Juror of Wanting to Hang Schaefer, 1973)

He continued by saying, "it was a dirty lowdown procedure" in which the juror has the right to face his accuser. He said the juror, Forbes, was presumed innocent until proven guilty.

Judge Trowbridge added, "I will not allow the judicial system to be blackmailed by this cowardly, faceless, accuser." (Fryer, Caller Accuses Juror of Wanting to Hang Schaefer, 1973)

Judge Trowbridge continued with his tirade by calling the accuser a faceless, nameless, backboneless person who would like to screw up American justice.

He stated, "If the court were to discharge this juror on the basis of this anonymous, cowardly, unsworn accuser…. There couldn't be a trial held in America without the threat of this type of interference."

Ernie Davis was put in the stand to testify about any statements he might have heard Forbes saying.

Mr. Davis said Forbes told him he would “like to take the ….. and hang him from his ….” (Quina, One Juror Excused in Schaefer Trial, 1973)

Gerard Schaefer, the defendant spoke to Mr. Davis as he left the stand. He told Mr. Davis that he had guts for testifying about Forbes alleged statements regarding Schaefer.

Clyde C. Hissong was the next witness to take the stand. He stated he heard Forbes say Schaefer needed to be hung.

Schaefer also told Mr. Hissong, “Thank you for your honesty”, as Mr. Hissong left the stand.

Hissong nodded to Schaefer.

Next to testify that Forbes had made the statement of wanting Schaefer hung was John L. Potts. He told the courts Forbes had told him he thought Schafer was guilty and should be hung. Once again Schaefer thanked Potts for his honesty.

Bryant Summerlin another witness was called to the stand. His testimony included the night he talked to Forbes after he had been selected for the jury.

Bryant Summerlin said, “I hope you hang Schaefer.”

Summerlin said Forbes told him he couldn’t discuss the case and that the decision would be based on facts.

Bryant Summerlin's statement about hanging Gerard Schaefer cut no ice with Judge Trowbridge.

He told Summerlin, "Do you really think that was an appropriate remark for you to make? You could be held in contempt of court for attempting to obstruct justice." (Quina, One Juror Excused in Schaefer Trial, 1973)

Judge Trowbridge, after hearing all of the witnesses, called Joe Forbes into the courtroom.

He told Forbes, "I have a very difficult duty to perform. You've never been accused or tried. You haven't been allowed to tell your story. Though the court has heard some evidence, it is not reaching any decision on truth or falseness of these statements.

I know precisely how you must feel at this time and I sympathize with you. You are released from any restrictions placed on you."

Judge Trowbridge did however recommend legal counsel if Forbes wanted to do anything about the testimony against him.

Joe Forbes asked the judge if it were possible to reply to the announcement from the Judge. Judge Trowbridge allowed it.

Joe Forbes stated, "I don't feel bad about stepping down. I don't want to stand in the way of justice."

After he made his statement he adjusted his

wire framed glasses stepped out of the jury box and walked outside to the front of the courthouse. Once outside he told the media hounds he would seek the advice of an attorney. Forbes called the accusations "fallacies." In his mind they were myths perpetrated by others.

When the media hounds asked Forbes if he had reached a conclusion about Schaefer he stated "no comment."

So at the end of the trial, the court had to bring in an alternate juror. This was just one more thing in the circus of Schaefer.

While the media circus was hanging around waiting to see if a verdict would be delivered that night they talked to Pat Quina a reporter for the New Tribune. She had interviewed Schaefer many times while he had been in Martin County Jail and Chattahoochee. Pat told the media hounds that she felt the jury would come back with a not guilty verdict.

Schaefer was sitting inside the courtroom around 10:30, when he commented to the media "the whole place is packed and all these people…. All these people, their (sic) looking at me." (Quina, Schaefer Convicted of Killing 2 girls, 1973) He also saw children and wondered what they wanted.

He added that he had no foreboding of doom. He told those around him, he didn't do it.

"I just know I didn't do it. I know that so much, that I'll be surprised if they come back with a verdict other than not guilty." (Quina, Schaefer Convicted of Killing 2 girls, 1973)

This was the part of the reality in Gerard Schaefer's mind. He really felt he would be vindicated.

When he was asked what his feelings had been when the state witnesses were testifying against him he said, "The experience is almost like you're on the other side looking at something else. It's like it's not really happening to me. They say all those things about me, but I don't feel any hate. I sympathize for the Places and Jessups. I feel sorry for them, but when persons start pointing their finger at me, I feel angry. It's a frustration. I know I never met them and that I didn't kill anybody. It's extremely frustrating. (Fryer, Schaefer talks about Himself, 1973)

Gerard Schaefer really believed the State, the Place and Jessup families were wrong.

While talking to the news media Schaefer would from time to time reach over and take his mother or wife's hand. He told them Teresa was the true image of a good wife. He stated she had complete faith in him. She never missed a court appearance and she never missed a weekend visit. This act for the media was again his way of gaining sympathy from them. He wanted the media to know he was a kind, considerate, person. One who couldn't possibly harm another human.

Then He played the, I am an avid reader card. He told the reporters he was very well read. He said he had read the "Winds of War" most of Leon Uris books and had completed "The Rise and Fall of the Third Reich" for the second time. Schaefer tried to show his intelligent side. He wanted people to understand just how smart he was. But as the trial got closer he changed to lighter reading. He read westerns. Again, this was a subtle tactic to let the media know he didn't appear worried about the outcome of his trial.

He quoted a writing of graffiti on the wall of his cell "This is the land of lost content. I see it shining plain (sic), the happy highways where I went and cannot go again." Was this his way of saying he knew he was going to prison? Or was this his way of saying that he was not worried about the outcome. This saying would appear in his book Killer Fiction.

Schaefer then took time to compare his confinement in the Martin County Jail to his confinement in the St. Lucie County Jail. He stated the St. Lucie County Jail personnel were more pleasant than when he had been at Martin County. He said they had been kind and very nice, even though his encounters with them had been brief. He continued by saying they were more humane at St. Lucie County jail but the food had been better at Martin County.

Schaefer continued to reflect on his time in jail. "When being in solitary confinement, the salvation is having peace within yourself, not that I'm a loner, but merely an individual. I cut my own path.

CHAPTER THIRTY-TWO

SEPTEMBER 27, 1973

11:06 P.M.

THE VERDICT

September 27, 1973 3:45pm the jury was handed the case to deliberate. At 4:00 they sent a note to the judge about the license plate. They were instructed to use their own recollection about that piece of evidence. They were then instructed to move to another room, because a bomb threat had been called into the St. Lucie County Sheriff's office.

St. Lucie County Deputies received a call from a man who declined to leave his name. He wanted to know if the Schaefer trial was still in progress. When the deputy told him to hold on so he could check the man told him never mind. The unknown caller told the deputy a bomb had been planted in the courtroom and would be going off in 20 minutes. The courthouse was evacuated. The second interruption consisted of the judge asking the jurors at 7P.M. if they had reached a verdict.

Judge Trowbridge told them that if they were not close to a verdict they would be allowed to take a dinner break. The foreman of the jury Mrs. Betty Haugh told the judge they probably needed to go to dinner.

None of the spectators ever left the courtroom. Everyone wanted to know the outcome.

The jury had testimony from everyone but Gerard Schaefer. They reviewed each piece of evidence presented to them during the trial. They had survived a bomb threat and several phone calls threatening their lives if they didn't come back with a verdict of guilty during their deliberations. Now they were ready to let the world know what they had decided. The time was 11:06pm.

The defense team, the judge and the State Attorney's office had been notified that the jury was done. Gerard Schaefer had rolled the dice per a comment; the comment where he said he would not be convicted because he could not be tied to the scene, and now it was time for the reckoning. The spectators, Schaefer's mother and wife as well as Schaefer held their collective breath while the paper was handed to Judge Trowbridge to read before it was read out loud. What would it be? Guilty or Innocent.

Judge Trowbridge after donning his purple judicial robe and calling the court to order said,

“This has been a long trial and it is an emotional situation, but let me warn you that if there is a person in the courtroom now, who can’t handle the emotional impact of the verdicts, I suggest you leave the courtroom at this time.” (Quina, Schaefer Convicted of Killing 2 girls, 1973) The only person who chose to leave the courtroom was George Jessup, Georgia’s father.

Deputy Court Clerk Douglas Dixon took the paper and read the verdict to the court. The sound of breathing stopped. The jury found Gerard John Schaefer guilty of two counts of first-degree murder in the deaths of Georgia Jessup and Susan Place. Gerard Schaefer showed no emotion as this verdict was read. He had propped his head against his left hand while he sat calmly at the defense table. He glanced around the gallery and flashed a tight-lipped expression at his weeping mother and wife. The electricity in that courtroom was so thick one could almost see it.

After the verdict was read, Schaefer was heard to say, “They didn’t prove it.”

As the verdict was read, there were smiles on the previously strained faces of Mrs. Shirley Jessup, and Mr. and Mrs. Ira Place. Teresa Schaefer, the defendant’s wife threw her head back as if she were trying to get her breath and broke into tears. She cried silently mindful of the Judge’s admonitions.

After the verdict was read, the jury of six was polled as to their decision. It was unanimous each juror felt Schaefer was guilty of the two crimes of first-degree murder.

As the verdict was read Gerard Schaefer showed absolutely no emotion. He just knew in his mind that he would find a way out. He really believed the jury would come back with a not guilty verdict. He had never been placed at the scene so he thought he would be able to beat the rap.

The judge told the courtroom the sentencing date would be October 4, 1973, the jury was thanked for their time, and the court was dismissed.

It had been the habit of Doris Schaefer and Teresa Schaefer to move to the first row of spectator benches so they could lean over the rail and talk to Schaefer during the courts recesses. However, when they moved to the first row after the verdict of guilty was read by the Deputy Clerk, Law Enforcement officers moved quickly to escort Gerard Schaefer from the courtroom. He was not allowed any conversation with his wife or mother. However, he did turn his head in their direction and say, "I'll see you Sunday." That would be the next visiting day the prisoners at the St. Lucie County Jail were allowed visitors.

As Schaefer was led from the courtroom he turned to look at his mother and wife. His lower lip trembled as he saw the scene play out. It resembled the final scene in a bad B movie. The slow camera's close up of his wife's face tear-streaked and partially hidden behind a long white handkerchief. Mrs. Doris Schaefer, who appeared to as grief stricken had taken Teresa, Schaefer's wife in her arms and stroked her sun-bronzed hair while she wept.

As Gerard Schaefer was led away the reporters asked him several questions. He was asked about his feelings concerning the verdict. His response was he was surprised. He was asked if he felt he had received a fair trial and he replied, "I'm not convicted. They didn't prove I did it."

Schaefer was asked what he felt when he looked back at his mother and wife, and he responded by saying, "They know I didn't do it and I know I didn't do it. It was just circumstantial evidence." The sad reality was Gerard Schaefer really believed he didn't commit two crimes of capital murder.

Almost as an afterthought, Schaefer said he had been satisfied with Elton Schwarz's representation of his case. This would later prove false as Schaefer filed appeal after appeal against Schwarz.

It had been a long nine days since the beginning of the trial. It had been an emotional roller coaster ride from July 1972 when Nancy Ellen

Trotter and Pamela Sue Wells had first escaped the web of torture, rape and murder, which was Gerard John Schaefer. A jury of his peers had found him guilty. The sentencing phase would be October 4, 1973. Schaefer was facing life in prison with possible parole at the discretion of the State Patrol Commission. It would also be determined at that time if Schaefer would be a declared mentally disturbed sex offender. If he was determined to be a mentally disturbed sex offender he would be sent to a state mental hospital where he would stay until state hospital officials determined he was ready to be released. Then he would be returned back to the prison system.

CHAPTER THIRTY-THREE

THE AFTERMATH

After the jury had been thanked and the court dismissed, the aftermath began. One juror told the news hounds that he wanted to just forget about the whole thing.

State Attorney Robert Stone stated he was pleased by the verdict. He continued to state that he still believed Schaefer might be connected with the deaths and disappearances of as many as seven to nine other young girls.

"He is still connected to seven to nine murders, and possibly 28. I said it before, and I'll stand by that statement." Stone said. (Quina, Schaefer Convicted of Killing 2 girls, 1973)

He continued, "My personal opinion is that Schaefer belongs in jail, without the fringe benefits of hospitalization in a mental hospital. I would imagine that after a conviction, there would be quite a few convicted people who would rather go to a hospital, than a prison." (Quina, Schaefer Convicted of Killing 2 girls, 1973)

Mrs. Lucile Place, Susan's mother also spoke to the media circus. She told the news people she was happy with the verdict. She said she had told the truth on the stand and she believed State Attorney did an excellent job as well as Philip Shailer. She was asked if she had wanted Schaefer to get the death penalty. She replied by saying she had first had wanted to see him dead, however, she felt he would suffer more by being confined. She continued that death for him would be the easy way out. She said the important thing was he would never be on the streets again.

Mrs. Place said she saw the pain and suffering Doris Schaefer and Teresa Schaefer had suffered at the hands of Gerard Schaefer.

"I tried to put myself in their place and I know what they must have been going through, but my problems were so overwhelming that I felt my case was the most important at the moment."Mrs. Place admitted.

"If Schaefer could have had psychiatric help a long time ago, perhaps this all could have been avoided and Susan would be alive today." She continued.

When she was asked why she stayed in the courtroom during the reading of the verdict, Mrs. Place stated, "I knew I would have to face it one way or the other. I just knew in my heart that the verdict would be guilty, because the man is guilty."

She was asked her advice for parents or young

girls, she said, "… don't ever believe it can't happen to you. Don't ever allow yourself to believe it can't happen it can." (Quina, Susan's at Peace Now Mom tells News Tribune, 1973)

When the media interviewed Elton Schwarz they asked him if he was surprised that Schaefer had been found guilty his response was "Taking into the account the publicity surrounding the case, the date the case was given to the jury and all that transpired I'm not surprised." (Fryer, Schaefer talks about Himself, 1973)

He continued by telling the reporters that Schaefer still maintained his innocence and that he, Schwarz believed him. He said that he and Schaefer had anticipated the verdict. The reality was maybe Schwarz had anticipated the verdict; however Gerard Schaefer had no clue that he would be convicted.

Defense Attorney Schwarz told Bob Fryer, from The Stuart News that Schaefer's conviction was just a battle it was not the war. He was quoted as saying the next "battle" in the "war" would be the sentencing hearing on October 4th. Schwarz would be filing all the motions necessary to have Gerard Schaefer committed to the mental hospital.

Schwarz also told reporter Bob Fryer, that he felt the dismissal of the juror William Forbes affected the outcome of the trial. He felt Judge

Trowbridge should have declared a mistrial in light of the dismissal and the alleged comments, which Forbes had been made. Schwarz continued by saying his chief assistant Bruce Colton would be handling most of the appeal work. Bruce Colton, in 1985 would later become the 19th Circuit State Attorney. The same circuit where he had helped defended Gerard John Schaefer in 1973.

State Attorney Robert Stone on September 30,1973 told Linda Butsch a staff writer for the News Tribune that he would continue to investigate Gerard Schaefer in several other unsolved murders they included, Collette Goodenough, Barbara Ann Wilcox both 19 from Cedar Rapids, Iowa. Leonard Masar, age 46 who was found in a clump of palmetto trees less than a mile due east of the area where Schaefer had admitted tying up Nancy Trotter and Pamela Wells in 1972. Stone said he could link Schaefer to the disappearance and murder of Mary Alice Briscolina, age 14 and Elsie Lina Farmer age 13 both lived in Fort Lauderdale. He had been working with the Broward County Sheriff's office on that case. He was linked to the disappearance of Carmen Hallock age 23; Leigh Ann Hainline Bonandies age 25 and Belinda Hutchins age 22 all who lived in Fort Lauderdale. However, at the time of the article no charges had been filed.

October 4, 1973 Gerard Schaefer was given a

life sentence for the murder of Georgia Jessup and Susan Place.

CHAPTER THIRTY-FOUR

JANUARY 5, 1977

THE FALL OUT

The C- 24 canal is located just west of the Florida turnpike near the Martin- St. Lucie line in Port St. Lucie. This area had not yet been developed in this newly acquired bedroom community in 1977. There were paved roads that ran into dirt roads, but no houses. Along the canal was another wooded and remote area where mangroves grew thick and dense.

On Wednesday night January 5, 1977, a local man by the name of Ed Smith who lived on Flamingo Ave. Port St. Lucie along with some friends had gone to that part of undeveloped land to hunt hogs. Mr. Smith's house was not far from the canal. As was the nature of the men who hunted hogs during that time, they had their hunting dogs with them to sniff out the wild hogs that roamed the area.

One of the hunting dogs found a scent and followed it into the dense undergrowth. When his owner called him back, he returned carrying a bone in his mouth. This bone had no resemblance to any animal the hunting group was used to hunting.

Mr. Smith and his party marked the area by bending twigs on the limbs of trees so it would be easy to find, left his truck at the scene and went back to find a phone to call the St. Lucie Sheriff's Department.

A Deputy by the name of James Mosley was the first responder. He followed Mr. Smith back through the bush and undergrowth, the mangroves and the dense and dark population for several hundred yards. When Deputy Mosley arrived at the scene he found something that continued the horror blight for the 19th Judicial Circuit, law enforcement and the continuing saga of Gerard John Schaefer.

As the darkness settled like a warm blanket around the men Deputy Mosley saw something that became a sense of déjà vu. As the yellow light of his flashlight slowly scanned across the tangled and rotted undergrowth and roots of the mangroves, he saw something that he didn't want to see. He saw human bones and an orange crate. The orange crate was sitting aside almost as if had been used a spectator's seat. The scene was almost a duplicate of Blind Creek. Deputy Mosley swiftly called back up to secure the scene. He knew this find was big, he at the time just didn't know how big.

He radioed to the department for a team of deputies to be sent to work the scene. He told them to follow the glow of his flashlight. When the team arrived, Deputy Mosley noticed, that the team was parking just a few hundred yards from the scene. Mr. Smith had taken Deputy Mosley in the back way. The road would have been seen from the crime scene if it had still been daylight. Two more sets of parents would soon know the fate of their daughters who had been gone since Jan 8, 1973.

When the driver's license, passport and diary belonging to Collette Goodenough had been seized during the search warrant raid at Mrs. Schaefer's house in 1973 a massive search was conducted on Hutchinson Island for the two girls from Iowa. They were never found.

The scene was secured with deputies spending the night. The painstaking work of gathering evidence would begin at daybreak the next day.

The work at the second crime scene started much like the work at the crime scene of Georgia Jessup and Susan Place in 1973 at Hutchinson Island. The coordinator of this second crime scene was Det. George Miller of the St. Lucie County Sheriff's Department. He has been part of the investigation at the crime scene of Jessup and Place.

They shifted the dirt with the same type of handmade shifter, which was four pieces of wood with a screen wire stretched across it. They walked the area making sure all evidence was found. They patience paid off. Among the find was a jawbone with teeth still intact, some rib bones, foot bones, shoes and some electrical wire. However, there were no heads found. This was the same method of operation, which had been found on Hutchinson Island with Georgia Jessup and Susan Place

The St. Lucie County Sheriff's Department started looking through the flyers of girls who had been reported missing over the last few years. They had already sent the bones, teeth and other evidence to the Medical Examiner's office and sent the teeth to Dr. Eric Koppelman a forensic dentist in Vero Beach, Florida, which was located in Indian River County.

CHAPTER THIRTY-FIVE

JANUARY 1977

THE IDENTIFICATION

January 14, 1977, the Stuart News in Stuart Florida ran the headline, "New Schaefer Probe Could Be Launched with Link to Bones." The Gerard Schaefer saga was to continue.

A missing persons report on two girls from Sioux City Iowa had found its way to the St. Lucie County Deputy's office. The girls had been reported missing in 1973. The Medical Examiner's office would verify if the bones found at C-24 Canal on Jan. 5, 1977 was indeed the two missing girls. The ability to make this positive identification was helped along the by anthropology department at the University of Florida.

January 18, 1977 four days later, the Stuart News read, "Remains Found in PSL Those of Iowa Teen." The first set of bones and teeth to be identified was that of Barbara Ann Wilcox age 19 years old. Her remains were identified through the dental records that Dr. Eric Koppelman had received from Iowa.

Personal items belonging to Barbara Ann had been seized in 1973 when the search warrant had been served at Doris Schaefer's house, the mother of Gerard.

Ms. Wilcox had a traveling companion by the name of Collette Goodenough. Although the other set of bones and teeth had not yet been tied to Goodenough, her personal effects had also been found in Doris Schafer's house in 1973.Goodenough's passport, driver's license and diary were among the items seized.

As the story of the girls unfolded law enforcement determined they had left Sioux City, Iowa to visit Collette Goodenough's sister in Biloxi Ms. sometime in December 1972. They let her house on Jan 8, 1973. She had taken them to Highway 90 in Biloxi, Mississippi. They told the sister they were going to hitchhike to Florida. They apparently wanted to visit Disney World in Orlando.

No one seemed to know how or why they found their way to Port St. Lucie. A sleepy bedroom community filled with snowbirds (those northerners who come south for the winter), with no nightlife for the young people. Port St. Lucie rolled their sidewalks up at dark thirty. There were no hangouts for the young, no place to party. The question will always remain how and why were they here?

Gerard Schaefer had not yet turned himself in

to the Martin County Jail to serve his six-month sentence for the aggravated assault charge against Trotter and Wells. Judge D.C. Smith had given him from September 1972 to January 15, 1973 to spend the holidays with his wife and to get her situated in Fort Lauderdale with his mother.

When Collette's sister didn't hear from the two young women she assumed they had hitchhiked to Florida. No one appeared concerned when the two girls were not heard from. All of these events led to the kidnapping, rape, mutilation and murder of two young girls. The chain of events would lead to yet two more victims whose screams could not and would not be heard. The count was now at six young women who were screaming silently.

In the meantime Attorney Elton Schwarz continued to maintain the innocence of his client Gerard Schaefer in the deaths of Susan Place and Georgia Jessup. But, when he was interviewed by the news media in January 1977 after the bones of Collette Goodenough and Barbara Ann Wilcox were found Schwarz stated he felt as if his client would be charged with their deaths. Did he know something that no one else knew?

Did he believe in his heart that Gerard Schaefer was guilty of the heinous crimes he was charged and convicted of? Had Schaefer confided in him or had he just said enough to lead Elton

Schwarz to draw that conclusion?

Schaefer had already spoken to the assistant public defender, Bruce Colton, before his conviction of Place and Jessup and asked him if Bruce wanted him to confess. Bruce told him that he didn't want to know.

Was this statement the reason that Elton Schwarz believed he would be charged?

In November 1977, appeals were filed by Schaefer's attorney in the Fourth District Court of Appeals to argue the first of many appeals on Gerard Schaefer's behalf. The Attorney General Robert Shevin argued for the State.

The saga of Goodenough and Wilcox re-opened on May 1981 when a fisherman found a human skull floating near the C-24 canal shoreline. The skull was identified as belonging to one of the two young women who had been found there in 1977. The skull showed that the young woman had been shot at close range in a sad ritualistic manner.

CHAPTER THIRTY-SIX

THE CIRCUS OF SCHAEFER CONTINUES AT AVON PARK PRISON

The circus of Gerard Schaefer continued even after his conviction of two counts of first-degree murder in the deaths of Susan Place and Georgia Jessup. Even though the personal items of Collette Goodenough and Barbara Wilcox were found in the home of Mrs. Schaefer and although their bodies were discovered January 5, 1977 at C-24 Canal, Gerard Schaefer was never charged in their deaths.

During the process of identifying the bodies Chief Investigator Lem Brumley made it quite clear that while there was evidence found, there was not enough to bring the case before the grand jury. The belief was that grounds for charging Gerard Schaefer for two more murders was shaky.

Yes, there had been physical evidence at the residence, and the bodies were mutilated in much the same way as Jessup and Place. However, being able to place Gerard Schaefer with the two girls was almost impossible. The ME couldn't even determine a medical cause of death. There was no way to determine what happened to them other than they were probably murdered. It could be argued that Schaefer had found the personal articles, the driver's license, passport and diary.

The State Attorney's office knew a grand jury would not indict.

Gerard Schaefer began his second act in this three-ring circus. November 17, 1973 Teresa Dean Schaefer went to Avon Park and made her one and only visit to Gerard Schaefer. It was not a visit for the sake of a visit. Teresa served her husband with divorce papers.

The press went in to overdrive. They said that Elton Schwarz had been dating the 21-year-old wife of Gerard Schaefer and had handled her divorce. They said that Schaefer had suggested the divorce and marriage. Elton Schwarz and Teresa Dean Schaefer were married November 30,1973 six weeks after Gerard Schaefer went to prison for the murder of Susan Place and Georgia Jessup.

Meanwhile, Gerard Schaefer found another outlet for his narcissistic personality. He told anyone who would listen that he was exposing a conspiracy. That conspiracy was one of drug-dealing lawmen. Schaefer said that he had been framed by these lawmen because he was going to expose them and the Martin

County prosecutors. In the reality that was in Schaefer's mind, he had been framed for killing two "drug informants" because he refused to play ball with the all-powerful drug lords.

When this bit of reality didn't go the way Schaefer planed, he took another route. He found another outlet for his amusement and front-page news. In 1979, Gerard Schaefer declared that he was married to a Filipina "picture bride." This picture bride appeared during some point in 1980, moving in with Schaefer's father, Gerard, Sr. Out of the blue, a marriage license appeared, without a ceremony and this marriage was accepted by the authorities at Avon Park the minimum security prison where Schaefer was incarcerated. Because of the "marriage" there were a few conjugal visits were approved. However, as soon as the new bride received her green card in 1985, she became history.

CHAPTER THIRTY-SEVEN

GERARD SCHAEFER GETS BORED

AND FINDS EVEN MORE THINGS TO AMUSE HIMSELF

After the "Filipino" bride hit the high road, Schaefer once again decided he needed a diversion in his boring life. In the early years Schaefer did several things that put him in the spot light.

He decided he would work with the North Miami police. The sting was he would pose as a 14-year-old prostitute by the name of Dee- Dee Kelley. Dee- Dee would offer nude photos to pedophiles. The postal inspectors confiscated the responses to his ads. None of his correspondents were ever prosecuted. Instead law enforcement found another fish to fry. One that Gerard Schaefer had helped to create. That was his involvement with another con man and known pedophile by the name of Eric Cross.

Eric Cross had been sent to Avon Park because only the best behaved prisoners were allowed to be incarcerated there. Among the 1,100 inmates housed there during the 1970's and 1980's were 50-some odd child molesters. Eric Cross fit right in when he arrived in April 1982.

Almost at once he became a hero at Avon Park. Many of the prisoners had a one time or the other seen his work, the photographs of children in different poses and modes of undress. He had been known as the" King of Porn" among his peers in Europe. Even though he did the required chores, he was always plotting the next venture.

Finally he found a great venture. Eric Cross set up an agency for children. He started by contacting the Dott Burns Agency. He convinced Ms. Burns he was legitimate by his smooth con job. He had Ms. Burns write to him at a P.O. Box, which happened to be the prison PO Box. But, he needed access to a phone. All outgoing calls from a prison are collect. The operator tells the person who answers the phone that it is a collect call and calling from a correctional facility. Cross needed to fix that small problem.

Enter Gerard Schaefer. Eric told Schaefer about Viewfinder, Inc. and the plan he had to photograph schoolchildren with animals. He told Schaefer a lot of money could be made doing this. However, according to Cross there was one small hurdle. They needed a telephone. Schaefer had a plan. He just needed to talk to his father, Gerard Schaefer, Sr.

When Schaefer, Sr. made a visit to his son the plan was outlined. The plan as explained to

Schaefer, Sr. was that Eric Cross wanted to photograph schoolchildren for educational purposes by posing schoolchildren with animals. He showed Schaefer, Sr. letters he had received RARE, the Rare Animal Wildlife Effort which was an affiliate of the Audubon Society. Cross also had posters and instructional material he used in his presentation to Schaefer, Sr.

Cross had gotten this material from Jerry Liberman, the director of RARE, who said that Cross appeared to be an enthusiastic volunteer. He said that Cross had offered to donate half of the profits, which came to about $5 a photo. When Liberman found out the scam was to take lewd photos of children and pass them to other pedophiles he said they didn't have the time to check out every volunteer.

Schaefer, Sr. bought the same story that Liberman did. Cross told Schaefer, Sr. that he needed a conference line in order to conduct the business of Viewfinder, Incorporated. He told Schaefer, if he would install a conference line, he could call collect and then, Schaefer, Sr. could re-dial any number Cross needed dialed. He gave Schaefer, Sr. the song and dance routine that he would pay for these calls with money he received from his mother in Canada.

Schaefer, Sr. bought into this scam because he

said that Cross seemed like a really nice man, who was well educated, and well spoken.

The scam was set into place. They added another player. She was a chubby African woman named Ruksana Diwan. Gerard Schaefer, Jr. had been a pen pal of hers. They not only exchanged letters they exchanged stamps from the two different countries. Ms. Diwan was not all she appeared to be either. She told Schaefer she was a member of the Tanzanian Lions Club.

Ms. Diwan flew to Atlanta for an International Lions Club convention, and after she arrived she told Schaefer she wanted to "defect" from her socialist homeland. Schaefer gave her a place to stay at his father's house, in the downstairs apartment. Ms. Diwan began visiting Schaefer at Avon Park. She was not what Schaefer expected. She was short, rotund, in her mid20's, and light- skinned.

However, Schaefer was able to use this gift. He explained to her what the business of Viewfinder was and what he needed for her to do. He told her the money was going to be very good. She was ecstatic.

The phone line was installed and Ms. Diwan went to work. Several times a day Eric Cross would go to the phone booth outside in the prison yard. He would call Ms. Diwan who was waiting beside the phone in St. Petersburg, Florida. The long distance operator would say she had a collect call from Eric Cross at Avon Park Prison, which was only about an hour away from St. Petersburg. Ms. Diwan would agree to pay for the call. She would then re-dial the number Cross wanted.

Once she got the party on the line, she would say "Hold on a minute, I have Mr. Cross on the line."

Cross took this opportunity to talk at great length to Dott Burns who owned a modeling agency about his movie plans. He told her the star would get $1,000.00 a week and Burns would retain a commission for her part. She fell for it. She sent him more than 100 composites of young girls. Cross would tape his favorite to the wall of his cell. He would cut another one out and put it in his wallet.

Cross was very particular about the girls he chose. Some he rejected because they weren't pretty enough, others were to "mature". As he continued to make his calls he would tell Dott that he was in Los Angeles, or New York. One day it might be "colder than blue blazes" or the next raining cats and dogs. He would also tell Ms. Burns he was in an airport getting ready to hop a plane. That was his excuse for the reason her agency couldn't reach him. But Ms. Diwan had his back. She would drop by Ms. Burns' agency to drop off a letter or to pick up photos.

Cross decided he needed to expand his business so he placed an ad in the Tampa newspaper looking for a freelance photographer for a major project. He got over 50 replies. The one Cross selected was Dean Cason. Apparently Mr. Cason had done work for Dott Burns in the past and he was impressed when Cross told him he could head up the 50-photographer organization that would be taking all these pictures of schoolchildren with animals. Not even the attorneys for Burns or Cason knew the person behind this business was in prison at Avon Park.

Cross stepped up his plan another notch. He told Ms. Burns he had selected 20 finalists for his movie. However, he had a problem. The problem was several scenes required nudity. He explained some of the scenes were Swedish Sauna baths, where people would sit around before they jumped into frigid lakes. One of the scenes showed Japanese girls diving in the nude for pearls and a Brazilian Indian fertility rite. He told Ms. Burns that Americans might consider nudity abhorrent; however, this movie was to be made in Europe by a company called Susan's Magic Carpet. Cross told her that Europeans had a much more casual attitude about nudity, especially when came to children.

Cross told Ms. Burns that Dean Cason was to take some tests shots of the girls in the nude to see how they behaved in front of the camera and to see if they met his criteria. When he met with Cason, Cross was very specific. He told Cason he want the girls completely nude. He didn't want to see any "fig leaves." He wanted to see full views of the front and back. Cason was not sure he wanted to do this, however, Cross like Schaefer had the gift of persuasion. He talked and talked to Cason and re-assured him it would be fine.

Cross even went one step further, he called the parents and explained it all to them. He told them he would return all photos as soon as he had looked at them. Some parents out right refused. However, those that showed some interest, he wrote letters to and promised many things he knew he would never deliver. Finally the parents of seven girls agreed.

No one seems to know, or if they did know they were not telling how 50 high quality slides of nude young girls was able to make their way inside the prison. Not only did they get in, they got back out as well undetected. When the officials were questioned they said that they thought one of the smugglers was a staff member and the other was Ruksana Diwan. Ms. Diwan was thought to have hidden the slides in her clothing. However the slides got inside was secondary to Cross' reaction. He hated them.

One prisoner stated that Cross was "raging

mad." The slides appeared to be washed out, color was wrong, the lighting was bad and the poses were amateurish. He called them "Coppertones." A term used as simple unenticing nudity like the old Coppertone ads.

One prisoner who saw one of the photos of a child holding her hands over her genitals with a look of pained expression said he knew that child had not posed of her own free will.

For two days Cross paced like a caged lion raging at his lack of luck after so much work.

Out of all the photos only one shot was considered top quality in facial expression, lighting and nudity. Cross arranged for this photo to be shipped to a very well know child pornographer in Europe. The others he sent to a man by the name of Robert Lodge in Seattle, WA. , who it was believed copied them and sent them back to St. Petersburg where they were allegedly returned to the parents.

The fallout of this crime, which was committed in a prison, was the exploitation of young children not only by Eric Cross but their parents as well. Gerard John Schaefer was a party to this exploitation. He used his father and Ms. Diwan either as willing or unwilling participants. However, neither of the Schaefer's was charged in the scheme. Eric Cross on the other hand was given extra time to his sentence.

Schaefer was not content to sit back while Eric Cross became news. He decided it was time to get back on top. He found a new outlet for his narcissistic endeavors.

CHAPTER THIRTY-SEVEN

THE LETTER WRITING CAMPAIGN, LAWSUITS AND DEATH THREATS

1985

Schaefer went on a letter writing campaign to anyone including members of the media to discredit and threaten Elton Schwarz, Judge Trowbridge, State Attorney Robert Stone, State Attorney Philip Shailer, and Martin County Sheriff Robert Crowder. Elton Schwarz was investigated twice by the Florida Bar Association for any indication of conflict of interest by his marriage to Teresa Dean but they found none. The complaints were dismissed.

When this tactic failed Gerard went on another campaign. He threatened the lives of Elton Schwarz, Teresa Schwarz, Robert Stone, Judge Trowbridge, and Robert Crowder. He alluded to the fact he had put contracts on their lives. A former inmate who had known Schaefer for several years notified State Attorney Robert Stone and told him that Schaefer was making plans to kill him and the others, if he was ever released from prison.

When Elton Schwarz was asked what the content of the letters were he stated they were letters saying that Schwarz had not properly represented him because he was in love with Teresa.

His bragging to unknown persons that he was going to escape the minimum-security prison at Avon Park fueled this fire. Several confidential informants told the corrections officials that Schaefer was going to break out.

Schaefer had also been known to gain the trust of other inmates, gain their confidence so they would confide in him and then he would flip on them. He would tell their confidences to law enforcement or the department of corrections.

No one seems to know why or how Gerard Schaefer was sent to Avon Park after his sentencing. Avon Park Correctional Institute is located in Avon Park, Florida. It is located at the Air Force Bombing Range on Highway 64 at the end of a long dirt road. It was built in 1957 to house minimum and medium custody males. In 1977 it was changed to house closed custody males, those criminals who were habitual and high-risk violent offenders. Schaefer was listed as one of those who were high risk.

After the death threats to Judge Trowbridge, Robert Stone, Elton Schwarz and Robert Crowder, there was talk in the prison of an escape attempt. It appeared that Schaefer and another inmate were planning on taking an unapproved leave of absence from Avon Park.

A former inmate who had known Schaefer for several years told State Attorney Robert Stone, who in turn told DOC. When the Department of Corrections got wind of this unscheduled leave, they immediately transferred Schaefer. They sent him to a maximum-security prison and put him in solitary. He was transferred August 18, 1985 one day before a reporter from WTVX was supposed to interview Schaefer at Avon Park.

The reporter, Jim Holmes had stated the station wanted to interview Schaefer as part of a profile story on him. Holmes said the department of corrections had approved the story.

However, when Schaefer was transferred the station decided not to pursue the interview Elton Schwarz applied for a Concealed Weapons Permit for himself and his wife. Gerard Schaefer was shipped off to Starke. This is the home of Florida's death row. However, that didn't stop him from continuing to find ways to be on the front page.

In 1985 Gerard Schaefer filed a complaint with the Governor of Florida, Bob Graham, against his attorney Elton Schwarz. Schaefer's new attorney, Barbara Lithicum, filed the complaint.

The complaint stated that Gerard Schaefer was not given adequate legal assistance by his former attorney Public Defender Elton Schwarz. Schaefer also stated in his complaint that he was agreeable to the divorce and the marriage of Schwarz and Teresa because Schwarz had allegedly told him "he would be released from prison as soon as possible."

Schaefer began his next plan of attack. He filed a petition in circuit court stating he had been imprisoned illegally. The line of reasoning for this petition in Schaefer's reality was that First-degree murder was a capital crime. Because it was a capital crime, he was entitled to a 12-person jury as opposed to the 6-man jury who had heard his case in 1973. Attorney Dan Brawley who stated that Schaefer had done a superb job of researching and arguing his case handled this petition. He also stated that Gerard Schaefer had turned into a great litigant. This only added fuel to Schaefer's perception of himself. Elton Schwarz told the news media this argument had been in the courts before.

When the argument was finally heard before a Polk County Florida Circuit Judge, Schaefer's request to be released from prison was once again denied. Polk County Dennis Maloney ruled he had no jurisdiction to hear the cases. His attorneys told the media those same arguments had been heard and denied several times before.

This didn't deter him in the least. He just took another path.

In October 1982 Schaefer filed a $6 million lawsuit against his old nemesis State Attorney

Robert E. Stone. He alleged Stone used his power to try and have Schaefer killed in prison. Schaefer stated in his lawsuit that the attempt was in revenge for an investigation he was conducting in prison which would show how Treasure Coast law enforcement officers received payoffs from drug smugglers. When that fell through, Schaefer said he wanted to be given a lie-detector test to show his credibility of the claims that Stone was trying to have him killed.

In 1983 Gerard decided he would add one more thing to his ever-growing list of things to keep him occupied. He was falling off the front-page news again, none of the people he threatened appeared to take him too seriously, and his appeals were falling on deaf ears so he took another route.

He started playing mind games with law enforcement all over the State of Florida. He sent out letters to ask them to check their records to see if he was a suspect in any of their open cases. He didn't ask about unsolved just open. He was playing the game all narcissists play—the game of "catch me if you can."

In 1983 he wrote Lake County Sheriff's Department. He specifically asked Lake County about "those two who disappeared from the Ocala Forest. There are some cops and newspaper people figure I got em. What do you say we talk about it?"

He had bragged that he could give law enforcement 34 bodies or burial sites. He told some that would listen to him that he had started killing in 1963 when he was 16 or 17 years old. He was taunting and teasing, as only Gerard Schaefer knew how to do.

CHAPTER THIRTY-EIGHT

COLLETTE GOODENOUGH

AND

BARBARA ANN WILCOX

REVISITED OCTOBER 1985

While Gerard Schaefer was busy writing his letters, making his death threats, being moved from Avon Park to Starke Prison and filing his numerous appeals; Rick McIllwain was busy trying to connect the dots in the murder of Collette Goodenough and Barbara Ann Wilcox

On October, 1985, Rick McIllwain, an Investigator with the State Attorney's office in the 19th Judicial Circuit, made the statement they might have found the "missing link" needed to link Gerard Schaefer to the slayings of Collette Goodenough and Barbara Ann Wilcox.

If indeed the missing link had been found, Schaefer if convicted could have been given the death penalty.

In 1981 a skull had been recovered in the C-24

Canal after the waters had receded. The skull was identified as belonging to one of the two murdered girls.

Rick McIllwain told reporters he would have to revisit prior witnesses and if he couldn't find them, then he would have a problem.

As the news leaked out, the source of the missing link was an inmate at Starke. The inmate told investigators that Schaefer had confessed to the slayings of Collette Goodenough and Barbara Wilcox.

Meanwhile, Gerard Schaefer remained in solitary confinement at Starke Prison. He was prohibited from watching television, ate his meals in his cell, was restricted in what books he read, and he was allowed to exercise and shower once a week.

The Department of Corrections maintained he was there for his own protection. Schaefer continued to expound on his own belief that he was innocent of all the charges. He also continued to file motions in the court system to get released from prison.

Gerard Schaefer found a new way to get noticed. He complained of dizziness and was admitted to the prison hospital at Lake Butler Medical Reception Center from December 17, 1985 until December 30, 1985.

Gerard Schaefer had gained the council of yet another lawyer by his charming and charismatic ways. Attorney David Higginbottom, from Frostproof, Florida complained to Governor Bob Graham that the treatment of his client Gerard Schaefer was cruel and that the system was determined to kill him. Attorney Higginbottom's area of expertise was not criminal law...it was civil. He even went so far as to ask other lawyers to jump on the bandwagon, which was Gerard Schaefer. His mantra was, "If we don't continually fight for civil rights, we won't have them."

The question is who was fighting for Collette Goodenough and Barbara Ann Wilcox as well as Georgia Jessup and Susan Place?

CHAPTER THIRTY-NINE

GERARD SCHAEFER'S SIDE BUSINESS AND DEATH WISH

*I*n the meantime Gerard Schaefer began an entrepreneurship. He managed to start up and run a mail-fraud operation from his cell. He did this by working with partners in crime to post ads in sex magazines to solicit money from various kinky "tricks" aka johns.

The way he worked his scam was masterful. He would take different pseudonyms, which were always female names. He would become "Mistress Felice", who was a dominatrix, "Jessica Zurriaga", a prostitute, and "Marton Miller" who was a stern husband –killer on death row.

Part of Schaefer's charm and business in the mail fraud of sex was he his ability to be inventive. He would send the "slaves" of "Mistress Felice" his female underwear and they would pay in cash for the privilege of washing them and sending them back to her.

When he needed another diversion he would write other inmates at different prisons declaring his undying love for them all the while laughing at them.

Schaefer decided to add to his thriving business. He wanted to prove he was indeed somebody. He became the "jailhouse lawyer." But this title came with a twist. As Schaefer befriended and wrote briefs for his fellow prisoners, he gained their trust. He would get them to tell him everything, and to confess to all their past crimes. Then he used this information as barter to law enforcement. This barter in Schaefer's mind would win him his freedom.

Schaefer had gained the trust of an inmate who told him where the body of one of his murder victims could be found. Schaefer told law enforcement, which put his newfound friend on death row. But it didn't win Schaefer any brownie points with law enforcement. However, it put his life on the line. He became known as a snitch and not one who could be trusted. Was this an extension of his childhood games when he always got killed in the game? It is possible as well as probable.

Gerard Schaefer didn't stop there. He befriended the notorious Ted Bundy who, when he met Schaefer admitted that, according to Schaefer, "had been inspired to kill two victims on a single day in 1974. Was this a true statement or was it yet another reality that was in Schaefer's mind?

He said that Ted Bundy was in awe of him and

that he (Schaefer) was a hero to Bundy. He was quoted as saying; "You cannot imagine how I felt having the famous fiend in awe of me." (Plarski, Killer's Book:Fiction or "How-to" Ex-Martin Deputy Call Novel a Product-'It's Not Me', 1989)

According to Schaefer he and Bundy debated and discussed the fine points of murder such as "the maggot problem" and how to clean up the upholstery after the dying victims urinated in their cars.

Schaefer was not content with just Bundy; he befriended Otis Toole who was convicted of a killing spree from out west to the south. Toole allegedly confessed to Schaefer the killing of Adam Walsh. Schaefer used his friendship with Toole to again gain possible notoriety and his bid for freedom.

Otis Toole told all who would listen he was the one who killed and beheaded Adam.

However, whenever the authorities questioned him he would deny it. It also couldn't be independently proven. In fact it had been proven that he didn't know anything and couldn't have committed the crime.

Gerard Schaefer formed a plan. He wrote to John Walsh, Adam's father posing as Toole demanding $50,000.00 for Adam's remains. He said he wanted John to be able to "get them buried all decent and Christian." When Walsh ignored Schaefer's generous offer, Toole bailed on Schaefer's get rich scheme. The only one who got any pleasure out of this event was Schaefer. He got great sadistic pleasure from inflicting pain on the Walsh family.

CHAPTER FORTY

MOTIONS GET FILED

A NEW ATTORNEY TAKES OVER

JANUARY1986

Attorney, David Higginbottom who was from a small town in Polk County, Florida, took Gerard Schaefer on as his own special project. He was running for the 10th District of the U.S. Congress. Schaefer would create great press and Higginbottom had a platform on which to run, that being civil rights of convicted criminals.

Higginbottom felt that Gerard Schaefer not been properly represented with the charges and conviction of Jessup and Place in 1973. Higginbottom told the news media he felt that Schaefer had received a raw deal. He stated that both prosecutors and his defense team had made mistakes in the case. He said the defense team never got the consideration they deserved.

He continued by telling the press that Schaefer had fallen through the cracks of the criminal justice system and just kept on falling.

Higginbottom went on with his tirade of the lack of judicial justice for Gerard Schaefer. He said there had been some mistakes made at the trial; however, he knew it was understandable in any criminal proceedings. But he felt that the mistakes were more suspect.

Higginbottom told the press that Schaefer's move to Starke and his confinement to solitary was a ruse to shut him up forever. He appealed to then Gov. Bob Graham by saying the prison system was bound and determined to kill Schaefer. He said Schaefer was sent to Starke to keep him from talking to the reporter from Station WTVX and telling the world about his illegal conviction as well as the drug operations, which involved members of law enforcement in St. Lucie County.

Higginbottom played on the sympathy of the public domain when he said that no matter how heinous Schaefer's crime that he didn't deserve the cruel punishment of solitary.

Higginbottom who was civil lawyer made his political platform civil rights for criminals. His war cry was, "If we don't continually fight for civil rights, we won't have them."

Schaefer added to the drama of Higginbottom's grand standing by the continual blasting of his former attorney Elton Schwarz. "Here is a man who is supposedly watching out for my best interest but he's sleeping with my wife. He should have had the decency to come to me and say, "Hey, I'm having an affair with your wife and I can't reconcile my professional aim, which is to get you out of jail, with my personal aim, which is to keep you in so I can get your wife." (Press, 1986)

Elton Schwarz countered by telling the press "We did absolutely nothing wrong at the trial. I did everything possible in his defense. I'll be glad when this petition is resolved so I don't have to answer any more questions about it." (Press, 1986)

Finally, in 1987, Circuit Judge Rupert Smith was finally fed up and done with the circus of Gerard Schaefer. He denied the last of the 18 appeals Schaefer and his defense team had filed concerning Schaefer's belief that Elton Schwarz had given ineffective counsel in 1973 during the murder trial of Georgia Jessup and

Susan Place. Schaefer had included in those appeals the accusation that Schwarz framed him because he was going to marry Schaefer's wife, Teresa Dean Schaefer.

Judge Smith told Schaefer's Counsel David Higginbottom, "The defendant should realize, once and for all, the die is cast, the mold is made, and the loaf is baked. Therefore, the judgment is final and forever, as concerns the defendant, Gerard Schaefer, it cannot be uncast, or unmolded, or unbaked."

(Barszewski, 1987)

He also said there had to be a conclusion to the litigation and abuses of the judicial processes. The final blow came with a final statement when he said that Schaefer's motion in 1985 concerning effective counsel was peculiar in that Schaefer had waited 12 years to make that claim.

Gerard Schaefer was done in the system. He could no longer file appeals. He would no longer be on the front page. He had finally fallen off the pages of the papers across Florida. Schaefer took a new route.

But was he really done?

CHAPTER FORTY-ONE

1989-1991

KILLER FICTION,

BEYOND KILLER FICTION, KNOCKING ON JOE AND SONDRA LONDON

On January 24, 1989 Gerard Schaefer lost his so-called biggest fan. That fan met his date with the electric chair at Starke Prison. Ted Bundy's appeals process had finally run its course. This date in time brought back someone from Schaefer's past.

Just when the public and law enforcement thought it was done with Gerard Schaefer, he once again burst on the scene. This time he had help from a former girlfriend. Her name was Sondra London.

She was the former Sandra Stewart who Schaefer had dated in high school.

Ms. London had read the accounts of the arrest and trial of Schaefer in 1973; however, she waited until February 1989 before she contacted him in prison. Sondra London had found her way into the literary world of publishing. She had Gerard

Schaefer and they had a history.

Gerard Schaefer met Sondra at a high school dance. He had taken a young lady by the name of Dee Cunningham to this dance. When he spied Sandra Stewart, as she was known then, he said he walked right up to her and said, "Don't I know you from someplace?"

That was the classic pick up line. She denied knowing him. He went home and went through every spelling of Stewart in the book he could find. He finally found her and called her and asked her out. She accepted. Schaefer dated Sandra until the end of 1965 when they both went away to school. She went to Tampa and he stayed in the Fort Lauderdale area.

In 1989 Sandra used basically the same line when she contacted him at Starke. She wrote "Remember me?" She went on to pitch her idea for a book and his experiences. Schaefer was ecstatic. He told her that his case was "virgin territory". This statement played into her marketing idea for touting his work in her promotional materials as his "Virgin Sex Queen", as she used their old teenage love affair as her hook. He then told her he was "favorably disposed", to someone who had known him on an intimate basis.

Schaefer was also able to get around the monetary problem when he claimed all of the writings were fiction. The "Son of Sam" law disallowed for a criminal to profit off of his own crime. Schaefer felt he would profit by the book and then in his twisted mind or his reality he would donate his proceeds to charity.

He flattered Sondra by saying she had been a former great love of his life. He didn't admit to any hostility during their parting of ways.

When London met Schaefer for the first time at Starke after years of not seeing him, she noted he was nebbish: portly, pale, balding, and half –blind. She said he reminded her of a "middle-aged, deskbound clerk gone to seed."

Gerard Schaefer had a new audience. He bent over backwards to impress her. He claimed to be innocent. He told her drug-dealing cops had framed him and attorneys who were afraid of his integrity. He became the martyr with a big "M".

He wrote her saying, "I let Satan get control of me. I hated evil. I wanted to destroy Evil. I went and immersed myself in the battle but destroyed myself in the process. God saved me by allowing me to be framed by corrupt people."

Later he wrote, "My battle has been to overcome the problem (of serial murder). I believe I have accomplished this through Jesus Christ. My own personal belief in Jesus assures me of my future as a child of God, but that does not excuse me from helping my fellow man. My reward, if any will be a spiritual one" (Newton)

Three days later, on March 21, 1989, Gerard Schaefer wrote Sondra again. He had flipped to another page in his reality.

He told her "I am, factually, a captain in the Dixie Mafia… I have, factually, the power to have you killed. I have, in the past used these powers." (Newton)

Three days later he sent her another letter which stated, "I am a Syndicate man… When I put on my (mob) subchief's (sic) hat I am "Don El Tigre"… and I can scare the living shit out of you." (Newton)

Sondra appeared not to be afraid of this latest revelation. She told those who would listen that when she read the accounts of the trial in the paper and the prosecutors calling Schaefer's case, "maybe the greatest crime the history of the United States." (Plarski, 1989), it freaked her out. She made the statement that it didn't match the person she had known in school. London was eager to renew old friendships but later in 1993 London made a different statement about Schaefer.

She told a newspaper reporter of the Orlando Sentinel that she had known about the dark side of Schaefer at an early age. That even though he had treated her well, she knew about his urges to kill.

She also told the reporter that Schaefer's writings shocked her personally and they offended her. But she felt the book needed to be published because of the impact.

Ms. London had read with much interest in the papers about the manuscript, which described the murders. She wanted to publish his work. Some have said she fancied herself as another Ann Rule. Ann Rule had written the book "The Stranger Beside Me" which detailed Ann's friendship with the newly deceased Ted Bundy. Sondra may have fancied herself the next Ann Rule because of her history with Schaefer. Gerard Schaefer would be her meal ticket. She even contacted Captain Yurchuck to try and draw him into the story. She wanted to interview him about Schaefer. He declined.

She told the Palm Beach Post August 14,1989 that even though she found his writings to be lurid, gross, disgusting and terribly degrading, she was going to promote the book because she wanted to do a big story.

The first book titled Killer Fiction was released in June 1989. It included the actual transcripts of the manuscript used as evidence against Gerard Schaefer's trial in 1973. It described in vivid detail fifteen different stories written in first person. The main character spends the entire book engaged in sex with prostitutes. This sexual engagement was not only before but sometimes after he murdered and mutilated them.

Journalist JR Brun did an interview by mail with Schaefer and in the prelude to the interview he talked about the story line in one of the Stories called American Psycho. He said if one took the amount of sadistic details and multiplied it by ten one would begin to approach the level of intensity and revolting realism found in all of Schaefer's stories.

Gerard Schaefer in his twisted mind called his work good writing. He told anyone who would listen that his stories were meant to make one throw up, and leave one looking over their shoulder for a long time. He said that he did research by reading mortician texts and homicide investigations texts. He said he has also seen people die by stabbings and shootings while he was with the Martin County Sheriff's office for less than a year. This statement in itself seems ludicrous and a product of his own reality. The truth is Gerard Schaefer was only with the Martin County Sheriff's office 28 days before he was fired for the aggravated assault of Nancy Trotter and Pamela Sue Wells. He didn't have time to see many if any stabbings and shootings or do much in depth research unless it was first hand.

He told the Palm Beach Post, "You can't just sit down one day and write a convincing horror tale without doing some exhaustive research." (Plarski, 1989) That statement is correct. One can't write a convincing horror story unless one has a very vivid imagination – does extensive research or has firsthand knowledge of the crime and horror.

One of the sentences in the introduction stated, I don't care if people hate my work so long as they understand that it is a product. It's not me." (Plarski, 1989)

Sondra London said, "Schaefer writings look into the vivid, violent mind of the serial killer."

However, she told the Palm Beach Post that Gerard Schaefer continued to maintain his innocence. She also stated that Schaefer continued to state his work was merely fantasies. Then she back peddled and said she agreed with law enforcement in that Schaefer wrote extremely convincing about murder. She went on to say that it was incredible how he wrote about it.

A Hollywood agent Sondra London hired to try and sell Schaefer's book to Hollywood made the statement that reading Schaefer's book was like watching a traffic accident. He continued that it was terribly repulsive however he couldn't take his eyes off the book.

Prison officials were drawn into the continuing the circus. They read the manuscript. They refused to allow Schaefer to continue to write saying that the rules said an inmate could not receive obscene material in the mail. So they confiscated the manuscript draft, which London had sent for Schaefer's review.

"It was a graphic presentation of sexual behavior and graphic violence in violation of state law. "This was a statement made by the Department of Corrections. However, the manuscript was returned to Schaefer a week later. Sondra London contacted an attorney to fight for Schaefer to have the right to write this book. The Department of Corrections returned the manuscript. They said they didn't fear a First Amendment rights violation, but because parts of the manuscript had been used in Schaefer's trial they were bound by law to return it. By introducing the manuscript at the trial it became a legal matter and Schaefer was entitled to receive it.

Beyond Killer Fiction was the next release attributed to Schaefer and his writings. It was touted as a satire against Schaefer's own case. The story revolved around a rogue cop who slaughtered prostitutes in his spare time.

Gerard Schaefer and Sondra continued their correspondence. Schaefer wrote to London on January 20, 1991 and he reveled a part of himself he had up to this time had kept hidden.

He wrote, "I am the top serial killer and I can

prove it." (Newton)

He claimed to be an expert hangman. He told London in his letter to her that he could dispatch victims "so quickly that they wouldn't even pee on the rope." (Newton)

He also confessed to the fact that he had "never at any time required more than two strokes to behead a woman. Never. I was absolutely skilled at it." (Newton) Schaefer was very vague on the number of kills; however, he said his body count was between 80 and 100 victims. He bragged that he didn't know if killing pregnant women counted as two kills. He continued by saying that it got confusing. He told Sondra that he had been disemboweling one whore while the other one watched. The second one drowned in her own vomit. He wasn't sure if that one counted a valid kill.

Schaefer made it a point to tell London in March 1989 that he didn't have a sex problem. He said a sex problem meant one was unhappy and discontented. He was neither of those. He wrote to her again on April 9, 1991 and told her he was not a sex killer, He was unique and he could guarantee it.

Even with all of Schaefer's alleged confessions and his touting of being in the Dixie Mafia, Killer Fiction and Beyond Killer Fiction flopped in sales. Sondra London became strapped for funds. Gerard Schaefer had a solution. On January 18, 1991, he proposed marriage. He told her that a wife couldn't testify against her spouse. He went further by saying that she couldn't be forced to testify even if he showed her a box of severed heads.

The next day for whatever reason, Schaefer appeared to have a change of heart. He decided to blame London for his crimes.

"I will tell you here and now that plenty of your women died because you couldn't help me solve my various crises in 1965. I tried to tell you about it but you couldn't deal with it. You bolted, abandoned me; that's when it started." (Newton) 1965 was the year Schaefer and London parted ways.

Added to the already lagging sales on Killer Fiction and Beyond Killer Fiction, Prison officials confiscated mail between Schaefer and London. On May 16, a letter was opened and in it was the outline for new stories. A disciplinary report was found and Schaefer spent the next 30 days in solitary for "conspiracy to conduct business" from his cell.

In the meantime Sondra London was finding her own way to make money. The television show A Current Affair offered to pay her 1,000.00 for a segment on Schaefer. Schaefer agreed though not very wholeheartedly. Steve Dunleavy was the reporter who did the segment.

Dunleavy added to the circus of Schaefer. Instead of the “they framed me” route, Dunleavy took the opposite route. His interview with London had her saying to viewers, “he was normal, except he had a compulsion to kill.”

Robert Stone, the State Attorney for the 19th Judicial Circuit who had prosecuted Schaefer, was recorded as saying Schaefer was one of the worst serial killers ever. Dunleavy even added his own observation by calling Schaefer a “monster”, and a “deceased specimen.” He even added his own thought that Schaefer would “find his hell on earth.”

When Schaefer saw the interview he wrote London on April 12, 1992 and told her they were through. “You’ve tapped a Black Hole of genuine rage and it’s focused on you…. Just never speak my name to anyone, anywhere ever again… I’ve met a number of people from the Satanist underground. To express my appreciation for what you said (on TV) I’ve explained to them about your daughter. They’ll probably get in touch with her personally… If you want to make an issue of this then the kid is gonna (sic) be the one to pay the tab, am I clear?” (Newton)

Sondra London went yet another step farther when she published Knocking on Joe. This was a book about several serial killers in the prison system among them Gerard Schaefer. Schaefer when interviewed by JR Bruun stated he had no idea she was going to include his writings in the book. By this time he was angry at Sondra because she had dumped him for Danny Rolling. Not only did she dump him for Rolling, she became engaged to Rolling.

Danny Rolling had killed eight students at the University of Florida and had been condemned to death. Sondra saw an even better money making venture in Rolling. She stopped corresponding with Schaefer. She cut him off at the knees so to speak. Gerard Schaefer had once again fallen off the front-page news. He was not happy.

He started a campaign to degrade Danny Rolling. In the interview with Bunn he said that Rolling was a confessed butcher and sex killer. He stated Rolling had killed five school children and that he should be executed immediately. He slammed Rolling for reveling in the endless publicity. He said that compared to Otis Toole, Rolling in Schaefer's mind was a two faced phony. He stated his belief that Rolling was a phony was because he had no remorse for his actions.

One has to wonder if Schaefer was really talking about Rolling or himself. One also has to wonder if he was jealous because he had fallen out of favor with his ex-girlfriend a second time and wanted to get even. Schaefer hated loose women.

In his mind they were whores. Had he come to this conclusion about Sondra London? It is highly possible and very probable. Sandra had walked back into his life years after she had walked out. She had allegedly lost her virginity to him when they had dated in high school.

Schaefer went on a hate campaign to intimidate Sondra into taking him back into the fold. He said that what Sondra had written about him in Knocking on Joe was 'largely fabricated foolishness."

He went further in his degradation of London when he calls her a serial killer groupie for wanting to marry Danny Rolling. He told the interviewer JR Bruun that Rolling kept Sondra on a string just for his own amusement. He called London 45, old and fat. Schaefer said that Rolling like his women young and dead. Then Schaefer added insult to injury when he stated that what he wrote creamed her (London's) old cunt. He added she was a fan of his.

Schaefer was asked if he was sexually aroused when he wrote. He denied it saying he wrote for his audience and his own erotic amusement. Schaefer said he turned out product, which had nothing to do with his own personal erotic reality. That was why he referred to himself as asexual. He said most of his fans were the kinky types again citing his former publisher Sondra London as one of them.

Schaefer told Bruun he was a pussy hound, and was only interested in lively, living human females for sex. He said he wrote stories about weird sexuality, however he always made it a point to let his fans know it was always fiction.

Schaefer bragged about an alleged letter he received from a fan who was asking about whether or not people had an orgasm when they were executed. He continued by saying this type of information was not released by the mainstream publishing industry, even though there had been much research done in this area. He maintained there were many official reports, which detailed all different aspects of execution, from hanging, gassing, to death by electrocution. Then he went into his expertise, erotic asphyxia. He told the interviewer he had done an interview by mail with prostitute who specialized in erotic asphyxia.

Schaefer called this alleged prostitute Matron Mary and she had supposedly written to him under the name of Mary P. Davis. He described the term erotic asphyxia as the engagement of sex play where one hung themselves by a hanging noose to the point of orgasm. Schaefer said that this Mary P. Davis enlightened him in the art of kinky sex in general and erotic asphyxiation in particular. He said that this Matron Mary aka Mary P. Davis kept him well informed about them. He stated, "People are drawn to that which is forbidden and socially taboo. It is those taboos that I address in my fictional works.

My writing is very honest. I tell you in clear terms about those monsters lurking under your mind's bed and because I dare to face those monsters boldly, I am condemned as a madman by the reactionary forces of repressions who (sic) set themselves up as the morality police of our civilization." (Bruun, 2007)

But in the introduction of Killer Fiction Schaefer writes this statement, "I'm not going to tell you if it's a true story or not. I'd prefer to see you sweat." That was Gerard Schaefer's lethal legacy.

Gerard Schaefer told his interviewer that he had filed a lawsuit against Sondra London in the U.S. District Court to block the release of Knocking Joe. He stated he has met with police investigators who would probably charge Sondra London with felony theft by fraud. He said she misrepresented that she owned the work of Schaefer. He went on to talk about how his fans would send him excerpts of Knocking on Joe and ask him about his long association with Ted Bundy.

Schaefer appeared to feel that Ted Bundy was the epitome of a criminal celebrity. The fans allegedly would ask Schaefer about the various sadistic, execution procedures. He said his readers were interested in the offbeat. Schaefer said he was able to provide insight because he supposedly had the opportunity to discuss murder methodology with some of America's most heinous criminals. He continued to brag about his conversations with Ted Bundy, his conversations with the execution squad who put Bundy to death, his conversations with Otis Toole and Kenneth "Mad Dog" McKenna another murderer at Starke Prison.

Schaefer accused McKenna and Bundy of being necrophilia and that was how he learned the art of necrophilia. He also said McKenna used a black stocking to kill. However, in the manuscripts that had been seized in 1973, Schaefer talks about the black stocking as well as the necrophilia. He did not learn these things from Bundy, McKenna, Toole or anyone else he allegedly talked to at great length with in prison. However, he said he never lacked for a great storyline. He told the interviewer that his stories were fiction however; they did accurately reflect how those types of crimes were committed as underworld executions. He said he was a writer and he told a really good story and he resented an imputation that his stories reflected actual crimes that would be attributed to him.

So the saga of Gerard Schaefer and his writings would continue. He wrote for a magazine called "Justice Now".

One of his stories was called Murder-Demons: This story is listed here in its entirety. The drawings are Schaefer's – they were found in the manuscripts seized during the search warrant in 1973 at his mother's residence.

Torture for the sake of torture did not interest me. It was, in those days, important to me to feel good about what I was doing. Whores were agents of evil, and as a good Catholic young man I had no difficulty with what one might consider philosophical grey areas. There was good and evil; a well-defined line ran between the two. Whores were evil. Whores were to be killed. Once that decision was made, the problem became how to do it successfully. A great deal of practical study went into the matter. The whore had to be selected, transported, killed and disposed of. The best way to kill them was to hang them. It was convenient, quick, effective, silent and tidy - except for the excrements

The alternative method was usually the use of a plastic bag. The bag was tied over the whore's head and she died by suffocation. This method was convenient, silent and effective, but it was far slower than hanging and much messier. I got to the point where I'd push such women out of the car after tying on the plastic bag. It was less unpleasant for me that way. There were variations on the kills.

I'm speaking only in generalities here at the moment, so that you can understand that there was a plan and a purpose and this was never a situation where some sex-crazed madman was snatching girls from the public streets every time the moon turned full. Returning to this thing about torture... my experience was that whores see events in terms of sexuality. Please consider the speed involved in a kill. A transient road whore is agreeable to suck cock; she has no qualms when driven to a remote area. I'd pull the gun and handcuff her, get out of the car. I'd go around to her side and get her out. She might say, "What are you doing?" or "I'm not into kinky stuff." I'd take her back by the trunk, open it, take out the noosed rope, put the noose over her head, pitch the other end up over a limb, tie it to the trailer hitch, get back in the car, start it up, put it in drive and the whore would be pulled up. We are talking three minutes on an average, five at the very most, between cuffing and the suspension. The victim doesn't realize what's happening until she's actually dangling, it's that fast.

Many kills were completely impersonal. The victim had revealed herself to be a whore and my responsibility, as I saw it, was to kill her. The killing was usually done quickly without any sexual molestation, rape or brutality. I knew how to set the noose so that the victim would be rendered almost instantly unconscious. I'd read the journals of the nineteenth century hangmen and knew exactly the point to apply pressure to cut off oxygen to the victim's brain. Some killings were almost peaceful. The whore would shiver, convulse, kick a bit and then be still.

As you might expect, this sort of kill was fairly boring. There was no stalking, no challenging ruse, and no fun. The real enjoyment was in the hunt. The kill was satisfying, but the cleanup was work. There is a post-kill depression that must be overcome. The initial impulse is to throw the corpse in a ditch, a canal, a hasty hole, to be rid of it at once. Your average killer cannot deal with the actual harsh reality of the act. He has no sense of responsible purpose, no long-term commitment to what he's doing. A lust killer murders for sex, and once he's fulfilled his lust, he dumps the corpse and flees from the scene and from himself as well. He looks back on the event and feels guilt, rather than triumph.

There came a time when I decided to make the game more interesting. I did this by introducing the concept that it would be better if the whore understood she was to be hanged and concurred in my decision to destroy her and what she stood for. I felt that if she understood what the ultimate good purpose was, that our experience would be a fulfilling one of shared intimacy.

I'd read a number of accounts where the hangmen had sex with condemned females; the women were agreeable to the intimacy and acquiescent on the scaffold. I wondered how that might be: fuck the whore, and then hang her, with the whore knowing she would die at the conclusion of the sex. It was a remarkable concept, and certainly not unique to the world, so I decided to try it. Let me tell you here about one very special experience.

The whores were mostly sad, stupid, moralless (sic) young women who, when confronted with the finality of their situation, simply fell apart emotionally. They'd listen for a few minutes and then begin a downhill slide punctuated by tears, slimy snot and pissy (sic) pants. The nicer I'd be, the more I'd try to make them understand, the faster they'd dissolve into great bawling sobs. But there were some exceptions.

The very finest of these exceptions was a wonderfully attractive young call girl from Omaha who had just come down to Miami to try her hand at the snowbird trade. I was introduced to her by a friend who'd suggested we go visit her and get out dicks sucked. We went to her trick pad, and my buddy went with her and got sucked off. When I went with her, I declined the blowjob; instead I made an appointment with her for an all-night sex fest. She was agreeable, even enthusiastic. We set a date.

I was absolutely smitten by this sexy whore. She was lively, intelligent, and had a sensuous figure. I was enchanted. I wanted our assignation to be special. I went right out and bought her a brand new rope. I knew she'd look exquisite swinging at the end of it. I took great care in selecting it. As the date approached, I called her to confirm our evening together. I instructed her on what to wear. I wanted to see her in pink and black. She had long blonde hair fixed in ringlets that would look so nice against a black evening dress. Black heels and stockings with a garter belt. Pink bra and panty. A frilly brief. She assured me she'd look her best for me. Never before had I been so taken with a whore. I was furious. She was seducing me, and I was helpless before her daunting sexuality. She would have to suffer for that. Yes, suffer. I drove out to Davie and purchased an excellent horsewhip. I'd put her to the lash before hanging her! She'd pay for her seduction!

The following days I spent clearing an area in the center of a melaleuca (sic) copse. I hacked out an area the size of a large room with a narrow entrance trail. I assembled the gallows beam, nailing it up between two trees. On a second tree, I stripped off the small branches, hammered in a piton and hooked a pully to it. The tree formed a living whipping post. I dug her grave. Deep. Down to limestone bedrock. I hauled in two twenty-gallon buckets of water from a canal. I carefully surveyed the scene and then went back to town and purchased a stepladder. It was just what was needed. I arranged the noosed rope over the gallows beam. Brought in a pair of Coleman lanterns and extra fuel. Towels. Knives. Buckets. Accessories. Everything was perfect for the whore.

I picked her up at the Dade County trick pad. She looked stunning. I bought her prime rib at the Forge. She ate a hearty last meal. Baked Alaska and brandy. I wondered if she'd be able to keep it down. Sometimes whores would puke. It was hard to predict and always messy. We drove north on Route 27 through the night. I told her how beautiful she was, how much I'd been looking forward to our romance to come.

She yawned, burped, leaned against the car door and seemed to doze. She was bored. She'd heard it all before, many times. A beautiful bored whore. I knew I'd soon have her complete attention. She'd see me through new eyes. She'd be alert to every nuance of my speech. I watched her light up a cigarette and stare into the night. Her last night.

I soon had the car parked at the end of a

limerock (sic) road at the edge of a trackless swamp. She looked puzzled. I cut the engine, pulled out a small pistol and put it to her face. She gasped. I got her cuffed. She was mine. All mine. Forever. It had taken less than a minute. Her initial thoughts were of sex. A bondage scene, she thought. She told me she didn't do kinky stuff. I was agreeable. Drew her toward me for a kiss. She pulled away. She didn't want to kiss me. She demanded I remove the cuffs. Demanded! I just said no. She glared. Such a pretty fit of pique. All full of roast beef and ice cream and booze. I needed to soften her hard look so I said, "Flies love a cunt but prefer a dirty shit hole. Are you aware of that?"

She just stared at me. Blinked. The hardness was replaced by wariness. "What do you mean?" she asked cautiously. I explained it to her. She said, "Please take me home." The first "please" of the evening. She was learning manners. I wondered if she'd say "please kill me" before the sun set the eastern horizon on fire. I shook my head, took out my penis, and instructed her to suck on it. Then I opened a switchblade and told her that if I felt her teeth on my cock I'd slit her throat. Quickly. Expertly.

She nodded. Kept her eyes on the knife. "Please don't cut me. I'll do whatever you want." I told her to think of my dick as a straw, and to suck my balls dry. She slid over, put her face in my lap and began to lick my penis. She got it up and took it in her mouth. I pressed the blade to her neck, and held it in place with my left hand. With my right, I explored underneath her skirt, squeezed the panty covered (sic) labial lips. She bobbed her head up and down professionally, her tongue laved my shaft.

I slipped a finger under the elastic of her panty; her crease was dry. I ran a finger up her vagina. She made no response but to suck more fervently. My finger drifted to her anus, and pushed into its center. She tightened her sphincter. I pushed my finger all the way up into her and felt soft turd. Put my thumb in her vagina. I could feel the thin wall of muscle separating the two vaults. Warm drool ran down my balls. I could hear the smack of her lips, the slurp of hot saliva. My crotch was wet with her spit. I fingered her anus, thumbed her cunt. Time passed.

She came up off my cock with an apology. There was a ring of frothy white saliva encircling her mouth, a clown's greasepaint. I told her to get back on the job. She said she'd had enough she'd done what I wanted. There was an edge to her voice. I took my finger out of her butt, my thumb out of her twat. I reached over and rubbed my finger under her nose. She drew back, eyes large and snapping with annoyance. Then she saw me put my finger in my mouth. I began to lick it. She watched, enthralled, the spit wet on her chin, the corners of her mouth glistening. "Flies truly love it", I told her.

She made a noise deep in her throat, swallowing. I licked my finger again and asked her if she wanted to throw up. "Take me home", she said, halfheartedly looking away, sensing there would be no going home for her, ever.

"Gimme a little kiss", I ordered. She turned toward me and shook her head furiously, eyes downcast, almost demure. I pulled up my trousers and let myself out of the car, went around to her side and opened the door, grabbed her by the hair, and jerked her out of the car. I flung her into the weeds and put the beam of the flashlight on her. She rolled to a sitting position, skirt bunched around her waist, black garter straps against her soft white flesh between her stocking tops and panty. Eyes rivaling those of a jacklighted (sic) doe - all wide, wet, startled, full of uncertainty.

I pulled her to her feet by her hair, turned a beam of light toward a narrow path leading into the copse of trees. I gave her a push. She stood fast before the dark entrance. I came up behind her, put my arms around her and drew her to me. I licked her neck, her ear, the line of her jaw, pressed my hard cock into her rump. "I'm going to stick it in you. Your cunt. Your ass. I'll fuck you nice." I felt her tense. She took a step forward. I took one back. She pivoted and swung a kick toward my balls that missed and made her stumble. I laughed. Took out the knife. She screamed. I stepped toward her. Tripped her, rolled her face-down in the leaves, and pressed the blade to her cheek. "Shut up!" I snarled. She went silent.

Beneath me, the well-fueled engine of her body huffed and puffed. I could hear her panting; feel her breathing hard beneath my own body. She was damp with her exertions. Mosquitos hummed around us. Frogs sang a chorus in the swamp nearby. I smelled her perfume, the moist earth, the rotting vegetation around us. A jet whined far above, the whore whined below.

She sobbed, instinctively understanding the price of failure. "Please. Please. Please", she murmured. I put the point of the knife to the corner of her eye. Told her I'd poke it out if she screamed, kicked, or misbehaved.

Whispering, I asked her if she understood. She sobbed, nodded a little. I ran my hand up her leg, squeezed her buttocks. She lay still, unresponsive. I stood up. Brought her to her feet by her hair. Returned her to the car. I sat with her. The night was still young. She asked to blow her nose. I let her snort into my handkerchief. She wanted a cigarette. I lit one for her, stuck it in her mouth. She sucked on it greedily. I watched her, she watched me. Death watch. I let her spit the cigarette butt into the dash ashtray. She leaned back against the door. Great crescents of dark sweat stained her evening dress, her perfume mingled with the sour acid stink coming from under her arms, leaves and seeds ornamented her bodice, her knees were pushing through her nylons. She sucked in her bottom lip, closed her eyes, and laid her greatest fear before me like a gift. "I don't want to die", she muttered, a statement as true as the moon, the stars, the eternal abyss, the gray mosquito feasting on her cheek.

"You'll live to see the sunrise", I promised. "Why me?" she asked the night. "Oh, God, help me", she prayed, her voice catching in her throat. She lifted her eyes and asked, "What do you want from me?" I opened myself to her instincts and intuitions; let her touch the truth naked in my eyes. She saw her own fleeting mortality, the transient nature of her earthly existence; murder demons, capering. She lowered her head and began to cry, hopeless sobs that left me untouched. I'd seen it before, understood the way of the whore. The cascading tears, the streaming wet cheeks, forerunners to the viscous nasal snot that would leave her face and bosom beslimed (sic). The ultimate gambit.

I rudely seized her nose with my left hand and forced a jumbo Kotex napkin into her mouth with my right. I tied it in place with a nylon stocking. Her eyes were wide and blinking. Her throat working furiously. She suddenly blew her nose. Tendrils of mucus whipped out, clung to her cheeks, soiled (sic) her dress. She squirmed with fear and alarm. Her clever words silenced, her verbal ploys stifled, all her plans in disarray. There was a stench of sweat. Her flanks were sodden with it. Her tresses were becoming lank and greasy. There were twigs and leaves in her hair. I pulled her to me and wiped her nose, her chin, her mouth. I tasted her tears, kissed her eyes. Promised her that I would treasure her memory for a lifetime, that we would become one in flesh and in spirit. The whore began to weep anew, but with a refreshing sincerity.

My experience is that women have a predisposition toward deceit. Whores lie. They are creatures of expediency and calculated illusion. A commercial menstrual rag will stanch the incontinent flow of lies from a whore's mouth as well as the bloody slops from her cunt. Great truths are better communicated tacitly, with a look, a gesture, a smile.

I'd promised the whore a sunrise, then (sic) turned her world upside down. She looked comic and vulnerable hanging by her ankles. Her head was in an empty 20-gallon bucket, her shoulders hard against the metal rim. She was so quiet I thought she might be unconscious. The night had subsided, and a gray light filled the tiny glade. The sun would soon be up.

I picked my way over to her and shined my flashlight beam into her face. Her eyes were wet and alive, blinking against the sudden glare. Mosquitoes rose from the bucket in a swarm to settle on her clothes. Her exposed flesh was a galaxy of tiny red welts. The flying insects of the night had fed well. The day shift would fare even better.

In 1991 Schaefer sent a letter to a private company in this letter he stated he knew they concerned themselves with missing persons. This is a copy of that letter.

Dear Sirs,

I've heard your company concerns itself with missing persons. I'm enclosing a Time Magazine story about my case. I'm also written up in many other magazines and books. Since 1973 I've been linked to 170 dead and missing women on 3 continents. The links include 105 photographs of female victims taken either before or after death and 170 pairs of panties stripped from victims. Depending upon what book you read I am credited with as few as 34 kills and as high as 170. All sources agree that I am unquestionably the most prolific killer of women between the years 1963 and 1973.

The years went past and only 6 of the 170 victim's corpses were recovered. Very few of the victims were ever identified by some. There were 3 continents involved, over the 40 states and 20 from countries over a period of ten years. I've never talked to cops. Still don't.

Last year I had a letter from an old woman who read a crime tabloid story about how I'd killed roadside hookers by driving them out to a rented warehouse where they were murdered by hanging. The old lady wrote & wanted to know if I'd gotten her hooker daughter. As it turned out I had hanged the whoredaughter (sic). The old lady was glad to know the kid wasn't walking around with amnesia.

It's now 1991. I'm still not talking to cops but I suppose there are people who wonder about what happened to hippie daughter who hit the road and never returned. If your company searches for females missing since the 1963-73 time period it may be useful to be able to have me ready to take a look and let someone know if I got the person they're looking for. This would necessarily be a private sort of thing since I never talk to cops. Just a thing to set a parent's mind at ease about what happened.

I am completely infamous as a killer of young

women but that was long and if I can help a parent privately without police meddling, I will do so.

Please advise if you are interested

Sincerely,
GJSchaefer

PS The 105 photos were stolen by a police officer &sold to a tabloid magazine syndicate in 1973. I've seen 5 in print, 4 show girls hanging, 1 shows a girl sitting on a toilet. Because most of them were to (sic) lurid to publish in the USA they were published in European tabloids. I've unsuccessfully tried to recover the photos. The cop who stole the photos was subsequently fired.

Gerard Schaefer had delusions of grandeur. He also continued to play the game of "catch me if you can." He really believed he was smarter than law enforcement.

Schaefer sent out yet another letter to a company concerning his interest in capital punishment. In this letter he says:

Oct.15, 1989
Greetings,

You guys probably don't read newspapers so

here's a timely tip on a book you don't want to miss... more than 20 stories of murder and sex crimes drama; many of them set in Oakland Park and Broward County.

From your own jurisdiction you'll read about Sgt. Chuck Kemp, his lost(sic) for juvenile delinquent pussy, his cowardice in the fact of a homicidal madman and his eventual commitment to the State Hospital at Chattahoochee where he's found to be incurable.

Jolie Parsons, the teenage schoolgirl found raped and murdered off Oakland Park Blvd.

Kevin Goodheart, he taught at Northeast High by day, by night he was a child stalker.

Oakland Park: A cesspool of vice, murder and corruption; carefully laid out for you the way it really is. No sugarcoated placebo from the city P.R. dept, can match the situation in Oakland Park today.

These books do not glamorize murder by nortraze (sic) it as the vicious, disgusting act it is- and carries it to its natural social conclusion in the

State Electric Chair.... Read about executions as they are really conducted.... And learn first hand (Sic) about the Early Release Killers like Charlie Street who are heading South to kill cons... and why.

Sold only by mail, only by Media Queen Publiciations (sic); a reading adventure that will never be forgotten: Killer Fiction Rouge Cop... By G.J. Schaefer, a name you recognize.

Signed
G.J. Schaefer (Schaefer, 1989)

Schaefer changed the real Sgt. Chuck Hemp's name to Chuck Kemp. He also uses his (Schaefer's) sojourn at Chattahoochee in this so-called fiction book. He used the name Goodheart, which was a play on the name Richard Goodhart the supervisor who had fired Schaefer from the School system.

The book was called Rouge Cop – it featured the Adventures of Detective Dan Kelly, Rogue Cop. Dan Kelly was supposedly Gerard Schaefer.

The book was promoted as "A murder Serial by Ex-Cop &Convicted Killer G.J. Schaefer.

He wore that title like a crown of achievement.

The synopsis read:

Hits like the Impact of a 9mm parabellum (sic) slug. Written in prison by GJ Schaefer- ex-cop and convicted killer who know the Florida crime scene inside and out- Killer Serial: Rogue Cop is a dizzying spin along the edge of insanity in a world gone literally mad.

Detective Dan Kelly- he's the top crime buster in Metro Miami by day... but by night he's the Dark Prince of the City, with an avaricious finger in every racket from whores to murder for hire. Known on the street as Dirty Dan, this Rogue Cop metes out his own brand of bizarre justice to the criminal slime balls who are his closest associates.

Chief Pork Shepard- is a good old boy who can never get enough of Dan's sweat or his own glory. Always ready whit those clever remarks just when Dan needs them the most, the Chief makes sure the boys at the F.O.P. appreciate him keeping the streets of Miami clean for right-thinking folks.

The Reverend Rapist-whose Legion of Decency is out to protect the world from pornographic filth, uses his limo to conduct private sessions for girls too young to drive. His movie-star good looks come in handy when he's videotaped raping a pigtailed virgin from the BVM Academy.

Crystal Beavers Dan's corn-fed teenage sex slave-straight from an Iowa farm and her step-daddy's arms-wanted to star in Miami Vice but instead winds up in a scene of sexual depravity beyond her wildest fantasies.

Melina Stein, Queen of the Freak Trade-Miami's top madame (sic) and Dan's not –so-silent partner-intends to control Dan's sinister empire, and she'll sacrifice anyone who gets in her way.

Women of every flavor spice up the **Killer Serial** – from Morgana the Cruel, Mistress of the

Lash and Melina's closest pal, to Nurse Nancy Blue, Radiant Angel of Mercy, whose tender ministrations carry and unending stream of AIDS- ridden, crack-fiends gently, gently into that good night.

The Slug, Der Henker, Chuck Spear, Emilio and the rest- all circling like ravenous sharks through the deep waters, mad with the scent of whoreblood (sic). They soon find out what happens when their bizarre passions take them beyond the protection of the law- and into the hands of Dirty Dan, **Rogue Cop.** (Media Queen)

The names in the so-called fiction were very similar to Schaefer's victims the crimes were a carbon copy of the crimes perpetrated on his real life victims.

Chief Pork Shepard – Shepard was the last name Schaefer used when he picked up Susan Place and Georgia Jessup in 1972.

Crystal Beavers came from Iowa-which was the same state Collette Goodenough and Barbara Ann Wilcox were from. Crystal was the nickname Collette went by. The same name Schaefer used when he went to the home of Mr. and Mrs. Jessup after Collette disappeared.

Dan Kelly was Schaefer's alter ego. Schaefer had been a cop albeit not a very good one. He did stop many women in his job. He believed he was a top crime buster because he had received a commendation while at Wilton Manor PD.

In 1989 he sent Sgt. Chuck Hemp of the Oakland Park PD a letter. This letter was to brag about his newest fiction book. He more or less tossed names of victims in Hemp's face. He deliberately taunted Hemp with what he claimed was fiction.

CHAPTER FORTY-TWO

1990

THE COURTS GET TIED UP AGAIN

Gerard Schaefer was not yet finished with the court system in Florida. He filed another appeal in 1990 seventeen years after his conviction of Georgia Jessup and Susan Place.

The day of the appeal hearing Schaefer asked for a postponement. He told U.S. Magistrate Judge Luarana Snow he needed more time to prepare his case. She reset the hearing to September 18, 1990. She was going to allow him to present evidence and testimony about his appeal. This was a first for Schaefer in his appeals process.

He had appeared before the appeals court 14 times prior to this appeal. The appeal was the same one it had been in all of the prior hearings.

He was filing again that he had incompetent counsel at his trial in 1973. Schaefer's defense was his lawyer Elton Schwarz had railroaded him because he was having an affair with his wife.

The added kick to this hearing was Schaefer had agreed to waive client-attorney privilege so

Schwarz could be called to testify. Schaefer's new attorney Federal defender, Kathleen Williams played right into the reality of Schaefer. She told the court she was seeking Schaefer's medical records to show that he was seriously medicated at his original trial in 1973 and therefore he was unable to aid in his defense.

Assistant Attorney General John Koenig was not happy about this turn of events. He seriously complained to the judge by telling her about the delay and the attempt to introduce his medical records as evidence.

He said, "I didn't think this was going to be a retrial. Now they're trying to obtain evidence that wasn't even presented at trial." (Kane, 1990)

Koenig told the courts that Schaefer's appeal was based on the arguments that judges had rejected in the past.

The support group at that hearing included Sondra London his publisher and his mother Doris Schaefer. Sondra told the reporters that Schaefer had been in prison so long he was nervous about getting out.

September 18, 1990 was supposed to be just another day in the life of the judicial system. However, in the courtroom of U.S. Magistrate Judge Laurana Snow, it was anything but another day. September 18th was Schaefer's day in court to argue his 15th appeal.

Schaefer attorney, Assistant Federal Public Defender Kathleen Williams presented her argument for a new trial.

She told the court, "Never in the history of jurisprudence has a defense attorney married his wife's client. The conflict is clear.

Schwarz maintained continued to maintain the stance he had taken from the filing and hearing of the first appeal. He told the courts that while on the outside the quick marriage looked unusual that he fell in love with Teresa after the conviction and he did all he was able to do to keep Schaefer out of prison. He told the courts that at no time before the conviction were he and his wife Teresa romantically involved until after the trial. He added he was shocked when the guilty verdict was returned in 1973. He said that he felt the state was unable to prove a case against his client, which was beyond a reasonable doubt. Schwarz told the judge that Teresa had kept up a façade for so long by standing by her man that when it was over she was on the verge of a nervous breakdown.

He continued his testimony by stating that for years after the divorce and marriage between him and Teresa, there was a steady correspondence between him and Schaefer. Schaefer insisted that Schwarz handle his appeals.

Schaefer had added to the ten-year drama by continually sending out letters or what Schwarz called "bulk mailings" to attorneys, legislators, reporters and judges, claiming he was framed for the murders of Jessup and Place. He claimed there was a conspiracy and that conspiracy was concocted by State Attorney Robert Stone. Stone told the court that he had strong case in 1973 against Schaefer.

Assistant Attorney General John Koenig, Jr. said added his two cents worth to this hearing, he told the court that it had the appearance of conflict, however no conflict was ever established.

Williams couldn't provide any evidence of romantic involvement. But, she did argue that the romance unconsciously effected Schwarz's efforts. Her argument included the fact that Schwarz didn't object to the inclusion of certain incriminating evidence used against Schaefer. She further argued that there were too many questions in the case that had never been asked.

The underlining current in this hearing was the fact that Gerard Schaefer continued to be represented by Schwarz on his appeals. When Schaefer was asked why he waited so long to object his response was that it never occurred to him that what had happened could have affected his case.

The judge while stating that she was skeptical of the claims against Schwarz, she conceded that there did seem to be a conflict of interest. However, she didn't rule on September 18th. She told all in the courtroom she would make her decision within the next few months. She would forward her decision on to U.S. District Judge James Paine who would make the final decision.

Gerard Schaefer not to be outdone tried to open up the circus tent again. When he was allowed to voice his petition he told the court, "Elton Schwarz had a motive for all of this. My young wife, who was smitten by his attentions. Sex with a young girl. It's an ancient motive. Turn to your Bible. Book of Kings. David and Bathsheba. So it happens. It happened to me." (Filkins, 1990)

Schaefer tried to compare himself to Moredici who was husband of Bathsheba. He implied he was the victim.

October 1991, U.S. District Judge James Paine ruled that Schaefer had received a fair trial in 1973 and there was no conflict of interest in the relationship between Schwarz and Teresa Schaefer. Judge Snow said that in her 51page report that Schwarz had given Schaefer a fine defense. She stated that the evidence against Schaefer had been very strong.

Schaefer's attorney Kathleen Williams told reporters that she had not yet seen the report and would have to review it before any decision was made to challenge it.

Schaefer still maintained there was a conspiracy by the trial judge; the medical examiner and Schwarz conspired to convict him because he was about to expose a major drug conspiracy along the Treasure Coast.

CHAPTER FORTY-THREE

SCHAEFER TRIES A COMEBACK

1991-1994

Gerard Schaefer tried his best to make a comeback to the front page of the paper. He wrote from his prison cell to let the world know that he felt television stations should be allowed to broadcast executions. He told the papers that he was very well versed in what was done to people before, during and after the electrocutions. He stated executions were horrible and that the public should be exposed to them. He wanted the public to aware of the "reality of violence, whether it be brutal murder or state-sponsored execution."

He added to that statement, "I believe that if society condones executions then they should be publicized on TV because nothing that is done in the name of the people should be done in a secret setting."

Schaefer's narcissistic personality emerged in his letter. He wrote, "I am a university-trained writer who has been in prison 18 years. I've written several books that address violence, murder, prison life and executions in graphic detail, and touch on areas that are regarded as unmentionable in a family newspaper such as yours. Violence is a deadly serious matter and is on the increase due to society's penchant for glamorizing violent acts and people. Florida Prisons are Horror Houses because the media as no access to them and citizens cannot be expected to make intelligent decisions concerning capital punishments unless they are aware of what those punishments consist of in whole." It would appear that Gerard Schaefer was once again making a pitch for his so called book of fiction.

He wrote another letter again undated. In this letter he specifically tells a company that he is willing to help them find missing females.

"I'm known to have done killings in 40 states of the USA, 4 provinces of Canada, Several countries in Europe and Africa with over 20 women killed in one city. Anyone can confirm those facts revealed by the police. This is not to brag but to address the scope of the activity from 63-73.

What I am willing to do for you privately –as a social courtesy to the survivors of the female victims- is take a look at what you have and either confirm or not whether I was responsible for the case. I'm doing double life in prison so no prosecutor will want to rush a case from 1965 or thereabouts, and won't rush the case without proof beyond an admission.

Now to be more specific, you ask about the New England area. I killed women in New England from 1966 to 1970, Five year span, and I confess I don't know New England very well but I did work upper New York, Long Island, Boston area along the road to Cape Cod- good hunting there- and the road running north to Newburyport; also the area near Brockton. I can't say exactly when I was I was in those areas I traveled all the time. You <u>can</u> eliminate December, Jan, Feb, and March. Mostly it was summer and in 1968 the fall as well through late November.

The type of female I nailed were usually hitchhikers, sometimes prostitutes, so if a girl was last seen hitching in your report or had a history of hitching, or was trying to buy dope from dealers; then I might be of some help to you. I often killed in <u>pairs</u> of girls so you should focus also on girls who went missing together.

I realize these are generalities but this is 1991.

Since this has absolutely nothing to do with a Court of Law what I will do for you is take a look at any material you want to show me. My preference would be general data on the girl's physical description, the known facts surrounding her disappearance such as the town or highway where she was last seen and a few pictures- Xeroxes are fine. The reason I want minimal data is because should I recognize a girl I want to be able to indicate I had contact with her. I had conversations with my victims and when a girl is about to be killed she can get very chatty and some of those conversations are memorable. There was a girl who worked at a shoe factory around Brockton. She was concerned about missing her shift, until she realized she was going to die… Another was saying she was going to get married...another was pregnant.

I might see the factory girl's picture; recollect the pickup and be able to tell some little odd fact to confirm I got her while never revealing the details of the murder. I need prompting but not <u>too much</u> detail! You see my point?

I will not accept any money for this assistance. I will not return a body even for a cash reward. The help- if it will be help remains to be seen- is voluntary and private. You may not reveal to anyone that I am your source. Agreed? I will accept a booklet of postage stamps to facilitate our correspondence." (Schaefer G.)

In Gerard Schaefer's mind he was the expert. He was the one who knew it all. The question, which remains unanswered to this day, is did he kill in that part of the country or was he using this tactic as a bargaining tool or was he trying to get information for his own sexual gratification? Did he want to relive his kills over and over again? One thing is known his offers to help were never taken seriously by the recipients of the letters.

In 1993 Gerard Schaefer changed gears again. By this time there were numerous writings floating around and he was not happy because he was being titled as a serial killer. He wrote Sondra London on April 24 and told her he was ready to sue everyone. He told her he might not win but he would break everyone's bank and make the lawyers rich. He wrote her again in June and told her he had sold the book and film rights of the true story of his frame up to a major publishing house.

He signed this letter by saying to her that "The very next time you say or do anything that causes me problems…. I am going to encourage my dope addled Satanist pals in Georgia to go pick up your slut daughter and teach her some sex education." (Newton, Sexual Predators- Gerard Schaefer)

Schaefer was not finished he was just getting started especially when he found out that Sondra London had dumped him for Danny Rolling. She and Danny had announced their engagement. When Schaefer found out he flew into a rage. In February 1993 he fired off a nasty letter to London.

His true personality came to the forefront. "Hello, Whore. The word on the yard is that the Queen of the Sluts was… romancing Danny

Rolling.... Valentine, you're mine... I know what you're up to: money. Your gonna (sic) get Danny Boy fried (sic) while you make a buck off his misery. Right? Well, go for it! Just make sure you keep my name out of it." (Newton, All about Gerard Schaefer)

He used the Ku Klux Klan as his threat instead of the Satanist to kill her this time. As London's relationship with Rolling grew, Schaefer escalated his frivolous lawsuits. He pled poverty so he wouldn't have to pay filing fees. He wrote all of his complaints by hand. These lawsuits were filed over time and he sued just about everyone who had called him a serial killer.

Schaefer claimed alleged libel in some of his lawsuits; in others he claimed "civil rights infringements". He alleged that published "false charges" were stalling his parole opportunities even though he had been told by the parole board that he would not even be eligible for parole until the year 2017.

Schaefer had lost the ability to commit murder, so he found other ways to amuse himself. He had the illusion of being able to control his enemies, the ones who publicly called him a serial killer. He sued, Patrick Kendrick who had the nerve to accuse Schaefer of 36 murders, when Stone had only accused him of 34.

He sued true crime authors Joel Norris, Michael Cartelis, Jay Nash, Michael Newton and Colin Wilson. He sued Robert Ressler for writing about him and mentioning him in lectures on serial murder. He sued Forensic Dentist Richard Souviron who had identified Carmen Hallock's teeth in 1973 for providing photos and fragments of Schaefer's writings to a British Magazine. He sued Sondra London three times and lost all three times. Sondra fought back using his 500 pages of letters which carried threats and murder confessions. When he was finally barred from contacting London he wrote a scathing letter to her publisher.

He wrote, "An Anointed Fourth Prince of the Hand of Death. All I need to do is ask this gentleman to have SL and her kid murdered and it would be done. SL is alive at this moment because I choose to allow it." Schaefer really believed he had more power than he had.

Schaefer never won a case. They were all dismissed a frivolous.

In July 1994 Gerard Schaefer was formally branded as a serial killer. The person who branded him was a judge in the Schaefer V Michael Newton case. He said that Schaefer had already made that claim in both public and private boasts. One of those public boasts came in the form of his bragging to Ten Bundy by writing in a story titled My Ticket to the Society of Fiends. "You were good, Ted, unless you can go over a hundred- WELL over a hundred- you're not in my league"

To add insult to injury while he was in the prison library working on yet another appeal to waste the courts he was given a taste of the shades of things to come. He wrote the appellate court a letter explaining why he was withdrawing his latest appeal.

"While working in the prison law library Plaintiff was attacked by another inmate and stabbed repeatedly in and about the face, body and hands. Due to the trauma sustained incidental to this attack, Plaintiff is now unable to prosecute his appeal; therefore Plaintiff withdraws the appeal in this case."

CHAPTER FORTY-FOUR

THE LOCAL CHURCH MINISTERS AND GHOST HOUNDS

ENTER THE CIRCUS TENT

1993

As if the circus, which was Gerard Schaefer, wasn't enough in St. Lucie County Florida, the local church ministers had to get into the act. Five local ministers gathered at C-24 Canal near Leafy Road in Port St. Lucie to hold hands and pray around the alleged hanging tree that bore the bodies of Collette Goodenough and Barbara Ann Wilcox.

The tree was a 100-year-old, 50 foot oak tree located on 30 acres of ground between Leafy Rd and C-24 canal. The property was covered with palms, palmettos, oaks scrub and the ever popular and alluring Spanish moss.

The property was owned by the Treasure Coast Victory Children's Home. Which was a Christian-centered based home for abused and neglected children.

Neighbors in the area had stated that for years

they had seen people with black hoods, painted faces and women in black negligees walking on the property. The stories became embellished with other stories of ritual chants and animal sacrifices.

Two 16-year-old boys who had been skateboarding in the area ran to a nearby home and had the owner call 911. When the officer arrived he heard a strange story.

The young men who appeared to be scared out of their wits told the officer they had been chased by hooded men with painted faces. They said not only were they chased, but as they were chased they heard voices saying they wanted to drink the boy's blood.

When interviewed Lt. Chuck Johnson with the Port St. Lucie PD stated that the area had been used for years as a place of satanic worship. He told reporters that Port St. Lucie was the home of the only official satanic church in Florida

Enter, the Rev. Smith, Alan Weierman president of the Treasure Coast Victory Children's Home, Rev. Frank Mucci, assistant pastor at the Calvary Worship Center, Rev. Chuck Longworth of the Covenant Tabernacle in Fort Pierce, Rev. C.J. Campbell of the Community Christian Center in Port St. Lucie and Raymond Hall a church member at Calvary.

The six men gathered around the gnarled,

twisted 100-year-old oak tree held hands and blessed it with shouts of "Hallelujah," "Joy", and "Amen". They added "Evil spirit be gone, Holy Father, and Praise the Lord." The Rev. Smith said they were spiritually breaking the curse and they were invoking the word of God to protect and preserve the property. He added they were sending a message to those people that is was not acceptable to do what they did on the property.

The century old oak had an inverted black cross, painted on one side of his large trunk. After the exorcism and blessing, Weierman took another can of spray paint and made the cross right side up.

After the site was blessed and the alleged satanic worshippers banished the Ghost hounds began to descend upon the area now known as Hammond Park.

The ghost hounds claimed they had heard screaming coming from the woods and seeing hooded figures chase thrill seekers from the area. They also told the story about the attempted tree cutting.

Apparently after the area and the tree had been exorcised a tree cutting crew had been brought in to fell the possessed tree. They came with chainsaws all of which malfunctioned as they tried to cut down the tree. The tree cutters left and returned with handsaws. Those didn't work either; all the teeth broke as they sawed away at the tree. Next they tried an axe, the handle kept coming off. Finally in frustration, the men decided to leave the tree intact. It became known as the Devil's Tree. People reported feeling cold spots in certain areas of the park, many refused to go into the wooded area and only the bravest would attempt to go at night.

Is the area haunted? Are Goodenough's and Wilcox's silent screams no longer silent? Do their restless spirits roam their bloody deathbed? This writer doesn't have the answers. But who is to say they are not still around waiting to be at peace waiting for their screams to be silent no longer.

CHAPTER FORTY-FIVE

1995

JUSTICE IS FINALLY SERVED

After Schaefer had written his letter to the appellate court withdrawing his appeal in 1994 due to being attacked in the law library, things quickly went south. He had made many enemies in the prison life he had adapted to. He had become known by the other inmates as a rat and a pain freak as well as a manipulating snitch.

Schaefer constantly complained he was fearful of as many as seven or eight other inmates.

After the attack Schaefer's life became a living hell. The other inmates would splash him with urine and pelt him with feces. Twice his cell was set on fire. As if that was not enough there was an investigator with the Fort Lauderdale Police Department who decided to open up some unsolved cases. He felt the time was right to approach Gerard Schaefer about three females who had been missing for over twenty years.

On Friday December 1, 1995, Investigator Tim Bronson called Starke prison to set up a meeting with Schaefer. That meeting never took place.

By Sunday December 3, 1995 Gerard Schaefer was found dead in his cell by the guards. Sometime before the TV Series Hercules and Xena the Warrior Princess came on the killer inmate was busy seeking retribution by placing 43 stab wounds in Gerard John Schaefer. Schaefer and another inmate had gotten a cup of coffee. The inmate was standing at the door of Schaefer's cell talking to him when another inmate came up and stated he needed to talk to Schaefer. The other inmate left and the second inmate went in shutting the door behind him.

The media hounds went crazy again. Schaefer had finally returned to the front-page news.

Judge Trowbridge told the media that if the death penalty had been on the table he would have sentenced Schaefer to death in 1973.He told the Palm Beach Post that Schaefer had finally gotten the death sentence he ultimately deserved but he couldn't be given in the courtroom. He continued by saying that he didn't know all of the circumstances of Schaefer's death, however he schemes did continue in the prison system and he suspected that one of them backfired.

Robert Stone said that Schaefer was the most sexually deviant person he had ever known. He said that Schaefer had made Ted Bundy look like a boy scout. He noted that Schaefer's IQ was well over

130 and he was more dangerous than other notorious serial killers. He said that Schaefer had ever possible sexual hang up that existed.

One of the psychiatrists called Gerard Schaefer a sadomasochist with sexual perversions. Another described him as a paranoid schizophrenic. They all agreed that he was incurable.

A reporter who was first introduced to the circus that was Gerard Schaefer in 1977 said he had the coldest eyes she had ever seen. When Schaefer was killed Nancy Smith the managing editor with the Stuart News remised about the Gerard Schaefer she had interviewed in the early days.

She said that every time Schaefer's name came up she remembered the first time she had been told about him, the gory details of the bodies without heads, personal belongings and Schaefer's wife Teresa who divorced him and married Elton Schwarz.

She said that in 1981 Gerard Schaefer wrote her a letter telling her he hadn't gotten a fair trial and that she had the power to help him. Ms. Smith had no desire to help him; however, she felt he just might have something new to tell. So she went to Avon Park alone.

Ms. Smith told the reporter that when she walked into the prison she was told that Schaefer was a crafty one. She was told that Schaefer would have her believing that he was nothing but a misunderstood choirboy.

Schaefer was indeed in full charm mode when Ms. Smith walked into the visitation room. He jumped up, pulled her chair out for her and apologized for her having to make such a long drive. He not only smiled softly, but he talked and walked softly. She found him intelligent, intense and informed. He had spent so many hours in the law library that he could have been passed as a law student.

But behind the soft-spoken, charming, likable man were the cold dead eyes. She noted his eyes were fixed quickly on something and they hung there, turning into a motionless, vague stare. She said that at one time they even made her shiver.

Gerard Schaefer's reason for Ms. Smith's visit was soon apparent. He wanted her to know that the girls Georgia Jessup and Susan Place had been members of a satanic cult and had been murdered by one of their own kind. How ironic that he should mention that after the article about the Devil Tree in Port St. Lucie where Collette Goodenough and Barbara Ann Wilcox had been found in 1977.

Ms. Smith said she received three letters from Schaefer after she did a three part series on him and he always started his letters with "Dear Nancy, my savior" and he signed it "Gerry". Had he reverted back to the Jerry Sheperd of 1973 when he killed Georgia Jessup and Susan Place?

She told the reporter that up to the day he was murdered he thought he had convinced her that he was innocent. She finished the interview by saying that the day she saw him he performed for her. The performance was as much for him as it was for her- and she was convinced – convinced they had the right murderer.

Another interview was with Jim Mills Schaefer's former supervisor with the Martin County Sheriff's department. He said that Schaefer had the propensity to stop women while he was on duty. He said that Schaefer had four to five times more traffic stops than the other deputies. He also meticulously wrote down the tag numbers and phone numbers of all the women he stopped. Mills said that Schaefer had bragged about things he used to do but none of the cops paid any attention to his bragging.

Lucille Place when interviewed about the murder of Schaefer was noted as saying, "He got what was coming to him, I feel relief, I really do." (Moore, 1995)

Gerard Schaefer's sister Sara told the Palm Beach Post that she and her mother believed that the killing was in retaliation for her brother's promise to cooperate with law enforcement in the continued investigation of the murder of Adam Walsh. She said her mother had received a letter the prior Tuesday where he told her that he would tell authorities what he knew about the Walsh case in return for possible gain time. Gain Time was time given to inmates who behaved, were model prisoners or had information.

She said that law enforcement thought Schaefer could help them locate the body of Adam Sara told the paper that her brother had information on Otis Toole who had previously confessed to the killing of Adam and later recanted it. She felt that Schaefer's death was related to his alleged testimony, which was supposedly approaching. Sara last statement to the media was "Did anybody say he was on the golf team and he got a scholarship to college and he was a volunteer for service organizations? No, they said he wrote killer stories, and liked to stalk women and he'll never lose that label."

Bob Fryer who had covered the Schaefer circus from the time of his arrest for Jessup and Place until his conviction and all of his appeals made the statement that Schaefer's murders had ended a small town's innocence. The city of Stuart was no longer known as the Sailfish Capital it became known as the town of a cop serial killer.

Shirley Jessup the mother of Georgia Jessup

stated, "I'd like to send a present to the guy who killed him. I've always believed he was going to get his. I just wish it would have been sooner than later."

Doris Schaefer said, "We still cry. I'll never get over this. He really didn't deserve this, contrary to what other people say."

She had always believed he had been framed for the murders of Jessup and Place.

Sheriff Robert Crowder stated that Schaefer's death seemed like some sort of poetic justice but the secrets of what happened to his other victims died with him.

CHAPTER FORTY-SIX

THE MAN WHO ENDED GERARD SCHAEFER'S LIFE

After all the legal maneuvering was finished, the crime scene worked and all evidence gathered at the cell which had belonged to Gerard John Schaefer, and the bloody white shirt and pants with Vincent Rivera's name printed on them; the murderer was named.

A psychiatrist had called him "the most dangerous fellow I've ever seen." He was also described, as having the highest potential for homicide of any person the psychiatrist had known. The person who took the life of Schaefer was a two-time murderer who had absolutely nothing to lose by taking Schaefer's life. His name was Vincent Rivera.

Rivera lived on the same wing as Schaefer and 76 other inmates in what was considered an open population area. That meant the inmates cell doors were always left open and the prisoners were free to walk around in that wing.

Even though Rivera worked in the food

service part of the prison the shank he used had not come from that area.

However, the day before the murder he had shown the homemade shank to a fellow inmate and stated he was going to kill Schaefer. Another inmate told the investigators that Rivera had wanted to murder Schaefer on the night of December 2nd, but he aborted the attempt because the guards searched him. Rivera passed the shank to another inmate before he was searched.

Still another inmate stated that Schaefer had made a sarcastic comment to Rivera who had said something to him about taking two cups of hot water.

The comment was "Jesus you can't even go on up and get a couple cups of hot water without somebody bitching about it"

The inmate said that Schaefer had made the statement in the tone of voice he normally did, showing how rude and inconsiderate people were at Starke.

After the murder still another inmate stated, "When I looked into Schaefer's house he was laying there between his bunk and his locker, dead as a doormat. He had letters thrown all over the top of him. Postmarked letters that had been-looked like they had been – taken out of the locker and thrown around." (Saitz, 1996)

Rivera had made his appearance at Starke Prison in February 1991, one month after he was sentenced to 45 years in prison for stabbing a 25-year-old Tampa man and suffocating a 45-year-old Tampa woman in 1990.

Dr. Melvyn Gardner who had been threatened by Rivers when he confessed his crimes through cell bars as two deputies stood guard, believed him. Rivers had said he would kill Dr. Gardner when he got loose.

Rivers was not in prison long when he started collecting disciplinary reports. By the time he was transferred to Starke two years later he had 43 reports in his jacket. The reports included fighting, possession of weapons, disobeying order and destruction of state property. He had been moved from Avon Park to Charlotte Correctional Facility because he was a problem. He was moved from Charlotte to Starke for the same reason.

Rivers was disciplined for performing an obscene act and possession of contraband. This was in April before he killed Schaefer in December.

Vincent Rivers was six feet tall and weighed 230 pounds. However, it wasn't his size that bothered those who came in contact with him. He had been diagnosed with severe chronic bipolar disorder and an antisocial personality disorder. His lawyer said that Rivers had told him that would be easy for him to kill him using the shackles he was wearing at the time of the interview. The lawyer believed him.

In late January 1996 Vincent Rivers was indicted by a grand jury for the murder of Gerard John Schaefer age 49 years old.

CHAPTER FORTY-SEVEN

SEPTEMBER 1996

TAMPA TRIBUNE

MORE BODIES

September 29, 1996 an article appeared in the Tampa Tribune, which discussed the disappearance of two young women from Pinellas County in October 1966 from the Ocala National Forest.

Pamela Nater age 20 of Clearwater, Florida and Nancy Leichner age 21 of Largo, Florida had been on a scuba diving outing with several friends. They had left early that Sunday morning and traveled to Alexander Springs in rural Lake County, Florida. In 1966 Lake County was still considered rural and sparsely populated with the Ocala National Forest wrapping itself around the county like a protective blanket. The Seminole Indians fought president to be Andrew Jackson and Johnny Weissmuller perfected his Tarzan yell at Alexander Springs and in 1966 two young women with their entire life ahead of them made the Springs famous.

Nater and Leichner were last seen wearing

their bathing suits walking away from the picnic area down a nature trail. Nancy had on a 2-piece suit with a blue bottom and a blue –red striped top. Pam was last seen wearing a 2-piece bathing suit with blue and white pinstripes and a boys Gant or Hugger short-sleeved shirt. Nancy left her prescription glasses, and both women had left their purses and shoes. One of the many friends had seen them going toward the woods. Another friend had seen them later walking up the concrete steps to the parking lot. No one ever saw them again. There were no goodbyes, no screams, no bodies and no bones. Just the forest listening to the silent screams.

Three weeks later all searches were called off. There was a long list of suspects ranging from the boyfriends of the two girls to a handicapped young man who lived near the springs.

Thirty years later since October 2, 1966 there has plenty of speculation, but no firm evidence. Investigators never believed they ran away.

These two girls had come from different backgrounds and were not close friends. They only knew each other because their boyfriends were divers. There would have been no reason for them to run away together. One of them at some time would have contacted a family member if that had been the case. This was according to State Attorney Gordon Oldham.

A former investigator named Keith Owen said that drowning and alligator attacks were not an option either. He stated that even as rumors and speculation about alligator attacks were running rampant, it was impossible because a gator could not attack two people at once. He said they could not have drowned, 30 divers had been in the water and they had dived the springs for years. Could they have gotten lost? Owen didn't think so. He said that he felt they would not have left the marked trails on their own.

One theory remained. That theory was the two young women had been abducted and murdered.

This theory has left holes in the lives of those they left behind. Dorothy Liechner, Nancy's mother couldn't talk about her daughter. Every time someone in the media comes to her with a question she had one of her own.

She asks "Is there anything new?"

When the answer is negative her response is always sadly the same. "I didn't think so."

She has said over and over again that she didn't think she would live long enough to know the answers and that even after thirty years it was still very painful.

The pain of losing a child is one thing- the pain of not knowing what happened to that child is indeed another. None of that pain ever goes away.

However, not knowing always leaves an open wound, which never leaves.

At the time of the disappearance a boy reported seeing the two girls on a trail with a man around 2 P.M. Part of the description of the man was he had parted his hair on the side.

When Sheriff Willis McCall was finally called in to help with the search, he spent most of the time focusing on the people in the diving club. They were all considered suspects especially Craig Mackie because he and Nancy had been engaged and she had broken it off and currently dating another member of the club, Ben Dauterman.

In 1972 in Volusia County, Florida an inmate by the name of Karl McGregory confessed to the murder and disappearance of Nater and Leichner. But, when he was questioned fully he couldn’t correctly describe the women or the area of the springs. He couldn’t even remember how they were killed. Another dead end for the cops. Fifteen minutes of fame for McGregory.

In 1973 State Attorney Gordon Oldham who was the State Attorney for that district went to St. Lucie County and questioned Gerard Schaefer. At that time he was eliminated as a suspect. They also interviewed a man wanted in South Carolina for a murder charge and two Texas men who were suspected of killing two young women in Michigan.

Score zero for cops and score four for the bad guys.

In 1984 an Ocala man wrote to the local law enforcement by post card and said a black woman whose dad died was the culprit. He reason was she had hated whites.

Another caller said the two young women had been beamed aboard flying saucers. Still another said an eccentric man was holding them as captives in a remote cabin. Some of the tips were they were murdered because they were part of a narcotics sting, they were strangled by a maniac who dumped acid on their bodies, they ran away and joined a convent and one of the best ones was when NBC sent still photographs of two women who had been on "Let's Make a Deal" on Dec 27, 1966. They looked like the missing women, sadly they weren't.

In 1994 nurse who lived in Leesburg, Florida called law enforcement after reading newspaper articles about the postcard tip. She told law enforcement that she had been the child in the car the day the girls were seen by the family of three. She told the same story that had been told in 1966.

Keith Owens who had worked for the State Attorney's office at that time stated that he felt the girls had been killed with a gun or a knife. He said whoever had done it could have killed them and buried them within five miles of the abduction and the bodies would have never been found in that forest. He also said that whoever had killed the young women was probably dead. He prophetically sated that it hadn't been the kind of crime that somebody would have only done once. He said maybe they died in prison or in the electric chair.

Little did Keith Owens know.

One lead, which should have been followed up on in the early days, wasn't. That lead was given to law enforcement by a family of three who had been driving into the springs about two o'clock about the same time the girls were seen with the man whose hair was parted on the side.

The family told law enforcement they had seen two women in the back seat of a car and two men in the front seat. The family said the women looked terrified. They said it looked like the women were screaming. Their screams were silent to those outside of the car. The car was last seen leaving the springs and turning toward Astor Park. Astor Park was located on the outskirts of Ocala National Park where the friends had gone to dive.

CHAPTER FORTY-EIGHT

1997

THE SITE OF THE FAMED DEVIL TREE AND CRIME SCENE OF GOODENOUGH AND WILCOX REVISITED

*I*n 1997 the crime scene of Collette Goodenough and Barbara Ann Wilcox was given new life. After the local ministers gave the site an exorcism in 1993 it became the playground for Halloween pranks. But in 1997 that changed.

The City of Port St. Lucie held a public hearing on December 16th. At the hearing it was announced that they had bought the property where the Devil sat and was going to transform it into a public park. The park would have nature trails, picnic tables and a boat ramp.

The city used grants from the Florida Recreation Development Association Program and a grant from the Florida Communities Trust to purchase the lots.

They also got grants to protect the environment and develop the land as a passive park, which included baseball fields or tennis courts.

This park would finally take on a different personality. Instead of one of horror and death, it became one of life and fun. A place where families could come and enjoy a day of fun and the silent screams would be heard no more.

CHAPTER FORTY-NINE

NANCY LEICHNER AND PAM NATER REVISTED

FORTY-ONE YEARS LATER

*I*n 2005 the St. Petersburg Times interviewed Collis Godwin who had been a deputy for the Lake County Sheriff's department in 1966 when Nancy Leichner and Pam Nater disappeared. He worked for Sheriff Willis McCall. That disappearance haunted him until he died. He always wondered if he could have done more. He felt those two young women could have been one of his daughters or granddaughters.

He had tracked lost campers and hikers as well as convicts all over the Ocala National Forest all those many years ago. He knew the woods inside and out. But for some strange reason he was not called into the search in 1966 until way after dark eight to ten hours after the disappearance.

By the time he and his tracking dog, a German Shepherd named Smokie was called to the scene, wind had picked up and the scene had been trampled and destroyed by the curiosity seekers and other searchers. Godwin and his dog were not able to get a good scent on the two young women.

Sheriff McCall refused to believe the women had been abducted. He held to his misguided theory that they had left of their own accord. He never stopped to think about the fact they left all of their personal belongings behind. No one followed up on the lead the family had given so many years earlier. Sheriff McCall refused to listen to any advice or belief other than his own.

It would take many years of working the case going through old records and just dogged determination for the case to finally be solved.

In 2004 the cold case squad of Lake County Sheriff's department re-opened the case. Sgt. Ken Adams with the Lake County Sheriff's department and John Tilly with the local State Attorney's office went back through old files. During the course of their search found out that Rick McIllwain who had retired from the 19th Circuit State Attorney's office as an investigator had a box of old files. In the box were several interesting pieces of evidence.

The most interesting pieces of evidence were some handwritten letters by an inmate at Starke who was a cellmate of Gerard Schaefer. In those letters dated between February and August 1985 he talked about Schaefer. His name was Charles Sizelove and he also had been a former law enforcement officer who had been convicted of fraud. This author wonders if Sizelove wanted to use these letters as leverage for less time to be served.

Sizelove wrote, "Jerry (Schaefer) talked about the two girls in Ocala and said time would take care of itself."

He said that Schaefer told him that he had taken the girls at knifepoint and gun and killed them.

He also wrote that Schaefer had told him how to dispose of bodies so animals would destroy the remains and that he had also told Sizelove that he had gone to school to learn how to dispose of evidence.

Sgt. Adams e-mailed Brent Hoover who was 11 years old, who all those years ago told law enforcement he had seen the girls with a man who had his hair parted on the side. He told law enforcement he was canoeing when he saw a man following the girls. They sent Hoover pictures and he identified Schaefer as the one with the same facial structure as the one he had seen that day long ago.

The Assistant State Attorney for the Lake County Area Ric Ridgeway agreed with the two investigators that the cold case of Nancy Leichner and Pamela Nater had indeed been closed forty-one years after they disappeared. He agreed that Gerard

Schaefer had indeed added these two young women to his cache of bodies. Their silent screams finally were heard. They had a voice.

THE SILENT SCREAMS

THE VICTIMS

CHAPTER FIFTY

NANCY LEICHNER

ONE OF THE FIRST KNOWN

SILENT SCREAMS

Nancy Leichner a blonde green-eyed beauty was born 1945 to Edward and Dorothy Leichner. She weighed a mere 115 pounds. She was 21 years old when she disappeared from Alexander Springs at Ocala National Forest October 2, 1966.

She lived in Clearwater, Florida with her parents.

She was a 1963 graduate of Largo High School. She worked for Honeywell. She made her own clothes and had plans to become a flight attendant.

Three years later she was gone.

She had a sister name Susan. A brother named Bob who was a mere 14 years old when she disappeared. He never got to really know his older sister.

One of the few memories he had is he would sneak in Nancy's room to play her rhythm and blues collection. One 45 record that he found was a 1957 hit by the Coasters which he played over and over. The name of that song was "Searchin."

Susan Leichner-Schonder, Nancy's sister kept her maiden name in hopes that someday Nancy would walk up to her front door and ring the bell. Her Brother Bob feels that the search was not conducted properly. He told the local paper they only searched 2% of the ground. They were in swamp with giant weeds over their heads and standing fifty feet apart.

Nancy's Father Edward died in 2007 without ever knowing what happened to his beautiful daughter that sun filled autumn day in 1966.

Nancy Leichner was robbed of her life.

She was left to scream silently into the Ocala National Forest. She had no one to hear her screams. She had no one to hear her voice.

CHAPTER FIFTY-ONE

PAMELA ANN NATER

THE SECOND KNOWN

SILENT SCREAM

Pamela Ann Nater was born May 30, 1946 to Herman and Alice Nater. She was a 20-year-old dark brown haired, brown-eyed beauty that cool autumn day in October 1966 when she walked away from the picnic area never to be seen again. She was only five foot three inches tall and weighed one hundred twenty pounds.

She loved the Beatles. She was going to be asked to be married to her current Beau Danny Dauterman.

Pam had graduated from Clearwater high school a few years early and became a nurse. She worked at Morton Plant Hospital.

Her father and mother posted at $25,000.00 reward for information about their daughter. In 2007 Mr. and Mrs. Nater were 87 and 85 years old.

They knew they were reaching the end of their time and still had no closure on the daughter they loved and lost. They both knew that someone someplace knew something.

In remembrance of Pam they kept the purse, comb and shoes their daughter left behind the day the forest heard her silent scream.

Mr. Nater remains troubled. He still believes the Lake County Sheriff, Willis McCall, should have done more. He felt that McCall only put on a show and gave lip service to the disappearance.

The case has been closed, but their daughter remains in the forest screaming silently.

CHAPTER FIFTY-TWO

LEIGH HANILINE BONADIES

THE THIRD SILENT SCREAM

Leigh Hainline was born in 1944. She lived in Fort Lauderdale Florida and worked as a waitress. She worked at several Fort Lauderdale restaurants. Her co-workers remembered her as being quiet and a loner. She had a sister named Caroline and a brother named Gary. She was 25 years old when she was last seen alive on September 8, 1969.The day she disappeared her husband called her family and told them they would not be coming to dinner because Leigh was not feeling well. A week later he reported her missing.

Leigh had been married only three weeks to her second husband when she disappeared. She had met him at the Mandalay an apartment complex for singles. She had been living with a friend her mother was not fond of.

Her marriage appeared to be troubled. Some said she often fought with her new husband. She had been heard telling her husband that she didn't need him.

He said she took drugs and drank heavily. Friends described Leigh as unhappy and mixed-up.

Her mother she was easily led. She also said that Leigh was unhappy. But she said that Leigh had been brought up in the church and was a pretty good girl.

She lived near Schaefer when they were in school. She went to public school and Schaefer went to the Catholic school. Leigh, Gary and Schaefer spent many hours together in the family pool, and playing tennis. She continued to play tennis with Schaefer even after she moved away from her parent's house.

The day she disappeared she left a note saying she would be back later in the day to play tennis.

She told her husband that Gerard Schaefer had offered her $20,000.00 to join the CIA. A few days later she left a note for her husband telling him she had gone to Miami, Florida. When Schaefer was questioned about Leigh he said she had called him and told him she was leaving her husband. He said she wanted him to take her to the airport where she was supposed to catch a flight to Cincinnati, Oh. He said he agreed to take her, but she never called him back with the time of departure. She was never heard from again.

One month later Leigh's husband filed for divorce. He was granted the divorce in 1970.

When the items were seized at Doris Schaefer's home in 1973 there was a locket seized and it had Leigh's name on it.

Leigh's mother told reporters that she never liked Schaefer. She said he did foolish things. He and Leigh's brother Gary went fishing on the ocean, Schaefer tossed the oars away. The two boys finally drifted to shore with the tide. She said that they never knew where Schaefer was. He was sneaky. She said he would drop in all the time.

Mrs. Hainline stated that Schaefer was too polite. That he was kind of a pest and she found him in the bedrooms all the time. She said he was always running upstairs to her son Gary's, Leigh's and a friend of the family's room. She said he was high tempered and that he talked all the time about hunting, fishing and golf.

A week before she disappeared, a private investigator found where Leigh had sent Schaefer a telegram.

Gerard Schaefer spent years alluding to the fact that he had killed her. He had admitted in many interviews that he watched her undress at night when they lived on the same street and were younger.

Leigh Haniline Bonadies' silent screams were never heard. Her skull with bullet holes was finally found in a new subdivision in Boca Del Mar in Boca

Raton, Fl. The subdivision was under construction in 1978. Her remains were finally identified in 2004. Her screams were finally heard.

CHAPTER FIFTY-THREE

CARMEN MARIE HALLOCK

THE FOURTH SILENT SCREAM

Carmen Marie Hallock was a brown haired beauty from Fort Lauderdale, who was 22 years old when she disappeared December 18, 1969. Six months earlier she was orphaned. Her mother had died without a will. She had graduated from North East High School in 1965 and attended junior college off and on. She had no set goals in her life and she had to support herself.

People who knew her stated she lived two different lives. Her family said she was warm and kind, however her friends were on the wild side.

Her friend last saw her after they had lunch with each other at Britts Department Store in the Coral Ridge Shopping Center. The restaurant was located just east of the Round Table Restaurant on North Federal Highway at Oakland Park Blvd, where Carmen worked as a waitress.

Carmen told her friend when they parted ways at 2:30 that afternoon that she had an appointment at 5p.m. that afternoon. She said she was going to find out about her new job. The new job was a position as an undercover narcotics agent that she had allegedly been offered three months earlier by a Broward County Community College teacher. Carmen had met the teacher while in her last semester at Broward.

Four days before her disappearance Carmen talked to her sister who begged her not to take the job. She told Carmen the job sounded very shaky. She said it sounded like the job of a high priced call girl. Carman's sister said that the person had told Carmen the job might take her out of Fort Lauderdale and she might have to go to Washington. Carman's friend added that she was told by Carmen the man told her he might be traveling to the "islands" from time to time. Carmen's sister also said that beside the $70.00 per month phone bill Carmen ran up she never told her anything else about the mysterious teacher.

Carmen refused to listen when her sister asked her not to go. She asked her sister what did she have to lose.

Carmen had called her sister in law on December 18th and told her she had an appointment with a male teacher from the local junior high school later that evening.

She also told her sister in law this male teacher did undercover work for the government. She said the so-called meeting could possibly get her employment that would include international travel and a very high salary.

By Christmas Day Carmen had not been seen or heard from. The sister in law checked Carmen's apartment and discovered she had her keys, driver's license, and car registration was gone. There was water in the bathtub and her dog had not been fed in several days. The day she disappeared she was wearing a black cocktail dress and black patent-leather pumps.

The sister in law couldn't find the high heels or the black cocktail dress.

Her car was found abandoned later in a nearby parking lot. She wasn't there.

A missing person's report was filed. But her silent screams weren't heard.

No one at the restaurant would discuss the man Carmen had last been seen leaving with. The assistant manager told reports that they were to leave the employees alone.

In 1973 when the search warrant was served on the home of Doris Schaefer there were three trophies found - two gold-filled teeth and a shamrock pin that belonged to Carmen. Schaefer was never charged in her disappearance. However, evidence points to him. He was a teacher during that time period. Her things were found in his mother's house along with trophies of his other victims.

Schaefer wrote a story and put it in a magazine. The story- Murders and Demons. If you as the reader passed over it in chapter forty-one go back and read it. It tells the tale of a young woman much like Carmen. The name Carmen has been mentioned in other writings. Her screams have been heard on paper.

CHAPTER FIFTY-FOUR

WENDY BROWN STEVENSON

AND PEGGY RAHN

THE FIFTH AND

SIXTH SILENT SCREAMS

Wendy Brown Stevenson was a brown haired; hazel eyed eight-year-old born June 20, 1961. She weighed 61 pounds and was four feet two inches tall.

She lived in Pompano Beach, Fl that was about fifteen miles north of Fort Lauderdale. The home of Gerard Schaefer's mother.

On December 29, 1969 Wendy was taken to the beach by her uncle.

She met her friend Peggy Rahn by accident.

Peggy Rahn was a blonde blue eyed, freckle faced nine-year-old girl born October 21, 1960. She had a scar over her right eye. She weighed 67 pounds and was four feet four inches tall.

Peggy was taken to the beach by a neighbor on December 29, 1969.

The two little girls met by accident and decided they wanted ice cream. They walked to the parking lot and were never seen again after a convenience store saw a white male in his twenties about six feet tall around 200 pounds buying the young girls ice cream.

When the clerk was given photographs he identified the two little girls.

Schaefer wrote a letter on April 19, 1989 and described killing the young girls after he was convicted of Georgia Jessup and Susan Place.

He said in his letter “I am annoyed by all this murder talk. Peggy and Wendy just happened along at a time when I was curious about (1930’s Cannibal Albert) Fish’s craving for the flesh of young girls. … I assure you these girls were not molested sexually. I found both of them very satisfactory, particularly with sautéed onions and peppers.” (Newton, All about Gerard Schaefer)

Their silent screams still resound in the universe. Their bodies have never been found.

CHAPTER FIFTY-FIVE

DEBORA SUE LOWE

THE SEVENTH SILENT SCREAM

Debora was a brown haired, brown eyed child born September 19, 1958. She lived in Pompano Beach, Florida a twenty-minute ride north of Fort Lauderdale. She weighed 125 pounds and was five feet five inches tall. Her upper teeth were crowded together one of her front teeth had a small chip in it. She had a small scar on her left leg.

She was last seen wearing a tan poncho, a yellow blouse and black slacks with vertical rose-colored stripes.

The last time Debora was seen was on February 28, 1972. She was seen walking to Rickards Middle School near 8th Street and Sunrise Boulevard in Pompano Beach between 7:30 and 8:30 in the morning.

At first law enforcement thought she had run away from her new home and back to Palestine, West Virginia. Her family had recently moved to Pompano Beach from West Virginia. Her family didn't believe she would do that. She had no history of being a runaway. She left behind all of her personal belongings.

Eva Newsome Debora's sister said that the police encouraged her parents to tell them that Debora was a runaway. She said in an interview they didn't want to be bothered. She also said the family finally got a copy of the Pompano Beach Police Department complaint form. It said that Mr. Lowe had stated Debora might be headed for Palestine, WV. The statement said she didn't have any friends in the area and was not allowed to date. Ms. Newsome believes that Debora may have been another victim of Gerard Schaefer.

Four years later Debora's father died of a heart attack. The rest of her family still holds hope.

Her silent screams are still being heard.

CHAPTER FIFTY-SIX

BELINDA HUTCHENS

THE EIGHTH SILENT SCREAM

Belinda Hutchens twenty-two years old, a cocktail waitress and married to a drug addict. She was arrested for prostitution in November 1970. She paid her fine in Fort Lauderdale, Florida. She had no more arrests.

But Belinda was not shy about showing off her extramarital affairs. Her husband Bill told police she had her own lifestyle. He told police that she started working at 14 years old at a go-go place in Baltimore Maryland. As she worked she learned the ways of the world in a hurry. She knew how to play the game in order to get ahead. She got married young to her first husband and then got divorced.

He told law enforcement he had met Belinda when she was 18 years old. He was working as a grease monkey at a gas station and she lived close by. He knew she was a working girl when they got married. But she allegedly stopped after the wedding.

Times got bad and Belinda went back to her

employment of choice. She cleared between $40,000.00 and $60,000.00 a year. Bill enjoyed the fruits of her labor; he was dark-haired and wore flashy clothes.

He told the Palm Beach Post in an interview in 1973 that he believed in prostitution. He told the reporter that a woman who became a prostitute in bad times for feed her family and her man – that she really must love that man. He said that no woman would go and be a prostitute for some man she didn't care for. He also told the reporter she refused to be pimped out. She didn't want some man selling her wares. She wanted to be a high-class hooker. She wanted to make the kind of money a high-class call girl was used to making. He said to her it was just a job.

Belinda came from very humble beginnings. Her family was poor. They lived in a small concrete block apartment in Fort Lauderdale. Her father who was of Spanish descent worked a menial jobs just to feed his family because of heart disease. Her brothers were also poor. Belinda helped her family survive. The last gift she gave her mother was a cuckoo clock.

Two of her brothers had died very violently before Belinda ever disappeared.

January 4, 1972 Belinda's husband and two year old daughter saw her climb into a blue Datsun sedan with a strange man driving. She was wearing a pink dress, with white high-heeled shoes and carrying a small clutch purse that contained her cigarettes. She carried no clothes or makeup with her and she left her Corvette and Cadillac parked in the driveway.

Relatives told reporters that some friends of Belinda had said she used to date a policeman named Schaefer and she would bring him with her when she visited them.

She was never seen again.

When the search warrant was served at Doris Schaefer's house in 1973 an address book was found. In that address book was the name address and phone number of Belinda's husband. When police went back and talked to him he identified the vehicle of Gerard Schaefer.

Belinda's sister in law and husband Bill identified a picture of Schaefer when it was showed to them by law enforcement after her disappearance. Her husband stated to reporters that he had asked her about "this guy Schaefer" and she had told him that the guy was okay.

Belinda left behind a 10-month-old baby girl with curly hair with no mother. The name Belinda was found in some of Gerard Schaefer's writings.

Her screams remain silent. Her body has never been found.

CHAPTER FIFTY-SEVEN

ALICE BRISCOLINA AND

ELSIE LINA FARMER

THE NINTH AND TENTH

SILENT SCREAMS

On October 24, 1972 two young girls aged fourteen years old named Mary Alice Briscolina and Elsie Lina Farmer was walking to local restaurant in Fort Lauderdale. They never returned home.

Elsie's family reported her missing that same day. Alice's family waited another week before she was reported missing. They thought she had run away.

These two young girls disappeared one month and one day after Georgia Jessup and Susan Place disappeared.

There was a construction site going on neat Plantation High School. That was where the silent screams of these two girls were finally heard.

Elsie's skeleton was found on January 17, 1973 and Alice's body was found February 15th 200 yards away from where Elsie's skeleton was recovered. Dental records identified them.

Gerard Schaefer was already in jail serving time for the two who got away. But later when he was in prison for Jessup and Place he wrote one of his many letters.

He admitted to killing these two young girls.

He wrote, "What crimes am I supposed to confess? Farmer? Briscolina? What do you think Murder and Demons is? Fiction? You want 'confessions' but you don't recognize them when I anoint you with them." (Newton, All about Gerard Schaefer)

When the search warrant was served at Doris Schaefer's house in 1973 there was a piece of jewelry seized which Farmer's family said belonged to her.

Their screams were silent no longer. They had a voice.

THE STORIES WITHIN THE STORY

CHAPTER FIFTY-EIGHT

PUBLIC DEFENDER

ELTON SCHWARZ

In 1949 Elton Schwarz traveled south from Ohio to Stuart Florida.

In 1954 Attorney Elton Schwarz hung his sign to practice law in Stuart, Florida that was the County Seat of Martin County. His first office cost $12.00 a month in rent. He had no air conditioning just fans and paperweights. He had no electric typewriters. Many times he was paid in cabbage, peppers and fish. There was little money in this little town.

He was only one of about a dozen who chose to practice in that sleepy coastal town. In the year 2004 he was the only one left alive of the original twelve. They only worked part time and there was no specialty law. They could seal a deal with a handshake.

In 1972 Attorney Elton Schwarz ran for the Public Defender's office of the newly formed 19th Judicial Circuit. He was appointed prior to his running by Public Defender Irvin Frank, Jr. who chose not to run for that office again.

Frank appointed Schwarz as an assistant in the Public Defender's office when a vacancy had been opened up with the resignation of Attorney Dean Tooker.

At the time Schwarz was 44 years old and a graduate of the University of Florida. He had been in the business of practicing law for 15 years with seventeen of those years in Martin County. He was quoted as saying to the press that the job needed someone who had substantial experience. He also felt as if the position was a real challenge. He just didn't know what a real challenge it would be in 1973

One of the first things Schwarz did when he took office was hiring three young men who were fresh out of law school. These young men were baptized by fire. They were pitched into the arena of major felony trials the first day on the job.

One of the young men was Bruce Colton. He became second chair at the Schaefer trial. He told reporters later that Schwarz gave those three rookie lawyers free reign and he had supported them.

Schwarz in his career as the public defender of the 19th Judicial Circuit handled some of the highest profile cases in the history of the Treasure Coast. He defended David Allen Gore who was convicted of six murders in St. Lucie and Indian River Counties.

He defended a woman who his daughter a member of the Stuart PD had arrested.

He established prison tours for high school students take as part of a criminology class. That was his proudest accomplishment.

Schwarz married Teresa Dean Schaefer, Gerard's wife in November 1973 after Schaefer had been convicted of two counts of first-degree murder. They were happily married until his death.

In the middle 1970's he helped a young black lawyer by the name of Willie Gary become established in the law arena. Gary worked as an assistant to the Public Defender's office before he took the bar exam. Willie Gary became highly successful he owns his own private jet and is very big in the Democratic Party.

In the 1980's Schwarz left the Democratic Party joined the Republican Party. He and Teresa were invited to the White House and photographed with then President Ronald Reagan.

In 1988 Elton Schwarz lost the election to the Public Defender's office to Phillip Yacucci, which ended his 16-year run as the public defender. In

1992 he ran again and lost. He called defeat gut wrenching. Schwarz returned to private practice and spent his time doing civil cases. He told reporters he had his fill of criminal work.

He began to decline in health probably due to an old habit of 10 cigars a day, even though he had been quit twenty years in 2004.

In January 2005- Former Public Defender Elton Schwarz died. His health had been failing and he had to continually inhale oxygen in order to breath. He was also wheelchair bound.

When reporters interviewed those whose life Schwarz had touched through the years he was given accolades of praise.

"I don't think people realized what a big part Elton played in the development of the criminal justice system in the circuit as it is today." State Attorney Bruce Colton. (Taylor, 2005)

Martin County Sheriff Robert Crowder said that Schwarz had encouraged him by telling a job would be waiting for him when considered law school in 1979.

Judge Trowbridge said that Schwarz had been a good public servant and would be missed. He also said that Schwarz had mentored many of the best and brightest attorneys as they learned the ways of the criminal court.

CHAPTER FIFTY-NINE

THE PLAYERS OF THE SCHAEFER SAGA

Elton Schwarz was just one of the many players in the circus that was Gerard Schaefer. Included in that Circus was:

Robert E Stone, State Attorney for the newly formed 19th Judicial Circuit in 1972. Robert Stone left the State Attorney's office in the early 1980's and went back into private practice. He continues to practice law today. Stone was threatened by Schaefer while at Avon Park Prison.

Jack is on the right

Jack Sewell worked the Schaefer case as an investigator. He helped form the 19th Judicial Circuit in 1972 became the Executive Director for the 19th Judicial Circuit and helped get Bruce Colton elected as State Attorney after Robert Stone resigned. Jack worked tirelessly for the State Attorney's office until 2003 when he retired. Then married the love of his life in 2007.

Philip Shailer- the Broward County State Attorney from 1969-76 who Co-prosecuted the Schaefer case with St. Lucie State Attorney Philip Shaileras lived in Fort Lauderdale with his wife, Midge, for more than 40 years. A graduate of Yale University and then Duke University School of Law, he has also held public office as Broward's Public Defender in the late 60's and as City Attorney of the City of Fort Lauderdale in the late 70's.

In addition to many years in private practice, primarily defending police liability lawsuits, he spent 10 years as Executive Vice President of Alamo

Rent-A-Car, which had its corporate headquarters in Fort Lauderdale. Now semi-retired, he serves from time to time as a mediator on circuit court civil cases.

Bruce Colton was appointed after Robert Stone resigned and was elected to the office in the 1980's. He has prosecuted many high profile cases including police officers in his seventeen-year history. Bruce's son had followed his father in law enforcement. He is now an officer for the St. Lucie County Sheriff's office. Bruce is running again this year for State Attorney he says this will be his last term. If that is the case the State Attorney's office will lose a fine asset.

Robert Crowder Martin County Sheriff who

rescued Nancy Trotter and Pamela Wells from certain death is now the Martin County Sheriff. He is also running for re-election. Crowder was threatened by Schaefer while at Avon Park Prison

Courtesy Palm Beach Post 1973

Judge C. Pfeiffer Trowbridge presided over the Gerard Schaefer trial. He retired from the Bench and went back on a part time basis. He eventually married Pat Quina and then he eventually divorced her.

Judge Trowbridge was known for reading the astrological chart of those he was going to sentence before he sentenced them and wearing robes on the bench, which were not standard. For months he wore a white wizard type robe with gold embroidered astrological signs on the cuffs and the hem. When he was reprimanded for wearing that robe he changed to a purple robe. He finally retired from the bench full time and worked part time. Today Judge Trowbridge is still going strong. Judge Trowbridge was threatened by Schaefer while at Avon Park Prison

Investigator Rick McIllwain moved from the St. Lucie County Sheriff's department over to the State Attorney's office where he worked very closely with Jack Sewell. He was instrumental in helping Lake County in North Florida solve one of their unsolved crimes from 1966 the disappearance of Nancy Leichner and Pam Nater. He had a box that had a letter from George Sizelove that said that Gerard Schaefer killed the two young women. Rick had held onto that box hoping one day someone would need it to solve more of the circus which was Schaefer. He retired in 2005.

Lt. Dave Yurchuck continued to work for the Broward County Sheriff's office until his retirement in January 1993. He then accepted a position with the North Port Police Department and worked there until 2004. He worked tirelessly on the cases in Broward County until they reached a conclusion. Lt. Yurchuck has two sons who have followed him into law enforcement. One on is currently a Sgt. with the Broward County Sheriff's dept. and the other one is a detective with the same outfit. Gerard Schaefer sued him as well as the Broward County Sheriff's office many times.

Det. Charles C. (Chuck) Hemp

Chuck began his police career with the City of Oakland Park Public Safety Department in South Florida, now District #12 Broward County Sheriff's department.

He served from 1962 until he retired in 1989. He received 17 decorations for outstanding work in the field and 3 Mayor's citations for valor.

During his time there, his assignments varied from Patrol, Narcotics, Vice, the Intelligence Unit, Organized Crime Unit, and 12 years as a Lieutenant in the Major Case Squad.

In 1989 Chuck received and accepted a lateral transfer as a Lieutenant with the State of New Hampshire Police Standards and Training Council. He was later promoted to Captain. His duties there involved teaching in the police academy and in-service training involving certified courses in Death Investigation, Internal Affairs Investigations and Crime Scene related topics.

He also served as the State's compliance investigator involving police officer decertification issues.

Chuck remained with the State of New Hampshire until 2001 when he retired and returned to Florida.

Chuck has a Bachelor of Science Degree in Police Administration from Nova University. He attended, and was Class President, of the 76th Session of the University of Louisville Southern Police Institute in 1986.

As an expert in death investigations, "Chuck" has lectured and taught throughout the country on that subject. He is an IAI Board Certified "Senior Crime Scene Analyst". He is also a licensed Scuba Instructor and a licensed Coast Guard Boat Captain.

Chuck is a member of the Southern Police Institute Alumni Association, the International Association of Identification and the National Association of Underwater Instructors.

He is Post certified in Florida, New Hampshire, Maine, Kentucky and South Dakota. He currently resides in Kansas City, Missouri.

Captain Hemp made Schaefer his life's work after his first interview with him.

Doris Schaefer was last known to be living someplace in Georgia.

Teresa Dean Schaefer Schwarz divorced Gerard Schaefer in November 1973. She then married Elton Schwarz that same month in that same year. They remained married until Elton's death. Schaefer threatened Mrs. Schwarz as well as her husband while he was at Avon Park Prison.

Sheriff Willis McCall was a soft pudgy-cheeked man who stood six feet one inch tall and weighed 215 pounds. He had an itchy trigger finger and wore a size 13 shoe.

According to reports he was not only the Sheriff of Lake County he was the law from 1944 until long after he left office in 1972. He believed in enforcing the law and order and he lumped criminal behavior and moral code in one single word.

He refused to call in the National Guard when the disappearance of Pam Nater and Nancy Leichner was termed more than two young women who ran away. He allegedly hated outsiders and despite pleas from the families he would not call in enough help to find them.

He was reported to have a bullwhip on his wall in his office and he was known as an iron-fisted sheriff.

In 1951 he had been investigated in the death of a black inmate and the critical wounding of another. After serving 28 years as the Sheriff of Lake County he was indicted and suspended for kicking to death a mentally challenged black prisoner in his jail cell in 1972. He was tried and acquitted in 70 minutes by an all-white jury. He ran for re-election and lost.

In 1994 Sheriff Willis McCall died at 84 years old.

Sondra London decided to break into the publishing business using the writings of Gerard Schaefer and then Danny Rolling. She became engaged to Rolling, which sent Schaefer into a tailspin. When the courts decided that Rolling could not make money off his crimes she broke off the engagement. She is currently still working in the industry. Schaefer threatened London and her daughter while he was at Avon Park Prison.

Craig Mackie the boyfriend of Pam Nater. He was suspected in the disappearance of the two women from the Ocala National Forest in 1966. He and Ben Dauterman had been best friends until that day. Ben used a wire and tried to get a confession from Craig. This caused a rift that has never healed.

Benny Dauterman the boyfriend of Nancy Leichner he was also accused by law enforcement in the disappearance of the two young women.

Dauterman quit diving and dating after that day. He lived with guilt for years. His guilt was self-guilt for taking the two young women to the Alexander Springs that Sunday in 1966.

Finally he moved on and got married and had a daughter. He is now retired and married to his second wife who he worries about when she goes out and doesn't call him.

Deputy Sheriff Collis Godwin spent the rest of his life looking for the two girls at Ocala National Forest.

CHAPTER SIXTY

ST. LUCIE COUNTY

MARTIN COUNTY

In 1565 Fort Santa Lucia was built by the Spanish at the Jupiter Inlet. The construction started on December 13, which was the feast day of the Roman Catholic Saint Lucia.

The first known colony was somewhere between Vero Beach which it to the North of Fort Pierce and Stuart which is to the south was established by Pedro Menendez de Aviles. The old Spanish maps called the area Saint Lucia.

The present day Saint Lucie County was known as East Florida in 1810. By 1821 it became known as St. Johns County. In 1840 St. Johns was split into several counties and the current area became known as Mosquito County. The leaders decided, ten years later, that Mosquito County was too large so they split it into two more counties. It was at this split that St. Lucie County came into existence.

Then thirty more years went by and in 1880 the borders again changed. A new county known as

Brevard County was added. July 1, 1905 St. Lucie County, Florida became formal. Fort Pierce became the county seat.

In 1917 some western acreage was cut out of St. Lucie County and it was named Okeechobee County. In 1925 another piece of land was cut out of St. Lucie County and it became Indian River County. During that same year a southern part of St. Lucie County and Palm Beach County was cut away and it became Martin County.

Martin County is located north of the West Palm Beach Boca Raton Area south of Fort. Pierce. It is located on the Atlantic Ocean and is the southernmost county in the Treasure Coast region. Okeechobee, St. Lucie and Palm Beach counties border it. The county was named for the governor from 1925 to 1929 John W. Martin.

The county seat is Stuart and one of the cities is Hutchinson Island. Martin County and St. Lucie counties were the home and the killing fields of Gerard John Schaefer.

The killings, which Gerard Schaefer perpetrated in Martin and St. Lucie Counties, opened a doorway for even more killers to ply their trade in the two counties years later.

FINAL THOUGHTS

CHAPTER SIXTY-ONE

THE BRILLIANCE AND DARKNESS THAT WAS SCHAEFER'S MIND

Gerard Schaefer was on one hand an intelligent, articulate, well-versed man. He was charming and good-looking. His IQ was well over 150. He held two degrees from College. He was charismatic with the ability to lure women to go with him wherever he wanted them to go. His face was one of an innocent. He smile was enduring.

But his eyes told the story. His eyes could penetrate the very heart of his victims. They could cause a woman to fall deeply into the orbs of trust and then be drowned by evil which lurked just below the surface ready to rear its ugly head like a poisonous snake ready to strike with its lethal venom. If one looked closely one would see the other side of the darkness, which was Gerard Schaefer.

He was a liar, manipulator, self-centered, selfish, self-serving, and murderer. The perverted side of his personality overrode his intellectual side.

He couldn't accept and wouldn't accept criticism.

He couldn't and or wouldn't accept rejection. He had delusions of grandeur. He was a narcissistic, psychopath who hated most if not all women. He believed he had a mission and that mission was to rid the world of the whores who contaminated the world and the men in it. He would pursue that mission with a determination which was unequaled and focused.

Schaefer told one of his psychiatrists that unless they were intellectual or virtuous he had absolutely no use for them.

He felt for the most part they were whores and welcomed the release of death.

He believed he was smarter than he really was. When the psychiatrists under the order of the court were evaluating him, he tried time after time to manipulate the interviews. At one point he would be in tears and just a quickly he would be dry-eyed. He told the psychiatrist in one interview that talking about his parents upset him.

But then when he talked about the relationship he had with his mother he said that she wouldn't allow him to fight his own battles. He told the psychiatrist with a smile that the doctors in his group therapy had told him his mother had castrated him.

Schaefer told one doctor that at age twelve he

started tying himself to a tree; struggle to get free while getting excited sexually then he would do something to hurt himself. When the doctor asked him why he hurt himself he said that he would fantasize about hurting women. This was he said due to his anger at his mother for not allowing him to fight his battles.

After the girl he had been dating from 14 years old to 17 years old went off to college he became angry that she left him. He told the doctors that when she came home he took her to the beach and got her all hot and bothered then rejected her. He said it had been his way of hurting her for hurting him by going off to college.

Schaefer had stated he bound, gagged and put a noose around Nancy Trotter and Pamela Wells' neck because they "laughed at him." In essence they rejected him and his alleged advice about hitchhikers.

When he was 19 years old he had another relationship with a girl. After five months she left him. Once again he was rejected. He reverted back to his self-inflicted pain. He became an even more determined masochist. He would hang himself by the neck and masturbate. He continued to do this type of behavior when he had trouble concentrating in college. At one point he struggled so hard that he did almost kill himself. He said it was one of the best sexual releases he had ever known.

Schaefer added another layer to his evil and twisted mind. He added the practice of killing and mutilating livestock according to his doctor. Not only did he kill and behead them, he had intercourse with them. The strange part of his "confession" about the killings of livestock was he told the doctor he had not remembered it before when he had talked to other doctors, but he had an epiphany with this particular one. There were reports in the town of Davie 15 miles west of Ft. Lauderdale of livestock being killed, beheaded and human semen left on them. It is highly probable that Schaefer was indeed telling the truth. When the doctor asked Schaefer why he remembered this incident at this point, Schaefer told him he was crazy. He told the doctor he was not normal and that he badly needed help for his hostility. Then he played the "I'm going to kill myself" card. He had told another doctor that he had delighted in drawing gory pictures of himself, which would give him great excitement. He was very pre-occupied with death, he would dream about killing people. Gerard Schaefer was no one's fool. He had all the angles and he used them to his advantage.

He felt he could do as he pleased and never answer for his crimes because he had a problem. He told Pat Quina a reporter for the Tribune that he could have killed, but if he did he didn't remember doing it. It was as if he really believed he had selective memory loss. But yet he continued to talk in therapy about his pre-occupation with his adventures in sex, his rejections and his determination to retaliate.

He even played the look at what I did card by showing the doctor his arm, which had a slash on it. He told the doctor he had tried to kill himself in 1968 or 69. He was smiling as he told the doctor he had tried to find his vein and that he had been depressed about his sexual perversions and the desire to kill. In 1966 Nancy Leichner and Pam Nater disappeared from Ocala National Forrest in Lake County, Fl. Was this his first kill? Did he feel remorse or was he just playing his mind games with the doctor in order to be committed so he would not be charged with two capital murder crimes.

When Schaefer discussed his marriages he said that his first marriage ended in divorce because his wife was frigid. Was the problem with his wife or was it with him? He told her to put out or get out. She left. He said he had no such problems with his present wife. The question is why?

Schaefer believed he was a savior for the whores of the world.

When Schaefer was arrested for the murders of Georgia Jessup and Susan Place reporters interviewed some of his classmates from his old high school St. Thomas Aquinas. The answers were not complimentary. They ranged from "he was kinda (sic) weird" to He was kinda (sic) out of it." One old classmate stated he was never part of the group. She also said that he was the last boy she would have dated and she didn't know why. She just knew she didn't like him.

Another female classmate didn't even remember Schaefer, but the records showed they were in school together. Another one said he was a loner and had no close friends. He was not part of any clique. She said she had no recollections of any athletic activities while he was in school, although he stated he was on the golf team.

She said he would sit in class and do strange things like all of a sudden he would start talking to himself. According to this same female Schaefer only dated one or two girls in high school. She told the reporter that she didn't like him and she didn't like him dating a friend of hers. However, she expected them to get married.

Even Schaefer's own mother appeared to understand there was something about her first born son which shouldn't be there; something dark and sinister.

She told Det. Chuck Hemp of the Broward County Sheriff's Dept. that she knew something was wrong the day the search warrant was served.

She recalled a day when she had returned home to find the crotch completely cut out of a pair of her underwear. She knew who had destroyed them. She placed them in a paper bag and drove to the Sheriff's office. However, according to Det. Hemp, once she arrived in the parking lot, she could not make herself go in. She untimely left. Det. Hemp said that she had been torn between knowing what he was and the fact that he was her son. This decision led to even greater consequences. Lives were lost needlessly.

Schaefer was already exhibiting signs of the darkness, which was Schaefer, the darkness that out shone the brilliance. This darkness is clearly shown in the writing, which was seized at his mother's house in Fort Lauderdale.

"In order to remain unapprehended (sic) the perpetrator of an execution style murder such as I have planned must take precautions. One must think out well in advance a crime of this nature in order for it to work.

We will need an isolated area, assessable by car and a short hike away from any police patrols or parking lovers. The execution site must be carefully arranged for a speedy execution once the victim has arrived. Ideally would be 2 sawhorses with a 2x4 preferably by car. A grave must be prepared in advance away from the place of execution.

The victim could be anyone of the many women who flock to Miami & Ft. Lauderdale during the winter months. Even 2 victims would not be difficult to dispose of since women are less wary when traveling in pairs. In any case it maybe more preferable to bind & gag the victims before transporting them to the place of execution. Then again depending on what torture or defilement is planned for them other items may be useful.

Bars of soap& water. These are useful if you would want to wash a woman before her execution. Induce her to urinate and then wash her. Soap provides an excellent lubricant for anal intercourse. Beer is useful to induce urination and make the victim groggy and more cooperative. Soap can also be forced into the rectum to induce defecation of bowels. Possibly she may want to defecate since people generally have a desire to do this when they are scared. A douche bag may be helpful in degrading her further and is also useful in a soapsuds enema which would be a great indignity, especially if one victim was made to urinate or defecate on the other. This would be a gross indignity. Nylon Stockings are useful to tie the hands and feet of the victim. The victim should be made to strip at least to her underwear. If stripped completely nude an attempt can be made to excite her sexually. This effect would be especially interesting if the victim had her neck in the noose and hands tied behind her back. A white pillow case should be placed over her head and her mouth gaged (sic). Her panties should be pulled down enough to expose the genitals and clitoral stimulation applied. During the height of her excitement the support would be pulled away and she would dangle by her neck. She may be revived before death if desirable and subjected to further indecencies. After death has occurred the corpse should be violated if not violated already. The body should then be possibly mutilated and carried to the grave and buried. All identity papers should be destroyed and the place of execution dismantled."

This manuscript was used at Schaefer's trial it clearly showed what happened to Georgia Jessup and Susan Place. It was listed as Exhibit 4 Item F.

"I am a University Student in Sociology. I am doing a research paper on capital punishment. I was impressed by statistics I read claiming that your country has legally executed almost 2,500 person since 1911. To me, this gives you a considerable amount of expertise on the subject of legal life taking. According to my facts your method of execution is hanging. I have a number of questions regarding hanging and the persons who are the recipients of this form of execution. I would appreciate it greatly if you would be able to help me

in my information gathering or direct me to possible sources of information. I do not intend to make moral judgments as to the right or wrong of capital punishment but merely intend to make my readers aware of the condition surrounding this one particular method of legal execution –hanging. Between the years 1911-70 are these statistic available as to the name, age, sex and crime of the persons executed. Is hanging considered to be the most human method of execution or is this method a carryover from the British? What are the chances of instantaneous death for the victim? Do most victims "accept their fate cooly (sic)" or display signs of fear and terror or create a scene?"Are any measures taken in regard to bodily excretions Such as in England where women were required to wear waterproof underwear (sic). Can you give victims, hangings, etc. that I could use in my account of the procedure involved on the morning of an execution both in regard to the authorities and the victim? Are there any sketched or photographs available of the gallows? Executioners, paper?

I want to thank you for your time and trouble and if you are unable to help me, could you please direct me to the correct source of direction." (Schaefer G.)

This letter to the unknown company clearly showed that Schaefer was doing his homework. He was asking specific questions and looking for specific pictures. The information he asked for was the same pattern used to murder Georgia Jessup and Susan Place as well as Collette Goodenough and Barbara Ann Wilcox.

Gerard Schaefer maintained his writings were only fiction. However, all of his writing clearly portrayed the way he thought about young women who were easily influenced, coerced and manipulated to do his bidding. Even though he maintained his writings were due to his ever-present creative mind, the characters were very closely related to those women whose screams were silent. He named one of his characters Carmen, and one Belinda. In his book Killer Fiction he became the cop under the character's name of Dangerous Dan. The killer character was called Chuck Hemp. He was named after Det. Hemp of Broward County. Schaefer also named one of his character's Jerry. He used this name when he picked up Georgia Jessup and Susan Place. There was a character with the last name of Goodhart. Some have said the character's name was based on Collette Goodenough.

However, a supervisor had fired Schaefer in the school system by the name of Richard Goodhart. He told Schaefer that he would never be allowed to teach in the school system again. In Schaefer's story, which includes Goodheart, he talks about the character Kevin Goodheart who is a teacher at Northeast High School by day and by night he was a child stalker. Schaefer in his brilliance placed himself as the teacher he had tried to be with the name of Goodheart. This character was the darkness, which was that part of Schaefer. Schaefer was linked to Stevenson and Rahn and their disappearance and murder.

One of Schaefer's characters was Jolie Parsons. She was a teenage schoolgirl found raped and murdered of Oakland Park Blvd. There is such a road located in Fort Lauderdale. Oakland Park Blvd is located off NE 21st Terrace. Susan Place was a teenage schoolgirl whose body was found on Hutchinson Island. Her death was the one of two Schaefer was charged and convicted of in 1973.

Schaefer named places like Power Line Rd in Broward County, which is the same place he would go to practice, his hanging sex acts. He described clothing worn by Carmen Hallock in Murder's and Demons.

He spent his interview on A Current Affair in the 1990's playing mind games with the interviewer alluding to the fact that he killed the victims. He bragged without confessing. He smiled as he said, "I am not going to tell you if they are true." The smile was a cold, dead smile never reaching his eyes, which were penetrating and daring. He dared the interviewer to say he believed Schaefer killed. He played the "catch me if you can." It had become a game and he was calling the rules.

Roy Hazelwood a well-known FBI Profiler and the author of "Dark Dreams" which examines the criminal mind talks about the mind of a narcissist. He said "The narcissist demand constant admiration. He does not hesitate to take advantage of other to achieve his goals, and he is indifferent to their feelings and needs. Essentially he believes that he is he only one whose satisfaction counts in this world. Everyone else is just a prop in his background scenery." (Hazelwood, 2001)

Gerard Schaefer's props were not only Nancy Ellen Trotter, Pamela Sue Wells, Georgia Jessup, Susan Place, Nancy Leichner, Pam Nater, Carmen Hallock, Leigh Hainline, Elise Farmer, Collette Goodenough, Barbara Ann Wilcox, Lisa Brisconlia, and others remain nameless, but also all of the law enforcement who lived this nightmare of torture, rape, murder and degradation of the lives of these young women. Schaefer's props were used for his sick and horrific self pleasure that being his need to feel self-important and above the law. As well as the need to gain sexual gratification at the expense of the lives of young women who were easily led with low or no self-esteem.

Schaefer spent his years in prison not only

filing lawsuits against everyone involved in his case, but also writing and reliving his crimes of disgusting proportions. He truly believed what he wrote was valid literature. He really believed his work was worthy of publication.

He believed his fame was built on the lives of his victims who still silently scream through the years. He probably relived these crimes in order to bring his past sexual gratification to the forefront- to relive the look on their faces when they understood they were not going home. They were instead going to die a slow, painful and disgusting death. It is highly probably that he vividly remembered the look on the young woman's face, as she had to watch while her friend was brutalized and murdered. He probably wanted to relive over and over again the pain and fear he saw in the eyes of the young woman as she was helplessly brutalized, sodomized, tortured and finally murdered. This gave Schaefer not only sexual gratification but the feeling of absolute power as well.

In Schaefer's book "Killer Fiction" he wrote a section called: Doing Doubles

In this section he wrote about talking to Ted Bundy and how Bundy was bragging about nabbing Ott and Naslund two of his victims. They were two victims from the University of Florida. Schaefer just had to brag about his conquest of Susan Place and

Georgia Jessup.

He wrote that he had been in the ghoul game for almost 10 years and he knew what to expect from the "juicy" young creatures after they had been killed. He knew their bodies would swell up with the body gasses and expand until they burst. He knew the smell would be beyond the vilest smell anyone has ever smelt. He was aware that the blowflies would swarm over the eyes, the nose, mouth and any other open cavity. Schaefer lived to see the bodies expand and blow apart. It is even probable that he helped that process along by slitting the stomachs from pubic bone to breastbone. When he called his victims "juicy" he meant it in every way.

He continued by saying that he had been doing "doubles" with an occasional triple when the opportunity presented itself. However, Bundy was only able to kill one at a time. He said that Bundy was trying to play copycat and not doing it very well.

He bragged that doing doubles was more difficult; however it presented him with twice the fun. He said there could be very lively conversation about which victim would die first. The conversation could be very animated between him and his bimbolinas (sic) bound by hand and foot and ready for a date with the skinning knife. Schaefer wrote that he reviled in the fact that these two girls didn't mind telling him why the other should die first. He added that by giving the victim false hope was a lot of fun.

"For instance you have the Jessup and Place girls and you decide that one will live and one will die. But which one will be the lucky one? Ask them and they will tell you in graphic detail why each is the best of the litter for you. Sex? You cannot imagine how companionable such a little teenaged vixen can be until you have one at your complete mercy. My, how they do ask for the privilege of doing whatever might please your amorous interests. Anything at all they are agreeable to." (Schaefer G., Playing Doubles, 1991)

Schaefer then proceeds to degrade Susan Place even more. He claimed she was a heroin addict without any visible means of legitimate income. He asked the question "How do you think the girl earned money to support her narcotics habit?" (Schaefer G., Playing Doubles, 1991) He appeared to be laughing to himself when he wrote the answer. The answer was "Yes, with her sex, so she was indeed quite knowledgeable and skilled for a young lady of 17." (Schaefer G., Playing Doubles, 1991)

Then he wrote about Crystal aka Georgia Jessup. He describes her as a beachfront hippie and that she was skilled in her own right. He asked the question “what should a fella (sic) do when confronted with so much agreeable young flesh?” (Schaefer G., Playing Doubles, 1991)

Schaefer with tongue in cheek and with a gleeful pen answers his own question by telling the reader that one does the best they can. He says one should ask questions that would make a Tangier whore blush. He continues with his sardonic sense of humor by saying that with “their asses on the line so to speak, were quick enough to answer each and every question and assure me that if they had never tried it that they would be quick to learn.” (Schaefer G., Playing Doubles, 1991)

Schaefer bragged about his ability to the mastery of his skill in being able to convince his victims that death was in her best interest and in the best interest of society. He wrote brief instructions on exactly how to do this as an expert. He explained that one must be self-disciplined and maintain personal control. That one must have a carefully laid out plan and then is able to execute that plan. Unlike Ten Bundy who just flew apart and went on a rampage before he was aware of what he had done. Then Bundy would have such a mess of blood, gore and guts all over the place. Schaefer on the other hand felt he was so meticulous he would never lose control. He would never beat the victim’s brains out. He would never kill them in a place he could not clean up or cover up.

Schaefer had other instructions for disposing of the bodies so they would never be found. He stated "the Police only become involved when they have a corpse." (Schaefer G., Private Graveyards, 1991) He explained that he specialized in victims who were into offering or buying drugs. With that being said, his car became a superior death chamber. He would "arrest" the doper, put her in handcuffs, wrap a length of cord around her ankles, shove a Kotex in her mouth then tie it firmly with an Ace bandage.

Once he had accomplished this feat, he tied a plastic bag over her head and face tying it with a scarf. His victim would be dead in five to ten minutes. Even though Schaefer wrote this fiction it is highly probable he used this method to kill some of his victims.

Schaefer in his narcissistic psychopathic mind wrote that he was sure Ted Bundy was disappointed that he had not taken enough time to smell the fear of those "pretty blossoms" as they were sent to their grave across America. He sarcastically wrote, "At least the ladies who fell into my hands enjoyed an interesting death and, after all that is something." (Schaefer G., Murder for Fun, 1991) He bragged that he didn't go about bashing in pretty heads. He found it to be brash and impetuous to the extreme. Gerard really believed he was doing his victims a favor. He was really taking care of them. He believed they were part of his world and they relished being released from the life they had chosen.

Roy Hazelwood wanted to interview Gerard Schaefer. The word Serial Killer was not a by word in the Criminal Justice System. No one knew what it meant. Sure it had been going on since Jack the Ripper. However, killings were not linked as they began to be with the Circus of Schaefer. The FBI had no department that profiled this type of criminal behavior. Law Enforcement was in unchartered waters.

Hazelwood wanted to talk to Schaefer, to get inside his head. He wanted to find out what made him tick. However, Gerard Schaefer had other ideas. This became another opportunity for him to paraded his narcissistic personality, and once again become the big dog, the front-page headliner, the one others talked about. It was his time to rise and shine again. So he played Hazelwood for a very short time. Roy was kind enough to send me two letters that Schaefer had written him.

These letters show his ability to swing any situation in his direction.

June 20, 1989
Dear Mr. Hazelwood,

Sandra London has informed me that you would like to meet with me to discuss serial murder and sexual sadism. She tells me you like to talk about such things, Ted Bundy was the same way; we had marvelous discussions on just these topics.

You probably already know that I am internationally recognized and respected as the greatest mass murderer of women in this century. Dr. Joel Norris reports in his illustrious text on serial killers that I killed over 20 victims in the Oakland Park Area alone. The Palm Beach Post Newspaper credits me with 34 murders. I roamed over 25 nations on 3 continents during a 10 year period. I enjoy travel.

In addition to being heralded as the foremost killer of women in this century I am also known as "The Sex Beast." The media has reported that I hang women, have sexual experiences with their rotting corpses and then hack them into pieces with a machete. This is said to be an indicator of sexual sadism. You'd probably know more about that than I would.

I am writing to meet with you under certain basic conditions and ground rules. I will not submit to being interviewed in chains. The sadists who operate this prison are fond of degrading and humiliating men. I will not accept such humiliations as a condition of conduction a session with you; so make the necessary arrangements respect to that.

I am not a haphazardly inclined man. I am neat and orderly, a University graduate; a trained police officer like (sic) yourself. Ms. London will tell you, I'm sure that my philosophy is that anything worth doing is worth doing as best one is able. I approach your request for a meeting in that manner; so in order that I might provide you with maximum return on your time I would like you to send me the following pertinent data.

 # 1 A Listing of the names (and jurisdictions) of the 34 women already known as my victims.(sic) I realize that in the 34 figure is from 1973 and that 28 of those victims are from South Florida.

In an effort to be helpful to you let me tell you here that I was on the road every summer between the years 1964 and 1972. I visited almost every state the USA and rode the Trans- Canada Highway west from Quebec. I was particularly attracted to California and Colorado. A teletype to all police departments asking for data on unsolved murders 1May- 1October, 1964-1972 would probably be helpful in establishing a basic list. Prosecutors (sic) state that my M.O. is strangling or hanging; shooting by small caliber weapon- sometimes combined with mutilation, beheading, etc. I was in England and Europe during the summer of 1970;

also North Africa. Try inter-pol (sic) on that; New Scotland Yard.

Missing persons would have to be a separate inquiry.

The second thing could be a bit more sticky (sic)

A list is easy to acquire. You have a time span, A basic M.O., a cooperative suspect. You can get right to work on a list and provide me with it. But what do we do about inculpatory (sic) statements? I know about Miranda. I know about voluntary admissions. I know that cops are liars and weaselers (sic)

I don't know how we can discuss sexual sadism without getting down to factual cases and I hate to waste time dancing around issues. I think a good place to begin is with a known victim. Anybody will tell you that I killed Mary Alice Briscolina in October 1972. They'll also tell you that I killer her pal, Elise. The Plantation Police Dept. will ship you the file I 'm sure. Plantation Police, Broward County, Fla.(sic)

I want you to make a copy of the file for Ms. London so she can also have the facts. I won't need a copy of the file; I have a good memory about Miss Briscolina. I want to start where the police say the greatest evidence is; with Briscolina/Farmer The cops have Eye Witness, the parents Ided(sic) jewelry taken from my home verification as belonging to Mary Alice; the corpses were found in close proximity to my mother-in-law's house in Plantation. It is an open and shut situation except as to why they had to die; how did they in fact die. The sadism part. (sic) How one has to watch while the other one dies; knowing she'll be next. That's what you want to hear, right? But how do we handle the inculpartory (sic) admissions? Tell me that first, OK?(sic)

One more condition: After we chat about Mary Alice and Elise Lina I want to take a polygraph test. I'm sure you have a good local man who can do it. This would be on the order of Truth Verification rather than lie dectetion (sic). In addition to the story of the Briscolina/Farmer case I am going to tell you about other cases. I will require truth verification on those cases as well. Four tests. None of this 'inconclusive' stuff either. We test first.

Your man using your box establishes truth or deception and I will get a letter from him as to his conclusions. Then we will get down to the next case.

Naturally there needs to be a spirit of cooperation here; so I'll take the first step toward that end. I'll give you Briscolina on the house. Simply on your own promise as an honorable FBI man that what we discuss will be confidential. If we do well together I'll go over the entire list with you on a polygraph machine. That seems fair, doesn't it?

And we can start on that matter as soon as I receive your listing of the 34 murders you know I did plus the ones you think I did across the U.S.A, Canada and Europe and Africa.

I'm well aware that this matter will take some time. Ms. London will tape and film all our meetings and be present to assure I am not threatened or abused as I have been in the past by the FBI.

Sincerely,
Gerard J. Schaefer

PS. While I am waiting for your list and our initial meeting I would like to read your various articles dealing with lust murder, autoerotic fatalities, etc.

The Lust Murderer
Death During Dangerous Autoerotic Practices
Investigations of Autoerotic Fatalities
Sexual Fatalities
Autoerotic Asphyxia Deaths and Social N.R.
Detective Magazines: Porn for Sadists?

You may send the 7 articles to me direct <u>under FBI Cover and Letterhead</u>. I will return them to you if you wish. My address is:

Gerard J. Schaefer
Prisoner #039506
Box 747
Starke, Fl. 32091

Being a law clerk, when I'm not in a torture dungeon, I try to keep up a date with all new material coming out on homicide investigation. I may have used your book on Autoerotic Fatality to win an argument in 1985. A fellow was claiming that women do not engage in autoerotic bondage and orgasmic asphysixia (sic). I said they did, and bets were laid. I produced a book on homicide investigations that showed a woman in autoerotic death bondage. It's fairly rare but not unknown. That may have been your book. I read everything that comes out. I talk to the freaks. Bundy was a wonderland of madness once he warmed up to you and the topic of killing women….. But, of course, I am fully recognized as the best. You've seen it time after time in print I'm sure. (Schaefer G., Letter to Roy Hazelwood dated June 20, 1989)

Gerard Schaefer had been in prison since 1973. But he had lost his place on the front page. When he was contacted by Sondra London to publish his writings in book form this was his ticket back.

When FBI Agent Roy Hazelwood contacted Schaefer regarding interviewing him this played right into his plan. It couldn't have been time more perfectly. He would use Hazelwood's interest in him to glean information for his own twisted use.

Schaefer played the “I am glad you consider me the foremost authority on serial killing and sexual sadism card.” What a stroke to his ego even if it was in his mind. He was going to be back on the front page. His narcissistic personality was in overdrive. He was important again and he played that hand so well.

Gerard Schaefer had become very proficient in mind games and control. That was how he was able to lure his victims in his web of torture and murder. He told just enough truth mingled with all the lies and subterfuge to gather more information or to see what law enforcement might or might not have on him. In his reply to Hazelwood he offers up Briscolina and Farmer. This was a teaser. They had been considered as unsolved even though Schaefer had been loosely tied to them. Schaefer dangled that carrot to see if Hazelwood would comply and send him the information he wanted for his own gratification.

This letter is filled with extreme narcissistic platitudes and attitudes. He brags about his kills. He taunts Hazelwood with his “catch me if you can” by daring him to ask for files on the names he has produced as well as unknowns and /or unsolved. Schaefer brags about his M.O. albeit thru the eyes of the press. He is proud of his accomplishments touting them like a flag.

He states he wants to take a polygraph test. That in itself is a double dare- a thumbing in the face act. He brags that he was a cop and that he knows how the system works. He makes it a point to say he knows about Miranda and that he expects professional courtesy afford him as a cop.

Schaefer spun his web of lies, half-truths and bragging with the ability of a true spin master. He wanted Hazelwood to think he was the notorious serial killer but yet, he doesn't want law enforcement involved. He delighted in playing both ends against the middle as he sends mixed messages like a tennis ball bouncing from player to player, each sentence a new serve just barely missing the foul line.

Schaefer bragged about the fact that a Dr. Joel Norris reports that he had killed over 20 victims in Oakland Park alone. He was not only playing "catch me if you can" with Hazelwood, he was trying to hook Chuck Hemp as well. Schaefer loved the limelight, the game. He wanted them to know he had the answers. But he would only trade for things that would benefit him and he would only trade if he was not "ratted" out to his nemesis, that being law enforcement.

Roy Hazelwood received another letter from Schaefer dated August 17, 1989.

Dear Mr. Hazelwood,

I found your letter most interesting. Taking it from the top let me ask you which of my literary properties you have? I've done hundreds of them.

Items on various sexual fetishes. I've quite a following among the practioners (sic) of what you call autoerotic sex hanging not because I 'm a practioner (sic) myself but because of my being somewhat of a recognized authority on sexual ritualism. Like yourself, I write to earn money. Honest work. Honest Buck. So to begin, which of my own stories or articles do you have on hand there and what source did you obtain them from?

The materials you sent me to read were interesting and in reading them I can see why you need my help. You really don't have much actual knowledge about the rituals you investigate, do you? Plenty of speculations to be sure but nothing concrete. I'm not surprised. All your people are deceased which indicated that they were craven novices with respect to understanding what they were doing. Then along comes some investigator and he can't figure what was going on with respect to the ritual which is the key to understanding the scene.

My specialty, as you may know from your reading about me, is Death Strap Bondage. I hold a Master's Status and was probably the only Grand

Cross Master in Florida during the 1960's I practiced in Europe and N.

Africa during the 70's and worked scenes in London. Was a member of the Calcraft Society until 1985. I've been retired from active participation (via mail) in these activities since turning 40.

I did notice that none of the fatalities in your study were clacraftians. From what was mentioned I can see a lot of Marwood-Berry influence and, of course the Pierrepoints. I've always told those Dekkerite Fools that they'd kill themselves messing with those later styles I see from your studies many do.

I'll give you one quick example here Your own sexual fatalities: Behavioral Reconstrution (sic)..... page 764-65

Case #1: A typical Pierrepoint #2 hanging, accidental death of course. No doubt a Dekkerite. I'd need to see the noose & placement of it to get a 100% positive make on his technique. Nonetheless it's a Pierrepoint. #2: Male.

A female hanged in that style uses a Holloway ring.

Do you understand the signifigance (sic) of the washer around the penis?

You obviously do not know your noosings (sic). I was amazed that you equated the numeral 13 with the wraps of a hangman's noose. Did the noose have

13 coils? Do you know what the 13 coils signify? Not everyone hanged qualifies for a 13 coil wrap.

Did you consider the date of the hanging? The fellow was obviously following ritual. Did you consider the aspect of the vernal cross? The 13 signifigance (sic) again.

The penis washer is not a masochistic device or feature.

Here you have a classic Pierrepoint 2 hanging and you don't even recognize it when you walk up on it.

Well, I guess that's why you need the help of a Grand Cross Master. How else will you ever learn the term? My last statement, I do selected tutorials, took years to learn ritual. He works the Philadelphia to Oak City Area. He hangs mostly crack hookers. Both of course. I'd know his work if I saw it, just know a Pierrepoint #2 when I see it.

I also recognize various cases you cite. In your work: Detective Magazines: Porn for the Satanic Sadist. Page 202. Case 1. That's certainly Harvey Glatman. The gal he tied up and strangled was Ruth Mercado.

The cop who worked it was Pierce Brooks who's now with some serial killer unit. Why the reluctance to say so in the story? Glatman was gassed in1958. He can't sue anyone.

As you recognize, I am an unusual person. I

may well be the first Grand Cross Master of Death Strap Bondage that you have ever encountered. I have been asked to arbitrate on ritual differences many times. Bondage Clubs sometimes write me about technique. I've been inactive since '86. Retired, I suppose. Sondra London and Media Queen Inc. signed me to do a series of books. I jotted off a quick book for them but the one she wants is the true story of my life as a Grand Cross Master during the 60's. Ms. London has a contract to handle my outside contacts with all my parties wishing to obtain information from me.

I've been credited by 34 confirmed kills. I've also been credited with the Sex Beast Murders. That's another 26; I've got official credit for 60 murders. A nice round figure: 58 women, 2 men. I've never courted any publicity or cooperated with bookwriters (sic). I've never regarded myself as a sadist. I was the disciplinarian for Kamarata's Stable and later Cappatturto's and Fazio's. This was way back when Callahan was a

Captain and Finno were working the jackets under him. All those stables operated under protection. You're FBI so I don't need to tell you the Mann Act and what happens to hookers who try to: steal. Snitch. Whatever. Back then the big round sex kick was snuff action. The ritualists (sic) wanted short cards and harness, berry drops, hoisting.

I was a Grand Cross by 1967 and a Master by 1970. There are some who say calcraftians are sadismos (sic). I disagree with that. The total picture is important so I don't think I qualify as sadist. Why in the world would you classify a Grand Cross Master as a Sadist? Out of ignorance, I suppose. You're the fellow who doesn't know the signifigance (sic) of a washer on a hanged man's penis. How could I discuss sadism with you?

As you realize, the hanging fetish is popular today. Due to my authoring many articles and stories on the hanging fetish and associated fetishes I get a lot of unwanted mail. I should say, I used to. Now I work through an agent, Ms. London. I write under 13 different names. If you read Bondage topics you've probably read my material. I'm one of the top bondage writers in the country today. I do cross-general writing- should you come across stories and articles by any of the following authors they are really me.

H. Benson Poole *Mistress Marsha*
Lacey Calhoun *Madam Felice*
Jessica Zurriaga *Priscilla Miller*

I've also written the following Bondage related works:

Harlots Hang High
True Crime Classics

Tyburn's Trollops
The Myth of Celebrity Enema
Mr. Marwood's Diapers
Sanitary Straps- Are They Necessary
Terminal Orgasm
The Holloway Ring and the The Women Who Wear it
Death Strap Restraints
The Penis Ring: 1875 Through Present

These titles are mine. They hardly qualify as ? in Sasdism (sic) however people read them and want more data. Most of my readers are submissives (sic) and 70 t0 80 percent are males: I haven't come across any more than two men who admit to murder by hanging the victims. One fellow works N.Y. State & New England, the other Philadelphia to N.Y.C. area. They hand prostitutes and crack whores. The cases get written off as suicides. Both persons have official backgrounds. I tutored both as to noosing techniques. Both travel a lot for their activities.

Well sir, I doubt I can assist you as a Sadist. I may be able to help you out so that you understand the rituals of the Hang-Shit fetish more thoroughly. I'll be willing to go over your literature on sex-hanging as you call it and correct any errors in your speculations. I'm still chuckling about your believing the metal washer on the penis to be a masochistic device. No telling what other misapprehinsions (sic) you may have going.

I'll send you a list of items I'll review for you next time... if you wish.

Sincerely,

Gerard J Schaefer

Articles from your file I will review next mail.

Your Biblography (sic) - Autoerotic Fatalities p. 411

Ford, 1957 Death by Hanging... J Forfan Sci 2:171-176

Resnick, H.L.P. Erotica Repetitive Hanging Arr. J-psy 26:4-21

Sass, Sexual Asphyxia in Females J Foren Sci 20:181-185

Usher, 1963 Accidental Hangings Newcastle Med J 27: 234-238

Walsh.... 1977 Legal Medicine Annual, 155-182- Autoerotic Asphyxia Death

These should provide good introductory case material so I can break down the various styles for you from Dennis to Decker.

Gerard Schaefer had apparently researched the

execution styles in England. In the letter to Hazelwood he talks about the Calcraft Society.

He bases this society on William Calcraft who was born 1801 and died 1879. He was the General Executioner in Great Britain and Scotland between the years 1852-1870. He was not well versed in his craft. Most of his hangings were botched at best. The person who was hanged most times did not die. Calcraft more times than not had to finish the execution by beheading the criminal.

Then he talks about Marwood-Berry influence. Marwood was William Marwood born in 1820. He was considered a famous executioner in England in the early 19th century. He was a follower of William Calcraft. He introduced the long drop method and the free running noose.

James Berry another famous hangman in the 19th Century did his work in Ireland. He was best known for his three attempts at hanging John Lee who became as the man they could not hang. The trapdoors failed to open three times. Lee was sentenced to life in prison.

Berry started his career as a 22-year-old Bradford Borough Policeman. He became an executioner in 1884 when he executed two men at Calton Gaol Edinburg.

Was there some underlying current in the fact that Schaefer was a cop and so was Berry. Did

Schaefer pattern his life after Berry?

Schaefer continues his who's who of executioners with the name of Pierrepoint. They were a family consisting of a father Henry, Henry's brother Thomas and Henry's son Albert they were the official executioners in England from 1901-1954. The father Henry started the family tradition. He taught his brother Thomas and Thomas taught Albert. Schaefer in his letter to Hazelwood told him that the Dekkerite Fools had killed themselves because they messed with the Pierrepoint style. That style was one of speed.

Schaefer again tried playing mind games with Hazelwood. He was trying to pull information from Hazelwood. He wanted to relive the fantasy that had become reality. But, he had no intention of giving an interview in regards to the crimes he was convicted of. Roy Hazelwood severed his correspondence with Schaefer after the second letter. He refused to be drawn into the Circus of Schaefer.

Gerard John Schaefer

CHAPTER SIXTY-TWO

THIS WRITER'S PERSONAL THOUGHTS

I am breaking a cardinal rule in the literary world. I am adding my personal thoughts to the end of this work. However, I feel this is necessary at this time. It is time the victim's screams were heard.

When I first heard about Gerard John Schaefer, I was being taken on a tour of Hutchinson Island in April 2006. I had made a life changing decision to move to Florida. As Jack and I were driving south on A1A he began the tale of terror that was Gerard Schaefer.

He pointed to Blind Creek and told me that he had been involved in a case in 1973 that involved a serial killer who had been a Martin County Deputy. This deputy kept teeth as trophies. As an author my mind went into overdrive. I knew there was a story. I just didn't know how much of a story and what an impact it would have on me as an author. I also didn't know how much of an impact it had on those who were involved in the investigation and conviction of Schaefer.

I had no idea how many law enforcement

personnel and how many counties it involved.

I started my research in the later part of 2007. I started with the way the case ended, the getaway of Nancy Trotter and Susan Wells. The more I dug, the more I found. The more I found the more I saw of the pure evil, which lurked behind the charming and charismatic mask of Gerard Schaefer. I saw the pain, the terror, and suffering of not only the victims, but their families and law enforcement.

I read the stories which he claimed to be fiction and saw his true feelings of enjoying the degradations, pain, suffering and ultimately murder and destroying of lives of young women. I felt their pain, humiliation, suffering, and ultimate acceptance of the fact they could only scream silently watching as one was destroyed knowing she would be next. I felt their silent cries of help knowing that none would come. I felt the pain of unspeakable terror knowing death and worse would occur before it was over. I felt the pain of knowing the things he did to his victims were completely out of their control. He had them unwillingly bending to his twisted and evil will. He was always in control. He was their master and they were his slaves.

It was true what he had told Trotter and Wells. There were men out there who would use them as sex slaves. He was one of them. He was the one they were to be afraid of. Schaefer relished their fear; he perpetrated that fear, fed off that fear and received sexual gratification from that fear. Gerard Schaefer lived for the feeling of a victim's fear it was his aphrodisiac.

The first apparent kill he perpetrated was the last one solved that of Nancy Leichner and Pamela Nater. Did he kill before 1966? He claimed he had. He told Special Agent Hazelwood he had started in 1964. Did he kill when he was in Europe and N. Africa? His writings would lead one to believe he did. Did Gerard Schaefer leave a trail of silent screams across several countries? He said he did in his letter to Hazelwood. Did he admit he was the "Foremost Killer of Women in this Century?" He did simply by stating he had been heralded as such. He stated it in such a way that it leads one to believe he was bragging.

In his letter to Agent Hazelwood dated June 20, 1989 he stated that he was credited with 34 murders. But he said he had roamed over 25 nations on 3 continents during a 10-year span. Then he went one step further and said he enjoyed travel. He again was bragging.

Gerard Schaefer believed he was the absolute best at doing what he did- kill women. But not just kill them- he enjoyed degrading them, torturing them and then raping them once they were dead. However, he also relished the fact that it was his "dirty little secret." He told an interviewer that he could never be placed at any crime scene. Yes, he had the evidence at his mother's house. Yes, he had pictures, and yes he had written stories. But, he couldn't be caught. He laughed in the face of the courts, he laughed at what he felt was the ultimate stupidity of law enforcement. He really believed in his ability to be smarter than the cops.

Gerard Schaefer relived and enjoyed every moment he was in the limelight due to the silent screams he perpetrated. He enjoyed great gratification knowing he would never be caught. Sure he was in prison for Jessup and Place. Sure Trotter and Wells got away. But he could explain all of that. With Trotter and Wells, it was a clean arrest he just got carried away. With Jessup and Place well he was convicted unjustly – he didn't do it--because he believed they were whores. The only evidence he had was what he created in his world. In his reality.

True serial killers such as Gerard Schaefer enjoy reliving the crime in fantasy. It is much more gratifying than the real life experience. He wrote his stories so he would always have his victims with him. In his sick and twisted mind he could re-read his accomplishments as many times as he wanted to. Every time he was interviewed by a reporter or saw his face on TV he relived the murders. He played each scene over and over in his head. He relished in the crimes of abduction, rape, degradation, torture, murder and mutilation with glee. These writings not only gave him gratification they made him feel important. He was somebody.

Georgia Jessup, Susan Place, Collette Goodenough, Barbara Ann Wilcox, Nancy Leichner, Pam Nater, Nancy Trotter, Pamela Wells, Carmen Hallock, Leigh Hainline, Belinda Hutchins and the others were forced into Gerard Schaefer's reality. They became his victims, his fun, and his gratification. He had no regard for their pain, fear, terror, suffering of the degrading of their bodies.

It didn't bother him that the families of these young girls would forever be in pain. They were victims as much as their daughters. Carmen Hallock's daughter was left without a mother at two years old. Did Schaefer think about that?

Probably not, if he did he probably believed in his twisted evil mind that the baby girl would be better off without her "whore" mother.

Gerard Schaefer not only made victims of the girls he brutally murdered and dismembered, he made victims of his own family. He left them to bear the burden of his actions and the consequences of those actions.

He left behind memories with those in law enforcement who worked his crime scenes, which they would rather not remember. Jack worked that crime scene. He saw the body parts, as they were uncovered in their grave. He watched as they were placed in plastic garbage bag in pieces. He saw their clothes and the remains of what were once two young girls with their life brutally taken from them. It affected him April 1, 1973. Today 35 years later he still feels the hurt and pain he felt when he first walked on the crime scene of Georgia Jessup and Susan Place.

While helping me research this book we were allowed to view the physical evidence found at the scene. It brought back many haunting memories and Jack was visibly moved. He stated it was as if time had been turned back to 1973 when he viewed the pictures of the scene and the physical evidence. When I went back to finish viewing the clothing and the tree roots with the hack marks on them, he could not go.

Chuck Hemp has spent his career honing his skills with death and crime scene investigations. Every one of those involved I talked to said the same thing. They all said Gerard Schaefer was indeed evil. More than one of them said he should have been executed long before he was.

As I close the book on Schaefer, I am saddened in a way. I am saddened that these young women suffered, and died way before it was their time. I am saddened that they have screamed silently for over 35 years. I have grown close to these young women. They have lived in my head for almost a year. I feel they had a hand in the telling of their story. They have been so much a part of my life it is hard to let go- but let go I must. I must give them a voice. Now, no longer will the victims scream in silence, they now have a voice, and with this voice, comes peace.

For the girls- sleep well.

Yvonne

RESOURCES

Barszewski, L. (1987, 28 October). Convicted Murderer's Motion for Relief Denied. *Miami Herald* . Miami, Florida, USA.

Butsh, P. Q. (1973, September 25). Schaefer Sister Confused on Stand. *The News Tribune* . Fort Pierce, Florida, USA.

Buun, J. (2007, September 30). The Beauty and the Sex Beast. *http://home.online.no/~janbrunn/writings/beauty.html* . USA.

Chattahoochee. (n.d.). Retrieved Jan. 21, 2008, from www.exploresouthernhistory.com/FLArsenal1.html: http://www.exploresouthernhistory.com/FLArsenal1.html

Donovan, D. (1973, May 20). Murder Suspect is Portrayed By Classmates as a Loner They Didn't Care to Know. *Palm Post* . Palm Beach, Florida, USA.

Filkins, D. (1990, September 21). Convicted Killer Seeks New Trial, Cites Romance. *Miami Herald* . Miami, Florida, USA.

Fryer, B. (1973, May 20). Accused Double Murderer Will Fly to Chattahoochee. *The Stuart News* . Stuart , Florida, USA.

Fryer, B. (1973, September 27). Caller Accuses Juror of Wanting to Hang Schaefer. *The Stuart News* . Stuart, Florida, USA.

Fryer, B. (1972, 12 24). Former Deputy Sentenced for Stringing up Teenage Girls. *The Stuart New* . Stuart, Florida, USA.

Fryer, B. (1973, August 23). Ground Rules Laid for Schaefer Trial . *Stuart News* . Stuart, Florida, USA.

Fryer, B. (1973, 7 8). Insanity Motion Withdrawn By Accused Double Killer. *The Stuart News* . Stuart, Florida, USA.

Fryer, B. (1973, August 12). Motion to Move Schaefer's Trial Continues. *Stuart News* . Stuart, Florida, USA.

Fryer, B. (1973, 6 24). No Decision made on Schaefer's Sanity . *The Stuart News* . Stuart, Florida, USA.

Fryer, B. (1973, August 10). Schaefer Asking to Be Committed. *The Stuart News* . Stuart, Florida, USA.

Fryer, B. (1973, 8 2). Schaefer Fears Assassination. *Stuart News* . Stuart, Florida, USA.

Fryer, B. (1973, September 30). Schaefer talks about Himself . *The Stuart News* . Stuart, Florida, USA.

Fryer, B. (1973, September 23). Schaefer Trial Grind to Halt As Witness Flies in from Nairobi . *The Stuart News* . Stuart, Florida, USA.

Fryer, B. (1973, 8 5). Schaefer's Bond Revoked . *Stuart Nes* . Stuart, Florida, USA.

Fryer, B. (1973, 8 2). Schaefer's Notions are Heard. *Stuart News* . Stuart, Florida, USA.

Hazelwood, S. G. (2001). *Dark Dreams.* St. Martins Press.

Kane, G. (1990, August 22). Judge Hears 15th Appeal in Murder Case. *The Palm Beach Post* . Palm Beach, Florida, USA.

Media Queen, L. I. (n.d.). Killer Serial Rogue Cop.

Moore, J. T. (1995, December 5). Serial Killer Stabbed to Death in Prison Ex-Martin County Deputy Got Two Life Terms in Deaths of Two Broward Teens in 1973.

The Palm Beach Post . Palm Beach, Florida, USA.

Murder Demons. (n.d.). *http://home.online.no/~janbruun/writings/murder.html* . Internet- Justice Now.

Newton, M. (n.d.). All about Gerard Schaefer. *www.crimelibrary.com/serial_killers/predators/gerard_schaefer/8.html* . Internet.

Newton, M. (n.d.). Sexual Predators- Gerard Schaefer. *Crime Library* . Internet.

Plarski, P. (1989, August 14). Killer's Book: Fiction or How-to? Ex Martin Deputy Calls Novel a Product:" It's Not Me" . *The Palm Beach Post* . Palm Beach, Florida, USA.

Press, A. (1986, August 11). Inmate Claims Attorney had Affair with His Wife . *The Orlando Sentinel* . Orlando, Florida, USA.

Quina, P. (1973, 6 17). Girls He Tied up Laughed at Him, Schaefer Says. *The News Tribune* . Fort Pierce, Florida, USA.

Quina, P. (1973, September 23). Girl's Relatives Testify at Trial of Schaefer. *The News Tribune* . Fort Pierce, Florida, USA.

Quina, P. (1973, September 24). Girls Tell of Schaefer Tying Them to Trees. *The News Tribune* . Fort Pierce, Florida, USA.

Quina, P. (1973, 5 16). Lawyer: Schaefer Desires, Needs Mental Health Care. *The News Tribune* . Fort Pierce , Florida, USA.

Quina, P. (1973, September 27). One Juror Excused in Schaefer Trial. *The News Tribune* . Fort Pierce, Florida, USA.

Quina, P. (1973, September 26). Prosecution, Defense

Rest Cases in Trial of Schaefer. *The New Tribune* . Fort Pierce, Florida, USA.

Quina, P. (1973, September 17). Prospective Schaefer Jurors Quizzed. *The News Tribune* . Fort Pierce, Florida, USA.

Quina, P. (1973, September 27). Schaefer Convicted of Killing 2 girls. *The New Tribune* . Fort Pierce, Florida, USA.

Quina, P. (1973, June 22). Schaefer Denied Further Testing. *The News Tribune* . Fort Pierce, Florida, US.

Quina, P. (1973, June 17). Schaefer Denies Guilt, Admits Problems. *The News Tribune* . Fort Pierce, Florida, USA.

Quina, P. (1973, September 18). Schaefer Jury List Pared. *The News Tribune* . Fort Pierce, Florida, USA.

Quina, P. (1973, September 27). Schaefer Prosecutor Pulls Out the Stops. *The News Tribune* . Fort Pierce, Georgia, USA.

Quina, P. (1973, June 11). Schaefer Said "Unable to Stand Trial". *The News Tribune* . Fort Pierce, Florida, USA.

Quina, P. (1973, May 15). Schaefer Sanity Hearing Friday;Gruesome Details. *The News Tribune* . Fort Pierce, Florida, USA.

Quina, P. (1973, June 17). Schaefer Says News Tribune Reporter Scared Him in First Meeting . *The Tribune* . Fort Pierce, Florida, USA.

Quina, P. (1973, June 22). Schaefer Warned after Outburst. *The News Tribune* . Fort Pierce, Florida, USA.

Quina, P. (1973, July 1). Schaefer's Mom: He's Not a Monster . *The News Tribune* . Fort Pierce, Florida, USA.

Quina, P. (1973, September). Some Jurors Pale at Schaefer's Trial. *The News Tribune* . Fort Pierce, Florida.

, Florida, USA.

Quina, P. (1973, 6 6). Stone Lists 97 Stuar
Case Against Schaefer. *The Tribune* . Fort F
USA.

Quina, P. (1973, September 28). Susa
Now Mom tells News Tribune . *The News T*
Pierce, Florida, USA.

Quina, P. (1973, September 21). Two
on Stand Monday. *The News Tribune* . Fort
USA.

Saitz, G (1996, December 23). Docu
Death of Murderer. *Stuart News* . Stuart, Fl,

Schaefer, G (n.d.).

Schaefer, G (1989, June 20). Letter to
Hazelwood dated June 20,1989. *Letter* . US

Schaefer, G (1989, October 15). Lett
Charles C. Hemp. Oakland Park, Florida, U

Schaefer, G (1991). Murder for Fun.
USA: Media Queen LTD, Inc.

Schaefer, G (1991). Playing Doubles.
Georgia, USA: Media Queen LTD, Inc.

Schaefer, G (1991). Private Graveyar
Fiction . USA: Media Queen LTD, Inc.

Stone Lists 97 Witnesses in Case a. (n

Taylor, J. (2005, January 22). 17- Yea
Defender Schwarz. *The Palm Beach Post* . F
USA.

unknown. (2002). History of the Bake
Development & Intent. *History of the Baker*
Development & Intent State of Florida Depa
Children and Families Mental Health Progr

Unknown. (1973, 5 27). Schaefer's La
Motion To Have Murder Charges Dropped. S

32002364R00253

Printed in Great Britain
by Amazon